Gift of

MENLO MOTHERS' CLUB

ON GUARD

ON GUARD

The Business of Private Security

by MILTON LIPSON

Quadrangle/The New York Times Book Co.

To and for Esther

Designed by Tere LoPrete

Library of Congress Cataloging in Publication Data

Lipson, Milton.
   On guard.

   Bibliography: p.
   Includes index.
   1. Police, Private—United States. I. Title.
HV8088.L55   363.2   75-8294
ISBN 0-8129-0518-0

Contents

Introduction

Private security makes an invaluable contribution to the public weal. Its absence would be disastrous to law and order, and the operation of the criminal justice system. It constitutes the largest available untapped, unstructured, dormant resource for the prevention and control of crime. Few people are aware of its full ramifications and potential.

Chance and long experience have enabled me to penetrate the haze screening private security and concealing its true proportions. This experience began with my employment as an investigator in the office of Congressman Fiorello H. LaGuardia, and after his election as Mayor of the City of New York, as an investigator for his Corporation Counsel, where for almost four years I investigated welfare cheats and corruption in the administration of welfare. During this period I attended law school and was admitted to practice.

From 1938 to 1946, as an Agent in the United States Secret Service I was given assignments in the New York and Washington, D.C., field offices, on the White House Detail, office of the Chief of the Secret Service and detached on occasion to act as an instructor at intelligence schools of the Armed Forces and the Office of Strategic Services. Anticipating the possibility that counterfeiting of U.S. currency might be used as a weapon by the Nazi-Axis powers, the Secret Service developed a Crime Prevention Program to make the country aware of counterfeits and their detection. I assisted in the creation of the "Know Your Money" campaign and materials, and later, to combat check theft, in the "Know Your Endorser" program. Both of these, in updated form, have been continued by the Secret Service.

After practicing law in New York City and Nassau County, New

York, from 1946 to 1962, I returned to investigations when I was appointed by County Executive Eugene Nickerson as Nassau County's first Commissioner of Accounts (Investigations). In a stormy four years, investigations we conducted resulted in changes and reforms, the collection of hundreds of thousands of dollars, and the prosecution of individuals who had defrauded the government.

Early in 1966 I became head of the worldwide security staff of the American Express Company, with the title of Director of Security. I was exposed to the problems of private security in depth through a staff of some 300, including 85 superior investigators recruited from the ranks of such prestigious organizations as the Federal Bureau of Investigation, the United States Secret Service, the U.S. Bureau of Narcotics, the Criminal Investigation branches of the United States Army, the United States Air Force, the Canadian Defense Forces, the Royal Air Force of Britain, the Royal Canadian Mounted Police, Scotland Yard (U.K.), Sureté Nationale (France), the Carabinieri (Italy), the Federal Police of Mexico and Turkey, as well as representatives of outstanding police departments of the major cities of the United States. In addition there were uniformed contract guards. I shared with many security directors of other companies the problems of physical plant security and potential employee defalcation. I also had problems unique to American Express in the protection of its money-like major products, its Travelers Cheques, money orders, and credit cards.

In this position I participated in some of the Interpol sessions, attending their annual meetings in quasi-observer status. I was accredited to attend the decennial Interpol International Congress on Counterfeiting. By invitation, I authored papers on traveler's checks and credit card frauds that were printed in the official Interpol and F.B.I. publications. I was a panelist and lecturer at meetings and seminars of such organizations as the Interpol Fraud Symposium in Paris, the National Association of Attorneys General, the National District Attorneys Association, the American Institute of Banking, the American Management Association, the International Association of Chiefs of Police, the National Retail Dry Goods Association, and other groups. As a member from 1967 through 1973 of the selection panel for the $10,000 annual award for the greatest scientific contribution to police work, which was given by American Express, with the cooperation of the International Association of Chiefs of Police, I had an extraordinary perspective into security problems.

Yet I have found everywhere there is a basic lack of understanding of what private security is, and what it is supposed to do. I have discovered that there are no academic institutions anywhere that have more than a cursory survey course on private security. Few, if any, of the graduates of the more than 200 institutions which offer programs and degrees in the fields of law enforcement, its administration and criminal justice, proceed directly into the field of private security. A quest for expertise is a venture into the unknown. Such organizations as Harvard University, Xerox, and American Express, to name a few, have had to go to the columns of the financial section of the Sunday edition of *The New York Times* in their search for senior security managers. Major consulting firms to business and government often become involved in security problems, but few, if any, have staff assistants or consultants versed in this branch of business. While senior law enforcement executives have knowledge of many of the techniques used by private security, and as such, form the major reservoir of talent for enlistment as leaders in private security, they rarely have a real visualization of its scope. A few are beginning to recognize private security as a potential resource in their defense against crime. Law enforcement's insistent problems with rising crime rates have not allowed for the time or financial means to organize the necessary cooperation.

There is clearly a serious need for systematic information on private security. I have in this book attempted to explain the nature, problems and opportunities of private security for the interested general reader as well as for those who need the information for more practical purposes.

ON GUARD

1 | The Business of Private Security

The private security business is booming. It flourishes in response to the economic impact of crime.

There is no accurate measurement of this impact. According to the United States Department of Commerce, the only comprehensive study of the cost of crime was made back in 1931, by the Wickersham Commission, and its recommendations for follow-up and studies were never acted upon.[1]

The Department of Commerce made an estimate of the economic effect of crime on business in 1972, but it qualified its figures by saying that they covered only what was labeled "ordinary crime." Burglary, robbery, vandalism, shoplifting, employee theft, bad checks, arson—these are ordinary crimes. The department specifically omitted in its estimate losses due to "extraordinary crime," which it defined to include airplane hijacking and embezzlement. It also specifically excluded losses due to "organized crime." "Ordinary crime," said the department, cost American business $16 billion in 1972.[2] In its second analysis, published in November, 1974,[3] the department reported the 1973 cost of "ordinary crime" to business to be $18.3 billion. Further, it estimated the cost for 1974 to be $20.3 billion.[4]

The 1968 *Report of the President's Commission on Law Enforcement and the Administration of Justice* estimated losses to crime for 1965 were $5.8 billion; the Small Business Administration, using a narrower definition of crime for 1967, put that year's loss at $3 billion; and for 1970, *U.S. News and World Report* gauged the loss at $10.8 billion.[5]

"White-collar" crime has been defined in the 1974 U.S. Chamber of Commerce *Handbook* as "an illegal act or series of acts committed by non-physical means and by concealment or guile, to obtain money or property, to avoid the payment or loss of money or property, or to obtain business for personal advantage."[6] The *Handbook* concludes that the annual rate of loss to United States business was "not less than \$40 billion." As to that amount, ". . . the estimate does not pretend to be the result of a rigorous, statistically valid survey and should not be regarded as 'the cost of white collar crime.' No one has ever really computed even a reasonably accurate figure."[7]

The *Handbook* specifically excludes the costs of price-fixing illegalities and industrial espionage, and it also omits the costs to business of crimes committed by physical means, such as robberies, holdups, burglaries, hijackings, and sabotage. To compare the conclusions of the Department of Commerce with those of the Chamber of Commerce is like comparing apples and grapefruit. Each uses a different base. It is reasonable to assume that if each enlarged its base so that it would be all-inclusive and equal, both would have to raise their estimates considerably.

Thus in the September, 1974, issue of *Fortune* magazine there appeared 15 consecutive pages of advertising sponsored by the American Society for Industrial Security and a select group of suppliers of private security services, machinery, and devices. The editorial copy interlacing these pages together adopted the figure of \$16 billion as the annual rate of loss by business to crime, and then qualified that estimate by saying: "But even that astronomical figure may not measure the true cost because it is estimated that actual crime is two to three times that reported to police."

Indeed, one page, a full-page advertisement for Burns International Security Services includes this statement: "Almost 2% of the Gross National Product. It's also the cost of crime against business in 1972. And that's just reported crime. Throw in all the pilferage and losses unreported for one reason or another, and you've got a figure that boggles the imagination."

Another barometer of impact of crime on business lies in the statistics on the number of instances of criminal attack and the various categories involved, published quarterly and annually by the Federal Bureau of Investigation since 1930. In the last 15 years these FBI *Reports* have reflected a sharply upward trend: crime grew by 208 percent between 1952 and 1969, with most of the increase occurring in the 1960s. The rate went up by 122 percent between 1960 and 1968.

There was a further rise of 17 percent in 1968, 12 percent for 1969, 11 percent for 1970 and 7 percent in 1971. A translation of percentages into the number of crimes reported indicates that in 1973, which reflected an increase of 6 percent over the previous year, there were 8,600,000 individual crimes committed. Available figures for 1974 indicate it was a banner crime year with a 17 percent jump.[8]

Figures and statistics are always open to various interpretations. IBM recently issued a six-volume study on data security. In it the company illustrated the risc in crime in three ways.[9] First, in 1971 there were 5,185,200 crimes committed against property, marking a 6.9 percent increase over 1970, an 82.2 percent increase over 1966, and a 199.1 percent increase over 1960. Second, in 1971 2,907 persons out of each 100,000 in the United States were victims of crime, a rise of 6 percent in the number affected over the previous year. Third, employees are reported to steal more than $10 million a day in cash and merchandise, or about $3 billion a year. This loss, they say, means that 15 percent of the price a consumer pays for goods and services goes to cover the cost of dishonesty.

In mid-April, 1974, the Law Enforcement Assistance Administration (LEAA) of the Department of Justice made public a report that casts great doubt on the accuracy of the FBI *Uniform Crime Reports*. LEAA had financed a study made by the Bureau of Census on victimization. The survey involved the interviewing of some 25,000 persons in 10,000 to 12,000 separate households and businesses in eight selected cities, denominated high crime areas. The study found that nearly half of all of the victims of assault, robbery, burglary, and larcenies of over $50 did not report the incident to the police. In the case of larcenies under $50, the unreported percentage rose to 80. The report contains the following revelation: "For commercial crimes burglary was up to 12 times more common in some cities than robbery, business burglary was, in general, at least three times more likely than household burglary, and business robbery up to 10 times more likely in some cities as personal robbery."[10]

The LEAA findings showed, for example, that in 1972, in Atlanta, Georgia, of each 1000 business establishments, 741 were burglarized and 157 robbed. In that same city, during that same year, of each 1000 households, 161 were burglarized and 102 were victims of a larceny. Detroit, Michigan, figures were comparable. Of each 1000 commercial establishments, 650 were burglarized and 170 were the target of robberies in 1972. An equal number of Detroit households suffered 174 burglaries and 106 larcenies. New York, Chicago, and Los Angeles were revealed to be statistically safer environments for business than Atlanta, Detroit, Baltimore, St. Louis, Portland, and Denver. In making these survey results public, Donald B. Santorelli, then director of LEAA, was quoted as saying that "for the first time in history, we now have an accurate measure of crime in America, at least in these cities."[11]

To these new statistics must be added the fact that, on a percentage basis, far fewer crimes against business are solved than are those of other categories. This can be inferred from the speech of Attorney General William Saxbe on September 23, 1974, to the International Association of Chiefs of Police. Speaking of cases "cleared" by law enforcement agencies for the year 1973, he announced the rate to be 21 percent of serious crimes. By definition, the clearance rate is the rate of arrests compared with the number of crimes committed. What Saxbe was saying was that for each 100 instances of reported serious crime, 21 arrests were made. The term "cleared," of course, does not mean that the arrested individual was actually convicted of the crime. In 1973 the clearance rate for murder was 79 percent; for aggravated assault, 63 percent; for rape, 51 percent; but for robbery it drops to 27 percent.

Logically, clearance rates are higher for crimes of violence because of the more numerous instances where the victim knows the assailant and furnishes leads to the investigating officers. Even in murder cases, where the victim is silenced, his address book and his friends are classic sources of clues for the homicide detectives.

Two major forces are brought to bear on the enormous rate of crime against business: the police and the private security guard. The army of public law enforcement agents—the sworn police—totaled 395,000 in 1969. This total included all the local police—those employed by cities, towns, villages, counties—as well as state police and highway patrols, and, in addition, all federal law enforcement agents.[12]

In the second force in 1969, working mostly for business, were an estimated 289,900 private security guards, plus some 120,000 "public (government) guards—all governments."[13] These guards, employed by governmental agencies, performed functions identical to the private security guards used by private business. The total manpower arrayed against the armies of crime in 1969, then, numbered 804,000, less than half of whom were public law enforcement officers. More recent estimates indicate the number employed in private security to be far higher. Richard C. Clement, first vice-president of the International Association of Chiefs of Police, and Chief of Police of Dover Township, New Jersey, said in a speech at the Annual Convention of the IACP in September, 1974, that private security personnel now numbered about one million, twice the number of those involved in public law enforcement.[14] The Office of Human Resources of Illinois circulated an equally high figure in a paper proposing a study to consider the licensing and regulation of private security in Illinois. "Private security personnel," it said, "outnumbers sworn public police four to one nationally and it is estimated in Illinois the number is at least three times the latter."[15] Early in 1974, in a memorandum distributed to members of the IACP Committee on Private Security, the assistant director of its research division, James A. F. Kelly, forecast that by 1990, private security would employ 1,431,000 individuals, as opposed to 775,000 law enforcement officers.

Conflicts in obtaining an accurate census are reflected in the cost estimates for private security. The total bill for all enforcement, both public and private, for the year 1969, has been estimated to be $8.7 billion: $4.4 billion for public law enforcement; $1 billion for public (government) guards; and the remaining $3.3 billion for private sector security.[16] The widely divergent estimates on the number of private security employees made since 1971 are all markedly higher than the one on which this 1969 cost estimate was figured. On the basis of the LEAA Census Bureau study on victimization, earlier estimates on the economic impact of crime—noted at the beginning of this chapter—will have to be reassessed.

A conservative reappraisal suggests that the burden of crime to the business world is in excess of all previously discussed statistics. In addition, those figures, which ranged from $16 billion to $20 billion annually, did not include the cost of insurance against the hazards involved. Earned premiums on burglary insurance alone amounted to almost $100 million in 1969.[17] According to my own calculations, the true cost of crime to American business—including the cost of internal auditors and through business taxes their share of support of both official law enforcement agencies and the criminal justice system (involving prosecutors, courts, and correctional institutions)—is in excess of $50 billion a year, an amount equal to more than 5 percent of the annual gross national product.

For years law enforcement and the criminal justice system have been under the magnifying glass of public scrutiny. They have been the subject of presidential commissions, political campaigns, editorial proddings, and research projects at universities and colleges. LEAA, alone, distributed more than $2 billion for the prevention and re- duction of crime in the last four years. By comparison, little is known of private security. During the entire period of soaring crime rates and losses to business, only two studies of real import were under- taken. The results of the first were presented by the Small Business Administration at hearings before the Select Committee on Small Business of the United States Senate in May and July of 1969.[18] The second was performed by the Rand Corporation and was financed by LEAA; the results were published in December, 1971.[19] LEAA sponsored the publication in 1973 of *The Source Book of Criminal Justice Statistics*. It contains 490 pages of statistics and data. Only two pages have material on private security. Despite numerous recom- mendations in the Rand study for further and continuing inquiry in the field, no funds have been forthcoming and no studies have been made under LEAA's, or any other group's, sponsorship.

Recognized or not, the private security sector blankets the nation from coast to coast. It exists in the metropolis, the suburbs, and in rural America. It thrives in the affluent "Gold Coasts" as well as in the ghettos and slums.

The largest part of private security is the full- or part-time direct employees of individual business establishments assigned to security functions. They are referred to in the industry as "in-house" em- ployees, as distinct from the "contract" guards who are not direct employees of the firm whose assets they are assigned to protect. Con- tract guards are modern mercenaries whose employers are the con- tract guard agencies, but whose individual services are purchased or rented. Contract guard agencies are sometimes called "rent-a-guard" agencies. That $3.3 billion estimate for private security in 1969 was subdivided as follows: $1.6 billion for in-house private guards and investigators; $920 million for security devices and alarms; $620 million for contract guards and investigation services; and $120 million for armored car services.[20]

The $1.6 billion for in-house staff reflects the employment of 220,400 individuals—198,500 of them assigned as guards and the balance, 23,900 as investigators or detectives.[21] This in-house group consists mostly of those employed by retail establishments, who, as guards and detectives, made approximately 500,000 arrests each year.[22] In many cases they process these arrests directly into the criminal justice system, with little or no intervention by official law enforcement agents.

The second largest sum spent, some $920 million, was for alarms, security devices, and machinery. All of these are designed to supplement or assist guards in preventing losses. The greatest part of these security devices are used and paid for directly by the business client, whether or not he employs an in-house staff or contract guards. Of the $920 million, $120 million was allocated for Central Station Protective Services. These are alarm systems, either automatically triggered or manually set off, that are connected by owned or leased wires to a manned central station. When an alarm is sounded, the central station notifies the police, and in some areas also has its own men respond. This service is regarded as the top of the line. The remaining $800 million spent for security machinery, equipment, and devices went for all of the other alarm contrivances which sound locally, flash lights, ring bells, and often activate automatic dialers that dial a preset telephone number and then deliver a pretaped message. The alarm devices include those triggered by pressure, magnetics, ultrasonics, and laser beams. The security machinery includes such mundane items as locks and fences and massive vaults. Other items of consequence are two-way radios, closed circuit television, and time-sequence cameras.

In 1969 there were 4,280 separate contract guard and investigative agencies doing business in the United States,[23] nearly four times the number of such firms in 1954. These 4,280 firms employed 67,500 full-time individuals: 8,100 were listed as investigators, and 59,400 as guards.[24] Despite the large number of such contract, rent-a-guard companies, the five largest firms (Pinkerton's, Inc.; William J. Burns International Detective Agency ; Wackenhut Corporation; Walter Kidde & Company (Globe Security Systems); and Wells Fargo Security Guards-Baker Industries, Inc.), did more then half of this segment's total billing. Their combined share amounted to 51 percent in 1967 and 1968, and grew to 53 percent in 1969.[25]

Guards and investigators, whether they are in-house or employed by contract agencies, generally perform the same function. Many companies use a combination of in-house and contract security. In such instances, supervisory employees and investigators are part of the in-house staff, and their services are supplemented by contract guards.

The remaining major function of the contract private security sector is that of the armored car industry, which, in 1969, did a business of $128 million and employed 10,000 full- and part-time workers.[26] This business involves the transfer of cash and other valuables in armored vehicles. Point-to-point delivery of items of value by a courier is also included. Unlike the guard and investigative branch of the industry, there is little or no division into in-house and contract segments. Only a handful of private companies operate their own armored cars.

Lower insurance rates are a key inducement for a business to use armored car services. Valuables moved in this manner are covered by the armored car's own insurance. A loss, therefore, is recoverable through the armored car carrier and does not affect the user's own deductible or insurance profile. In 1967 there were 344 armored car companies in the country. One of them, Brinks, Inc., a division of Pittston, did more than half of the total volume of business.[27]

All authorities agree that we have no solid figures on financial losses due to crime. The known indexes have all reflected a rapid increase. But even these known indexes do not account for the fact that some 50 percent of all crime has been and remains unreported. Clearly, the walls manned by both public and private security against criminal attack are insufficient. The breaches in security are widening and allowing the losses to increase. Fraud is among the many widening cracks. Each year, fraudulent insurance claims total $1.5 billion. It has been estimated that 10 percent of all insurance claims are dishonest and that they are responsible for 15 percent of premium charges. Other widening cracks are embezzlement and pilferage. Together they represent billions of dollars a year in losses, exceeding those due to robbery and burglary. Even in the banking system, fraud is said to have been a prime factor in the failure of some 100 banks in a 20-year period. Overall, 30 percent of all business failures each year are caused by employee dishonesty.[28]

Private security is a muchly overlooked resource that can and should be more closely tailored to combatting crime. Business losses and costs cannot be solved by merely releasing more money and men into the morass of doubtful statistics. Much of what is being done in this field is misunderstood and misdirected by leaders of business and government, and is wasteful of money and manpower. The aim of this volume is to clarify the extent and potential of the business of private security.

2 | Security Before 1830

No demarcations existed between the security groups of the ancients. Military, public, and private security needs have common roots. The security function seems to have had its beginnings with the need of the nomadic tribes to protect their flocks from marauding animals and to receive warnings of attack by warlike neighbors. The passage of time saw the duties of these guards take on more significance in the welfare of the tribes. The Bible reports the use of a guard or watchman: *shomer,* a word still in use in modern Hebrew. In Psalm 127, the power of a watchman is belittled when viewed in relation to the power of the Mightiest:

> Except the Lord build the house, they labor in vain that built it; except the Lord keep the city, the watchman waketh but in vain.

As early rules of kinship became tribal laws, with retribution and blood feuds, "an eye for an eye," there was an increasing need for the security of the clan and its encampment and for a force to uphold the rule of vengeance. These needs required armed men. The military to this day retains the function of peace-keeping, although that duty is now thought of as most appropriately fulfilled by police and private security.

Historically, security forces also had to protect the king and his treasures. In ancient Egypt there were the feared Mamelukes. Rome had its Praetorian Guard. Far later, the early sultans were closely watched by their Janissaries.

As tribes became nations, the small rulers became kings and emperors. Trade developed between them. Along with the business of government grew the business of commerce. Early chronicles of travel and trade in the caravels of ancient Phoenicia and in the caravans of the desert contain references to watchmen and guards.

Under the Romans and their Byzantine offshoot elaborate codes of law were brought into being. The equivalent of a police force was established from the ranks of the imperial soldiers. The hordes who overran Rome had no such detailed rules, or special forces to carry them out. The Western world slipped into the Dark Ages. Meanwhile, in the East the use of centrally imposed laws of conduct continued under the new religion of Islam. These laws, and the men who administered them, were primarily concerned with the subjugation and control of the conquered. Another security system, the use of eunuchs to protect the concubines, the wives, and the daughters of the rulers and the wealthy, is also related in stories of those times.

In the West, the Dark Ages saw the commingling of security functions, so that they were often carried out by one person describable today as one who wears many hats. The security guard was at once soldier, public policeman, and private guard. These different roles became sorted out over the centuries, and insofar as the public police are to be concerned, two different systems evolved: one in the common law environment of the British Isles and the other in the civil case environment of the Continent. These two systems are important because they affected the development of private security.

After the fall of Rome, there was a resurgence across its old empire in the West of the rules of kinship, of blood feuds, and of revenge. The killing of a member of a clan or a tribe resulted in a blood feud that required the surviving members to repay the wrong by committing an act of equal or greater scope on the wrongdoer, or on a member of his group. Clan or tribal guards were, from a modern point of view, multifunctional: soldier, watchman, and guard.

This communal responsibility took a different turn in Anglo-Saxon England prior to the Conquest of 1066. A system of "frank pledge" had evolved under which people were banded into groups of 10, with each member of the group jointly answerable in blood and in damages for the good behavior of the others. This system was imposed by the rulers to quiet private feuds and tribal wars, and was deemed superior to the calls for tribal or family revenge, blood oaths, and general scourging. It imposed peace, "the King's Peace." The Tens were later bound together in groups of Tens (10 Tens), and thus became Hundreds. These were later associated territorially, based on the boundaries of the ancient kingdoms, which still later took on the name of "shires." Eventually, the shire-reeve, the officer appointed by the king with the responsibility for keeping peace in the shire, had his title compressed to "sheriff." The Norman conquerors kept this system and added to it. An officer was designated to be responsible for suppressing violent crime and riot in each Hundred. He was called "constable," and he with the sheriff were direct ancestors of the modern sworn police.

The feudal period saw the emergence of some lords and barons as stronger and wealthier than their peers. Their increasing number of retainers, men-at-arms, tax collectors, clerks, and other personal servants spilled out beyond the walled castles. Towns began to grow with houses built mainly of wood, or sod, and thatched roofs. Fire, so necessary to life, and so difficult to contain, was a constant threat to communal existence. The night fire watch that came into being to guard against that hazard, served also to assist the security of the castle.

As towns expanded, new classes came into being, especially merchants and artisans. These groups banded themselves together in associations for their mutual benefit. The guilds, as these associations were known, in addition to rules governing membership, apprenticeship, and business practices, had mutual-aid programs. One such program asked for joint contributions on behalf of a member required to pay "weregeld," a payment in lieu of a blood feud. Others called for all members to help rebuild after a loss by fire, to pay for prayers for the dead, and to attend funerals. These mutual-aid programs became enlarged, so that all members contributed to make good the loss by one from robbery or shipwreck. The guild members united to perform the duty of watching their contiguous property in the heart of these medieval towns, serving as watchmen themselves, later assigning their apprentices, and thereafter hiring special guards. In these practices are the visible roots of both modern insurance and private security. As the need to suppress crime and disorder increased, the number of constables was increased. By his Statute of Winchester, Edward I in 1285 decreed that there should be two constables for every Hundred. These would serve without pay. His statute also provided for a regular system of night patrols, and required the assistance of all persons, under penalty of fine or imprisonment, to join in the pursuit of a felon when a "hue and cry" was raised. Every man was required to serve as a constable, though many merely paid lip service to the rule and employed substitutes. The quality of these substitutes was inferior, in that they were selected from the least capable workers, those who could be spared most easily from their regular tasks.

In many of its cities on the Continent, the guild system was as strong as it was in England. But while Edward I was decreeing an unpaid increase in the number of constables, King Philip I of France, not long afterwards, was starting a system of paid royal officers, independent of the judicial system, and answerable to him for the enforcement of laws against crime and riot. This group evolved by the middle of the fourteenth century into a formal military police, the *maréchaussée,* with nationwide power and jurisdiction. By the mid-eighteenth century, these forces were known as the *gendarmerie,* a national police force, carefully organized down to a block or small sectional level. There were *inspecteurs de police,* one for each *quartier,* regular detectives, functionaries, and a system of spies and paid informants. These were backed up by foot and mounted soldiers, separate from the regular troops, which could also be called up when needed.

These police forces in France operated on both a criminal and political level. If it had a political connotation, the most casual remark was reported. Landlords of hotels and lodging houses were required to furnish particulars on each visitor on the day the visitor arrived. Brothel keepers and prostitutes had to deliver reports on their customers and their idiosyncracies. The word *dossier* took on a special meaning. Corruption became rampant in this police system before the Revolution. *Inspecteurs de police* with official salaries of 4000 livres a year, were becoming millionaires through payoffs or through an interest in or control of gambling.

Under such a system there was little need for private security. Whatever private security did exist was compelled to act for the regular police. It was cheaper for those who required special protection to hire or bribe the regular police. Only the very wealthiest of the nobility were able to keep retainers who functioned as guards. The function of the police system of France was disrupted by the Revolution, but it survived nonetheless. In 1796 it came under the control of Fouché, who remained at its helm until after Napoleon's defeat at Waterloo in 1815. Under his direction it surpassed in pervasiveness its operations during the *ancien régime,* and played an important role in maintaining Napoleon's empire while he and the armies of France were engaged in wars over the breadth of Europe.

Many of the principalities of Europe set up police systems which followed the pattern of the French. They also used soldiers to help enforce the laws and keep their rulers secure. Some of these principalities had a surplus of trained men and officers, and many a prince found that he could market these men to the benefit of his treasury. Evidence of the rent-a-regiment business is found in the American Revolution in the use of Hessian troops by the British. The use of mercenaries was not then a recent invention. Evidence of such use exists as far back as ancient Greece. The best-known vestiges of the practice are the Swiss Guards, still employed to perform ceremonial guard functions at the Vatican. Their use by the popes predates the painting of the Sistine Chapel by Michelangelo, who designed the famous uniforms still worn by these guards. As rented, uniformed guards, these mercenaries were collateral ancestors of the modern contract guard.

England remained far behind the Continent in the development of public police. Though individual monarchs and their civil servants employed networks of informants, there was no civil force of police other than the sheriffs and constables. After the Restoration under Charles II in the seventeenth century, Paliament authorized a civil force of 1000 night watchmen, first called "bellmen" and almost as promptly nicknamed "Charlies." These constables, together with the military forces when needed, were the arms of law and order. Few constables served in person, nearly all appointing deputies, who were paid so miserably that it was said of them that "the office has fallen into the hands of the lowest class of retailers and costermongers who make up the deficient allowance of their principals by indirect sources of emolument, by winking at offenses they ought to prevent."[1]

The "Charlies" and their successors for the next century and a quarter were incapable of controlling a rising and blatant crime wave. Robbery and violence were rampant everywhere. Highwaymen infested the country roads, and exploits of men like Dick Turpin are still remembered in song and story. Rather than a sanctuary for the traveler, inns and hotels were often run by criminals, and thus served as a perfect place for a robbery. In London organized gangs of criminals became so powerful and operated so openly that the ransoming of stolen goods was a generally recognized procedure. This type of crime reached its zenith in the activities of Jonathan Wild. Under his generalship, the business of theft for ransom made him a millionaire in the coin then in use, and by modern standards, a multimillionaire. Most of the thieves of London brought their loot to him for fencing. His offices in a street called Old Bailey were known throughout the city, and victims would come there to buy back their own property. Competing thieves, or fences, were turned over to the courts by Wild, who thereupon immediately claimed rewards for their capture. There is no doubt that many of the constables of the period were members of the Wild organization.

Not surprisingly, persons who could afford it were compelled to hire their own watchmen, guards, and other protectors. These were private security employees in every sense of the word. Security devices of the period were utilized and man-traps and spring guns were installed on many an estate. The rich suffered less than the other classes, but even so the fortified strength of their houses and the protection of their armed servants did not allow them to escape unscathed.[2] Ample evidence exists that many of the so-called trusted servants and watchmen, in cahoots with thieves, engineered robberies.[3] It required no imagination for the thieves and fences who were paid to return what they had stolen, to take the next step and be paid for not stealing from certain businesses in the first place. This technique expanded into organized extortion and blackmail, and the banks of London were major victims.[4] Attempts were made to arrest and prosecute the most notorious of these criminals. Unfortunately, key trials in the early years of the eighteenth century resulted in acquittals because the prosecution failed to prove all elements of the crime as required under common law.

The intolerable situation was debated on many occasions by Parliament, whose reaction was to increase the severity of punishment for proscribed acts. A long list of crimes, including some now considered minor misdemeanors, became capital offenses. Increasing the severity of punishment failed to halt the rising crime rate, however. On two separate occasions Parliament passed laws aimed at Wild's fencing activities. Stymied only temporarily, he changed his tactics and became a "self-nominated quasi-public police department."[5] He would, for an agreed upon reward and receipt of a detailed description of the stolen property, undertake to locate it and restore it to its owner. This approach was also the target of an act of Parliament in 1718, under which Wild, after three trials, was eventually convicted and hanged in 1725.[6]

Contemporary descriptions of that underworld appeared in *The Beggar's Opera* and in Henry Fielding's novel, *Tom Jones.* Fielding's knowledge of the situation was acquired firsthand as magistrate at Bow Street in London. He and his brother John, who succeeded to that office after Henry's death, were among the leaders of reformers seeking to improve the police, judicial, and correctional systems of the time. Officers of their particular court, called "Bow Street Runners," were probably the only trained police officers in England at the time. The next magistrate on that bench, Patrick Colquhoun, suggested changes that were to be instituted two decades later. In one of his works, a *Treatise on the Police of the Metropolis,* printed in London in 1797, Colquhoun discusses the French system of national police and then rejects it as unsuitable for England. In this conclusion he was joined by most of the other reformers.

By the start of the nineteenth century, it was estimated that one out of every 22 people living in England was a professional criminal.[7] But the cumulative effects of a massive crime rate and the urgings of reformers were beginning to yield results. Distinguished legal scholars credit the last two decades of the eighteenth century with producing the most rapid and extensive growth of the entire English law on theft.[8] In part these new laws set the stage for the introduction of modern police. Enforcement is but one part of the criminal justice system. It is effective only when it is coordinated with the balance of the system: the law, the courts, and the correctional institutions. Otherwise, efforts at enforcing the law are in vain.

The early part of the nineteenth century found a criminal situation in England being fought by a futile constable organization based on underpaid, untrained, and often corrupt individuals. The private watchmen and guards employed by the wealthy and the businessmen increased to the point of being regarded as "an incidental civil force."[9] The status among the private security guards themselves varied, some having semi-official standing as constables. Corruption reached well into their ranks, too. Magistrate Colquhoun noted that nine-tenths of all the crimes committed along London's busy waterfront were by persons whose presence in the area was essential or justified, and he listed them as "watchmen, sailors, revenue officers and so forth." He noted that stolen goods were being transported in the same watermen's barges that did the regular loading and unloading of ships.[10] Another contemporary author said most robberies of warehouses and houses were "put up ones," committed by those employed or domesticated on the premises—a charge that included the private watchmen. The Bow Street Runners were often hired or paid by private interests, and police offices became police markets where individual officers were sought out and engaged to do what were essentially private security tasks. It was against this background that Parliament, in 1829, passed legislation that enabled the founding of what has grown to be London's Metropolitan Police System. We in the United States still have not resolved the problem of sworn police moonlighting on private security jobs, or the quandary of deputizing private guards.

Stepping back in time to follow security requirements on the western shores of the Atlantic, we find novel problems: frontiers and Indians. In Virginia, Captain John Smith, and in the Massachusetts Bay Colony, Captain Miles Standish, took their places as captains of the guard—the watch. The Dutch watch system, established in Niew Amsterdam, was transformed into an English system when the city became New York. Frontier life prompted a plan of self-help and mutual aid. The settler went to his field with his musket, and the nearby stockade sounded a cannon, bell, or gong to notify the entire community of danger. That call was answered by all. This system moved with the frontier on its course westward.

Some 80 years after it was first founded, in 1699, the Colony of Massachusetts formally legislated the creation of a regular "night watch." It was to operate from nine o'clock in the evening until the first light of the next day. The years that followed saw other large settlements along the seaboard adopt similar legislation. The spreading and moving frontier continued to maintain their sentries, or security patrols, on a voluntary basis. It was not unusual for wealthier settlers to use an employee, or even a bond servant, for that purpose. As larger cities came into being, their increasing business and its risks led to the creation of daytime guards, operating under the heading of "the ward." Friction was often the result of the fact that this group was usually controlled independently of the night watch.

The basic laws of the colonies were the laws of England, and these were well established by 1775. The courts of the new States were rooted in common law. Precedent, needed as a basis of argument or ruling, remained as it was before the Revolution. Recourse to reported citations from English law continued to be used, as it is to this very day. This continuity with English law prompted an active interest by American lawyers and lawmakers in the changing criminal laws and rulings in England, particularly the growth of laws on theft at the end of the eighteenth century. Scholars report that the statutes of the new States followed these new laws of England, which were copied and enacted almost without change.[11]

The French type of national police and its ramifications were also well known to many Americans who helped formulate the legal structure of the Republic. Benjamin Franklin, John Adams, Thomas Jefferson, and others had their personal experiences with the system during the periods in which they lived in France. Like their English counterparts, they never indicated any desire to install a similar system. The drive for local autonomy, implicit in the separate colonies and carried over into their successor states, also mitigated any consideration of a national police. But continued growth of American metropolitan areas, fed by commerce and industry and a steady flow of immigrants, brought changes by the 1820s. Crime in the cities had become a problem in the United States. It was one that continued to fester and it resulted, finally, in the adaptation of enabling laws that created police organizations roughly similar to the one started in London by Sir Robert Peel in 1829.

The southern colonies and their successor states, with their plantation systems, had special security problems connected with the capital investment in slavery. It was important to confine the movement of these slaves because this investment could indeed "walk away." The South was also haunted by the specter of slave revolts similar to those that had occurred in the Caribbean islands. Overseers and trusted slaves were used on individual plantations as guards over the others. Cooperative security patrols were organized by contiguous plantation owners. These patrols, and their leaders, were later given official or quasi-official status by deputization.

Thus, by 1830 in England, and within a decade or so thereafter in the United States, the beginnings of a separation of the security function into two spheres of responsibility were taking place. Public police departments, with their sworn duties, were charged with maintaining law and order. The burden of security for private property and personal safety thereon had to be redefined. The world of private security was to be limited.

3 | Private Security and the First Police Century: 1830 to World War II

The police force that was started in London in 1829 met with success. Its sponsors were pleased, and similar systems were installed in the other major cities of England, Scotland, and Wales. The political concessions made to obtain the legislation and appropriations that the new police would not carry firearms did not prove to be a handicap. Similar city police departments were started late in the next decade on the Continent in many of the principalities that later united as Germany.

The Georgian period, with its excesses, gave way to the strict public morality that marked the reign of Queen Victoria. The new police profited. Their exploits made good copy for the newspapers, and stories about them and their successes made them and their nicknames, at first "Peelers" and then "Bobbies" (after Sir Robert Peel, who was credited with their creation and early direction), household words.

The establishment of an effective sworn police system, however, did not lead to the automatic disbanding of private security. Watchmen continued to be employed in banks, countinghouses, factories, and on the docks. On the roads, the practice of arming coach drivers gradually disappeared. Servants returned their weapons to the household armory, and private security adapted itself to the new era of comparative law and order. The self-help of private security was replaced by a call for the attendance and attention of the sworn police.

In the United States the early part of the nineteenth century, after the end of the War of 1812 with England, was a period of expansion. Rivers and lakes—natural travel routes—were joined by canals and served to increase trade between the cities of the coast and the interior. This trade fed an import and export business with the rest of the world. The goods so moved needed protection, however, and watchmen were put on the barges, the docks, and at the canal locks. The new railroads, which developed and spread quickly, followed suit, employing men to watch the equipment and the freight it carried.

In 1844 the legislature of the State of New York passed a law enabling the City of New York to have a consolidated "day and night police." It was the first organized police department in North America. In the next ten years, similar departments were created in Boston, Philadelphia, Chicago, New Orleans, St. Louis, Baltimore, Newark and Providence. In 1856 New York and Philadelphia required that their men wear distinctive, standard uniforms.

There was then no national police force in the United States. There is none now. At the time New York State took its action, there were no Federal investigative agencies with nationwide jurisdiction. The United States Secret Service did not come into being until the end of the Civil War in 1865. The Federal Bureau of Investigation did not get its start until the end of the first decade of the twentieth century. Only the Customs Service had anything like coast-to-coast jurisdiction. That service had its start shortly after the beginning of the Republic, but its jurisdiction was confined almost entirely to the borders.

In the South, protection of slave property became important. Among the pressing political questions of the early nineteenth century were how to contain slavery in the states that recognized it, and, conversely, how to bar it from the territories that were asking for admission as states. The Missouri Compromise of 1820, which drew a horizontal line of slave and free territory across the nation, increased the efforts of the Abolitionists, who aided and sheltered escaping slaves on their route to the North, and on to Canada.

Insofar as the slave owners were concerned, these escapes had to be countered. They were a direct loss of a capital investment. Allowing a trickle of escaping slaves to become a flood would have marked their economic ruin, and left them with fields they could not cultivate.

The South's lobbies fought in the Congress for Fugitive Slave Laws to compel the return of their property and to penalize those who aided in its theft, or knowingly harbored the contraband. Their lawyers vigorously pursued their remedies in the courts, and the Dred Scott Decision was a landmark case in defining these rights.

But laws and adjudications were valueless north of the Mason-Dixon Line unless there was machinery to run down the escaping slaves as well as those who harbored them. To do this, a network of private investigators, motivated by monetary considerations, came into being. They operated for the slave owners, paying for information and rewarding informers. Depending upon the point of view, they were either ruthless headhunters, living on the backs of those yearning for freedom, or paid investigators earning an honest living. The Abolitionists and their newspapers tried to identify and expose these private investigators in the Northern communities, but not all of them were compelled to surface. Front men were often utilized to make the necessary court appearances, while the true investigator or informant stayed well in the background. Despite all of the searching interest in the Civil War period, scholars have skimmed over this pragmatic aspect of the South's efforts to retain or recover its slave property. There has only been conjecture on the use of this network of paid agents and informants as part of the espionage system that operated in the North on behalf of the Confederacy during the Civil War.

With police departments before the Civil War confined to the very largest cities, the rest of the country relied on its private security resources. The discovery of gold in California in 1848, and other precious metals later in Nevada and Colorado, required the immediate hiring of armed guard-watchmen. They were used at the mines, the vaults, and while the specie was in transit.

Private enterprise responded to the obvious need for security. Companies engaged in the business of carrying valuables and money came into being in the 1830s. Later, they began to carry other goods as well. They were known as express companies. Several such companies, under the leadership of Henry Wells as president, and William G. Fargo as secretary, joined together and formed an unincorporated association in March, 1850, known as the American Express Company.[1] Two years later, without giving up their interests in, or positions with American Express, Wells and Fargo started a second company, doing a similar business in the Far West. They gave the new venture their own names: Wells Fargo and Company. In the years that followed, the new company and American Express operated under a working agreement in which Wells Fargo had all of the business west of the Missouri River and American Express the balance east of it. Three quarters of a century later, Wells Fargo and Company came under American Express control.[2] The other big security-express company of that era was Adams Express. When gold was first discovered in California, Adams Express was the only stable organization undertaking to deliver it to the East. It was to compete with Adams in this new lucrative field that Wells Fargo was started.

Not surprisingly, the very existence of these companies, and the knowledge that they carried cash, bullion and other valuables, attracted the attention of thieves. With such attacks came the need for defense as well as for investigators. "Riding shotgun" was the terse description of the guard with a gun on his lap who rode alongside the stage driver. The need for security was accelerated by the discovery of gold in the west. These express companies, who invested their money and efforts in such faraway places as the Mother Lode country of California, were also actively pursuing markets in the fast-growing industrializing areas of the East. Railroads, with their rapidly multiplying miles of tracks, were becoming the principal haulers of freight and people. The express companies utilized railroad facilities from the very beginning, and their messengers and safes rode the roads. Express cars, entirely devoted to their needs, and later built to express company specifications, came into being. In this manner the problems of railroad security and express company security often coincided. Both had need for investigative help. The newly created sworn police served mainly in metropolitan areas, and their jurisdiction was strictly limited to their own territory. The local sheriff usually an elected, untrained official, was also restricted to county and state jurisdictions, and by the practical consideration that the taxpayers of his locality were not going to support his activities elsewhere. There were no Federal agents who could be of help. The private detective came forward to fill this need.

Illustrative of the rise of private security in America is the history of Allan Pinkerton and the company he started. Born in Scotland in 1819, apprenticed as a cooper, he set himself up in Scotland in the business of making barrels when he was but 19 years old. Four years later, with a newly acquired wife, he emigrated to Canada, but changed his mind en route and ended up in Chicago instead.

After a year as an employee, Pinkerton started his own barrel-making business in Dundee, Kane County, Illinois, some 38 miles from Chicago. According to some accounts, while searching for trees suitable for use as barrel staves on a nearby island, he came upon evidence of the operations of a counterfeiting gang. Currency was not issued by the United States Government then, but by state banks, which had the problem of combatting counterfeiters. (The first United States Government issue of paper money occurred during the Civil War in the printing of the so-called greenbacks and led to the start of the U.S. Secret Service in 1865.)

Pinkerton made contact with the local sheriff and the bank involved. He was instrumental in the capture of both the counterfeiters and their printing plant. There is no record of how the bank expressed its gratitude, but shortly afterward, he was appointed Deputy Sheriff of Kane County. Within the year he switched to a similar post, with the same title, in Chicago. This work was obviously more remunerative than manufacturing barrels.

In 1849 Pinkerton was appointed Chicago's first detective. In addition to real ability, Pinkerton had a flair for attracting a good press. Sometime in 1850, he started on his own as a private detective, and in 1853, was the subject of a story in the penny newspapers describing his ability, efficiency, and courage. It also told of his having been injured by an unknown gunman whose two shots lodged in Pinkerton's arm.[3] One early employer of Pinkerton's talents was the United States Post Office, and the story of his arresting a postal clerk and recovering $4,000 stolen from the mail made news. The article said that Pinkerton had no superior as a detective in this country, and doubted if he had an equal.[4]

Pinkerton, in the United States, was not the first private detective. In Europe, Eugene Francois Vidocq had started his private detective agency in 1832 in Paris. Vidocq, whose career began as a common police informer, later became a police officer and rose to the top of the French Police under Fouché. This was in 1811. He remained a senior French police official for almost two decades. His memoirs, published in France in 1829, was a best seller; translated into English, it enjoyed enormous popularity in both England and the United States. Pinkerton himself was the "author" of 18 books before his death in 1884.[5] The Police Gazette, which was started in 1845, was also a vehicle for many stories in praise of Pinkerton, his men, and their exploits.

By 1853 Pinkerton's Agency had a staff of five full-time detectives (one a woman), a secretary, and several clerks. He had arrived at the right time and place. Railroads had expanded faster then public law enforcement agencies, and local gangs were stealing more and more of their property. The railroads chose Pinkerton to help them cope with the situation. His contract with the Illinois Central Railroad, dated February 1, 1855, was for a retainer of $10,000 a year to guard their property and rolling stock.[6] Illinois Central was by no means his only client. The list included the Michigan Central; Michigan Southern and Northern Indiana; Chicago and Galena Union; Chicago and Rock Island; Chicago, Burlington and Quincy; and the United States Post Office. Each of his railroad clients issued free passes over their line to Pinkerton and his men.

In January, 1857, George Brinton McClellan, an engineer and West Point graduate recently returned from the Crimea, where he had been the United States Military Observer with the British Army, became vice-president and engineer in chief of the Illinois Central. From their first meeting, Pinkerton and McClellan started a close business and social friendship. Pinkerton also had some meetings with an attorney from Springfield, Illinois, who did some legal work for the same railroad: Abraham Lincoln. McClellan was later to become commander in chief of the Union Army—and the 1864 Democratic candidate for President defeated by Lincoln.

Lincoln, elected to his first term as President in November of 1860, was to be sworn into office on March 4, 1861. He and his staff were making their way slowly from Illinois to Washington, stopping for political consultations at the large cities along the way. One of the Pinkerton customers was the Pennsylvania Railroad. The president of that road requested Pinkerton to check out rumors of plans to assassinate President-elect Lincoln as he passed through the city of Baltimore en route to his inauguration. Pinkerton's operatives came up with material indicating that such a plot was indeed in the making. Pro-slave state feelings were running so high in Baltimore, that riots could easily be triggered should Lincoln proceed through its streets with the usual fanfare due his position. Such a riot would be an ideal cover-up for an assassination attempt. Vulnerability was increased by the fact that the Pennsylvania line did not traverse the city; passengers continuing south had to leave the northern terminus and proceed by foot or carriage across most of the city to the southern terminus.

With this information, Pinkerton accompanied the president of the Pennsylvania Railroad to Harrisburg in order to intercept Lincoln and his party, which had stopped there for a political function. A meeting there resulted in the President-elect, accompanied only by his secretary, John Nicolay, Pinkerton, and one of Pinkerton's operatives, proceeding to Baltimore on a train other than the announced one.

The transfer in Baltimore took place without incident. Word-of-mouth embroideries of the event erroneously had Lincoln slipping through Baltimore disguised as a woman.

The Civil War was not long in coming. Trained Army officers were welcomed back into uniform by both sides, and George McClellan was commissioned a general and given command of the Union Department of Ohio. He called on his railroad detective friend, Pinkerton, to assist him in the area of intelligence. It was not long before Pinkerton was a member of McClellan's staff, in full charge of the Ohio area.

When McClellan moved to take command of the Army of the Potomac, Pinkerton, with a brevetted rank of major, was taken along and put in full charge of all intelligence activities. In this capacity he is credited with the establishment of the Union's spy system in the South. It was created around a nucleus of his detective agency employees, informants, and contacts.

McClellan is recorded by history as an admirable organizer of armies. It also records him as being most reluctant to engage his forces unless he had assurances through intelligence of his own superiority in men and position. Historical hindsight indicates that he was often fooled; he claimed superiority for the enemy that did not exist. This was especially true after the Battle of Antietam, where an aggressive offensive by his army might have shortened the war. Lincoln relieved McClellan of command in early 1863. Pinkerton did not continue his services on behalf of the North; instead, he returned to his prewar private detective business.

Pinkerton's wartime record and contacts—along with the reputation and contacts he had gained before the war—helped him prosper. He was also helped by enormous publicity in solving thefts from Adams Express. Before the war the Adams Express Company, headquartered in New York, had been referred to Pinkerton by another private detective from New York. Adam Express wanted him to track down a missing package containing $40,000 that had disappeared from a train between Montgomery, Alabama, and Augusta, Georgia. Pinkerton had been able to prove that the thief was the Adams manager in Augusta, and in dramatic fashion recovered almost all the loot. Adams Express Company had joined the growing list of clients who retained Pinkerton and his organization, which by the start of hostilities in 1861 had grown to a staff of 15 investigators.

When he left Federal service, Pinkerton found that his old business contacts were still there. Many had prospered, and to serve them better Pinkerton began to expand, opening offices in New York City in 1866 and in Philadelphia a year later. In January, 1866, Adams Express Company was the victim of a $700,000 robbery in cash, bonds, and jewels taken from a safe in a locked company railcar attached to a local train making numerous stops between Rye, New York, and New Haven, Connecticut. Dogged inspection of every foot of the right-of-way by Pinkerton investigators disclosed that the thieves must have jumped from the moving train after throwing out their loot near the village of Cos Cob, Connecticut. The Pinkerton men found a bag containing $5,000 in coins in a patch of weeds near that point. Investigation led to a railroad employee, a brakeman, and then to the entire gang. Pinkerton recovered almost all of the missing valuables. The resultant publicity was commensurate with the size of the robbery.

Postwar industrial expansion, fed by an increasing flow of immigrants, also helped Pinkerton's business. With the growth came labor unrest and movements to organize workers. In the strife that ensued, the use of private security guards to combat efforts to unionize became commonplace. Pinkerton and his company were used by industry, especially the railroads and mining groups.

One particularly vocal—and violent—group in the mining field, for example, was an underground organization known as the Molly Maguires. In the pay of the mine operators, Pinkerton had an undercover agent, James McParland, join the Molly Maguires and live with them from 1873 to 1876. When McParland surfaced to testify against them, they were effectively destroyed as a group.

In the efforts to organize labor, both workers and management used every conceivable ploy, legal and illegal, to gain their end. The protagonists on labor's side were the workingmen, their wives and children. They manned the picket lines and were on occasion responsible for breaking windows, throwing bricks, pulling triggers, and planting dynamite.

On the side of business, the battle was fought by an army of mercenaries. Unlike the rent-a-soldier of the previous century, they wore no uniforms. But like them, they enlisted for a skirmish, a campaign, or a war, and they were the toughest men money could buy. Their field commanders were employees of private security firms. While industry's objectives were defined by the businessman-employer, it was the mercenary who fought for them on the scene of battle.

A landmark confrontation took place in July, 1892, on the Monongahela River at the Homestead Works of the Carnegie Steel Company, not far from Pittsburgh, Pennsylvania. The union, the Amalgamated Association of Iron and Steel Workers, and its predecessor, the Sons of Vulcan, had represented skilled workers at the plant for some time. After a bitter strike in which the workers had effectively barred access to the town of Homestead, repulsing both strikebreakers and sheriff's deputies at the railroad station and on the streets and roads leading into town, management signed a three-year contract due to expire July, 1892; only the skilled workers, some 800 of the 3800 employees, were represented by the union, however.

The Carnegie Company had come under the management of Henry Clay Frick, while Andrew Carnegie was in semiretirement in a castle in Scotland. Frick, citing poor business, refused the union's demand for a renewal of the contract. In fact, he demanded that the men take a cut in their $25-a-week paycheck—and the union offered to take $24. Frick, though, wanted them to take two dollars less. Anticipating difficulties, management had built a stout perimeter fence, topped with barbed wire, around the steel plant. The fence had portholes at regular intervals, and, as a biographer of Carnegie noted: "At strategic elevations platforms had been constructed on which searchlights were placed, another military precaution whose meaning was not lost on the Union men."[7]

Frick had also made appropriate arrangements with the Pinkertons, who had been playing a conspicuous role in labor crises on behalf of big business for several decades. They had been hired to furnish men to protect business properties in the course of some 72 strikes before the Homestead Plant battle. American railroads, for example, had found the Pinkerton "private armies" unfailingly useful in helping solve their labor problems.[8]

The rationale for their use was as follows: Under Anglo-Saxon common law the preservation of order is the responsibility of the sheriff. When necessity arises, the sheriff has the right to impress private citizens to form a kind of quasi-military force called a "posse." This is a relatively ineffective way to get things done, because of the natural reluctance of private citizens to become involved in such thankless and dangerous jobs. A Pinkerton aggregation, however, provided a "posse" without the need of serving writs on reluctant citizens. Two or three hundred professional "watchmen" imported from New York or Chicago could be sworn in as deputies. They were then available to act to prevent disorder as accredited law officers.[9]

Late in June, 1892, the Carnegie company negotiated with the Pinkertons to supply 300 men at $5 a day to be sent to Pittsburgh. The Pinkerton office also shipped 250 Winchester rifles, 300 pistols, and ample ammunition for both to the Union Supply Company, a Carnegie subsidiary in Pittsburgh. Local attorneys for the company asked the sheriff of Allegheny County to deputize the Pinkerton mercenaries, and the sheriff's answer was that he would do so after they had actually taken over custody and protection at the plant. But custody of the plant meanwhile had fallen into the hands of others.

On July 1, when no agreement was reached, the workers seized the plant and its fortifications. Again, as they had done three years before, they set up blockades at the railroad station and across the roads leading to the plant. They also set up a warning system to alert them to any attempt to wrest control of the plant. The mayor of Homestead was a plant employee and a striker. Understandably, management made no request for assistance to him or to any other law enforcement agency. Instead, at Pittsburgh, on July 6 at 2 o'clock in the morning they secretly loaded 300 Pinkerton men, each armed with a Winchester rifle, onto two river barges. They felt that the river avenue of approach was unguarded, and they knew the fortifications on the river side of the plant were minimal. A tug towed the barges on the two-hour run to Homestead.

The secret was not well kept. Estimates of the reception committee waiting at the dock are as high as 10,000. Both sides opened fire. Eight were killed—three Pinkertons and five strikers—and the wounded were many times that number. Abandoned by their tug, which hightailed it back to Pittsburgh, and pinned down by a withering fire, the Pinkertons surrendered. They were then escorted to the railroad station. The march to the station was indeed a gauntlet. According to one description of it, "the chief offenders were women, the wives of Hungarians, Slavs and Italians; the cowardly Amazons lining both sides of the advancing procession, beat the unarmed men with clubs, hurled stones and pieces of iron, until the march was changed into a mass of stumbling, falling, half-crazed, bleeding men."[10]

Four days later, without any opposition whatever, the plant was occupied by troops called out by the governor.

Two weeks later, Henry Clay Frick was shot three times. He was seriously, but not mortally, wounded as he sat at his desk in the company office in Pittsburgh. Frick's assailant, who was promptly captured, was identified as 25-year-old Alexander Berkman, a Russian immigrant—called an "anarchist" by the authorities—advocating views "so extreme that even the comrades of his own ilk had hesitated to associate with him."[11]

The Homestead battle and the attempt on Frick's life occurred in the midst of a presidential campaign. Benjamin Harrison, a Republican, was running for re-election. His Democratic opponent, Grover Cleveland, had been defeated by Harrison four years before when Cleveland himself had made a bid for a second term. The Homestead battle immediately became a campaign issue. It was alluded to by Cleveland in derogatory tones as it pertained to the steel company and the Pinkertons. With the tacit approval of President Harrison, his running mate for Vice-President sent urgent cables, using State Department codes, to Andrew Carnegie in Scotland, pleading that the strike be settled as an aid to the Republican Party. Meanwhile, 176 strikers were indicted for treason in Allegheny County, while the *New York Sun* editorialized: "Treason Against Whom? Frick?" And a subcommittee of the U.S. House of Representatives Judiciary Committee began full-scale hearings.

Among the results of the Homestead battle was the defeat of Harrison. Harrison was not the only loser, however. The union, unable to hold its men together in the face of Frick's adamant refusal to deal with it, ceased to exist by the end of the year. The Pinkerton Agency announced that the task of supplying "watchmen" in labor troubles was dangerous and undesirable, and that it would no longer engage in such pursuits. The House subcommittee, while it found no illegality in the employment of the Pinkertons by Carnegie, and said it had no jurisdiction to legislate in matters involving labor strife, said also, that the execution of laws should not be farmed out to private individuals in the employ of private persons or corporations.[12]

Early the following year, the Congress passed, and the President signed, a bill that remains law to this day. It is generally referred to as the Pinkerton Law.[13] It bars the employment of Pinkerton, or similar detective agencies, by the government.

Pinkerton, however, continued to attract investigative business of this type. Former Governor Frank Steunenberg of Idaho was killed in December, 1905, by a bomb affixed to his front gate. As governor he had been involved in calling out troops in connection with the strikes in 1899 at the mines at Coeur d'Alene. The bomber, who confessed upon his arrest, was one Harry Orchard, a drifter. Governor

Frank Gooding, who was in office at the time, had the state retain the services of the Denver office of the Pinkerton National Detective Agency to investigate and determine who, if anyone, hired Orchard to do the job. He also appointed James H. Hawley, dean of the Idaho Bar, and William Borah, later Congressman and U.S. Senator, to act for the prosecution.

The manager of the Pinkerton Denver office was the same James McParland who 30 years earlier had been the undercover agent who broke up the Molly Maguires. McParland persuaded Orchard to turn state's evidence, and with his testimony, three high officials of the Western Federation of Miners were indicted. Reputedly, they were leaders of the radical International Workers of the World—the IWW, whose members were known as Wobblies. Clarence Darrow, the Chicago lawyer, led the attorneys for the defense. The trials attracted a good deal of attention. And so did the "not guilty" verdicts.[14]

The Pinkerton Agency was again involved in a congressional review and resolution of censure in 1935. A senate subcommittee, under the chairmanship of Senator Robert LaFollette of Wisconsin, investigating labor espionage practices, found that 30 percent of the detective agency's total income came from this type of work. The Senate adopted a resolution that read in part: "The industrial spy system breeds fear, suspicion, and animosity, tends to cause strikes and industrial warfare, and is contrary to sound public policy."[15] Pinkerton's promptly announced that it would forego all future activities of this type and today does not accept investigations with regard to labor disputes from either side.

The history of the settlement of the American West, in which Pinkerton men also figured, is larded over by thick layers of dime novels, Grade B movies and TV horse operas. They all make the point that the American West had vast empty spaces, and that among the early arrivals were those who came to escape jail or to make easy fortunes by stealing from others. Claim jumpers in the gold fields, cattle rustlers on the range, and horse thieves in both areas were unfortunately very real, and their presence caused acute security and enforcement problems for the settlers. The great western expanses were taken over by frontiersmen who were well ahead of the soldiers, or the Federal officials of the territories. The hardworking men and women who braved the uncertainties of pioneering the West had to rely on self-help. They formed vigilante groups in San Francisco in the 1850s, and levied summary justice to rid it of some of those guilty of murder and robbery. One of the mining camps in the central California Mother Lode area was called Hangtown, commemorating the execution of three thieves by a committee of miners. "Necktie parties" took place throughout the West, usually in the belief that lynching was a form of speedy justice.

Private security played an important role in this turbulent period. Adams Express, Wells Fargo, Overland Express, and others did extensive business from branch offices dotted across the landscape. They represented that era's largest organized business ventures. They were trusted to carry the valuables of the growing population. When their coaches or offices were robbed, they used their own agents, or contracted with outsiders, to investigate and try to recover their losses. Black Bart, who was given to writing doggerel and holding up stagecoaches (28 in California alone between 1875 and 1883), was finally captured by J. B. Hume, a private detective on the Wells Fargo payroll who followed a trail of Chinese laundry marks. C. E. Bolton (Black Bart's real name), committed each robbery while wearing a flour sack to mask his face. Before he left, he would drop a note with a few lines of poetry. His most-quoted four-liner reads:

> I've labored long and hard for bread,
>   For Honor and for riches,
> But on my corns too long you've tread
>   You fine-haired sons of bitches.

It was signed "Black Bart, the PO8."[16]

Those regions that did have sworn law officers found that their representatives had limited jurisdictions that stopped at territorial, county, or state lines. Few crimes constituted violations of Federal law, under which help might be sought from the handful of Federal officials. Train robbery, for instance, did not become a Federal crime until after World War I.[17]

The Pinkerton National Detective Agency offices in Denver were opened to assist their railroad and express clients who were suffering losses. But their presence brought in new clients as well—banks and cattle interests who were also victims of the criminal element. Among the names in the Denver files of criminals are a number that have passed into American folklore and ballads. The Pinkertons were responsible for the eventual arrest and breakup of the Reno gang of bank and train robbers. They chased Frank and Jesse James across many miles and over long stretches of time. Two of these Pinkerton agents were murdered by the James gang. While the Pinkertons were responsible for harrying the James boys, they met their end because of the temptation to other gang members of the huge rewards being offered. The Pinkertons chased Butch Cassidy and the Wild Bunch across the West and down into South America where Cassidy had introduced Western-type bank robbery. The photographs of the various members of the Wild Bunch, reproduced on thousands of posters in both North and South America, were discovered as a group picture in a Fort Worth, Texas, photographer's studio by a Pinkerton agent. The gang had posed for it while hiding out in the area. They never expected it would be unearthed.

Working for commercial interests whose losses were considerable, the Pinkerton agents were able to convince their clients that the posting of substantial rewards would be in their interest. As a result, they built up a network of reward-eager sheriffs and informants. The Pinkertons welcomed tips and answered inquiries. Many of the peace officers forwarded descriptions and even photographs of their local outlaws' associates and friends. Hideouts were pinpointed, and information about potential travel detailed, all in the hope that a wanted man and possible reward might be involved. These tips were supplemented by information from bankers, railroad men, cattlemen, mine operators, and other potential victims of the lawless. The Pinkerton files kept, in what was for those days exemplary fashion, were a mainstay of law and order.[18]

By the time of his death in 1884, Allan Pinkerton had made important contributions to the field of investigations which he and his firm had dominated for 30 years. In an era when there was no central agency maintaining records on known criminals, he created files that set the pattern. Not only did he record the criminal's name and physical description, but he also included a description of his modus operandi. He made his records available to sworn law enforcement authorities who queried him for facts by telegram and letter. When his own organization was involved in an arrest, he would insist that the police strip each prisoner, so that his men could record each deformity, scar, and mole. He was a pioneer in the establishment of what later became known as a "rogue's gallery." His early photos were tintypes, but with the advent of the wet-plate process, Pinkerton turned to it, recording pertinent data about the subject on the reverse

of each photo. Many of the pictures used on "Wanted" posters originated from Pinkerton files. He probably was responsible for the start
of the contract uniform guard business, when his agency undertook
to supply six such uniformed men to guard businesses in Chicago in
1860.[19] The Pinkerton National Detective Agency was the first firm
to reach the $1 million-a-year level, as it did in 1868–1869. Pinker-
ton's death had little effect on his company's business, which continued
under the management of his sons.

Stories about the Pinkertons were greatly enhanced by the publication of Pinkerton's 18 books. The subject matter of each concerned an
exploit of his, or of his agents as detectives. Totaling some three
million words, these books were best sellers in the United States and
in Great Britain. Looked at today, they are period pieces in which the
villains are rogues and blackguards without any redeeming features,
while the heroes are stalwart, upright, ready-to-do-battle types with
superior intellect, clever intuition, swinging fists, and fast guns. The
basic plots were derived from known and unknown triumphs of the
Pinkerton Agency. Pinkerton told his son, Robert, in 1876, that he
had seven writers working on his stories. He would prepare an outline,
and the writers would flesh the story out to book length.[20] No one
that I know of has checked them against the works of Sir Arthur
Conan Doyle, which began to appear in 1887, but there is little doubt
in my mind that some of the Pinkerton stories were the inspiration for
certain plot lines of Sherlock Holmes.

The Pinkertons National Detective Agency remained a privately
owned company controlled by the descendants of Allan Pinkerton
until it went public in 1967. It was a proprietorship until 1925, when
it was incorporated for the first time. It changed its name to Pinkerton's Inc. in 1965.

Pinkerton's growth and use by business and industry was only a
small part of the total employment of private security. Railroad police
were brought into being by all of the larger roads. By the turn of the
century, states were passing legislation giving these forces a quasi-
public character. Their authority in many areas was equal to that of
sworn officers.

Mining of coal and metallic ores required large investments of
money and men. Company towns were established by mining companies near the pitheads. Company owned houses were built and
rented to miners and their families. Company stores sold food and

general merchandise to these employees, many even extending credit. In lieu of money, other companies paid their men with company scrip redeemable for merchandise at company stores. In such areas the company in-house guards, in addition to protecting the mine, its buildings and property, also patrolled the streets and were, in effect, the public police of the private town. Elaborate in-house security forces were created by the larger companies of the iron and steel industry, as well as by major shipping firms engaged in inland or international trade.

In 1909 the William J. Burns International Detective Agency was founded. Prior to launching this venture, Burns had earned an enviable reputation as an operative of the U.S. Secret Service. He had been involved in several cases that had received considerable play in the public press. One of them was the investigation of Abraham Ruef, the political boss of San Francisco, which culminated in Ruef's indictment and conviction. Others involved Homestead frauds, and the manipulation of timberlands in Oregon. When the Bureau of Investigation (later the Federal Bureau of Investigation), in the Department of Justice was organized, Burns was selected to head the group. The Burns Detective Agency, like Pinkerton's half a century before, was involved only in investigative and detective work at its inception. The American Bankers Association, which previously had used the Pinkerton Agency, retained Burns's services. It was later joined by the American Hotel Association. The Burns Agency did not get involved with guards or central alarms until much later in its history.

The first paper currency printed by the United States Treasury, the "greenbacks," was issued to help finance the Civil War. Following the axiom that the creation and collection of wealth stimulates attacks and therefore the need for security to guard it, the U.S. Secret Service came into being at the end of the Civil War. The early period of currency issuance had been marked not only by counterfeiting, but also by scandal at the original printing plant. A congressional investigation found that some male employees ran off sample bills from genuine plates to finance parties for some of the female employees of the plant.

As the only Federal department with trained investigators, Secret Service Agents were borrowed by other agencies, and even by the President, for use as investigators. This practice increased after the enactment of the Pinkerton Law in 1893. President Theodore Roosevelt encouraged the use of the Secret Service in the investigation of

Homestead frauds in the West, to the embarrassment of friends of members of Congress. One of the Congressmen friendly to interests so involved was William Borah of Idaho, who was well acquainted with investigators and investigations.

Legislation in the form of a rider to the 1909 Federal budget barred the Secret Service from lending more than two agents to any other department. Since the existing Pinkerton Law prevented the use of contract investigators by government agencies, a scarcity of such talent faced the various executive departments. It was filled that same year, 1909, by the creation of the Bureau of Investigation. This bureau underwent several changes over the years until it emerged in 1932 with much of its present powers as the Federal Bureau of Investigation (FBI).

All these twentieth-century changes had echoes in the official police world. The introduction of the automobile added to law enforcement problems, problems due not only to the sociological changes resulting from the accelerated movement from the farm to the city, but also to the car itself and the traffic problems it created. To keep up with the problem, police had to go from foot and horse patrol to the use of bicycles, motorcycles, and cars.

Official law enforcement also found itself involved with new communication methods. The telegraph, the telephone, and the radio were adapted to police use soon after their commercial introduction. The unauthorized tapping of telegraph wires was made a crime in California in 1862. Scandals involving the interception of stock quotations sent by telegraph wires were featured stories in 1864. News stories, intercepted by rival newspapers, were the subject of legislation in Massachusetts in 1874.

Nor did the telephone escape hanky-panky. Illinois passed laws banning telephone wiretapping in 1895. In 1905 charges by the *San Francisco Call* that the *San Francisco Examiner* was engaged in wiretapping its telephones for the purpose of stealing its news stories caused the California legislature to extend its ban on wiretapping of telegraph lines to include the telephone.[21]

The use of private security was influenced by actions of anarchists, the IWW, and the nihilists, both in this country and abroad. Their violent methods were featured in newspapers and magazines, and tended to make big business wary about lowering their security barriers. Acts of sabotage during World War I, at the instigation of the

Central Powers or their sympathizers, also provoked stricter security requirements.

America's entry into the war on the side of the Allies made security a governmental problem. All railroads and express companies were nationalized. Their private police became employees of the Federal government. Home Guards, made up of volunteers who for one reason or another were unable to serve in the regular armed forces, were uniformed, armed, and trained by the government. They were deployed to help guard public as well as private areas important to the war effort.

The end of hostilities did not restore all things to the way they had been before the start of the conflict. The railroads were returned to private ownership, the Home Guards went home, and the war-inspired sabotage stopped. But in their place came the threat of communistic socialism, primarily from Red Russia. Attorney General A. Mitchell Palmer's publicized raids on private homes and labor offices in search of Red agents kept the leaders of business aware of the threat—and the demand for private security high. Other events not directly connected with losses influenced private security. Important was the adoption of the Prohibition Amendment. It began a period in which there was an insidious deterioration of sworn police morale in many metropolitan areas. Businessmen, when they could afford it, preferred to rely on their own force. Another event that increased such reliance occurred in Boston in 1919 when members of the Boston police department, in attempting to form a union, went on strike. The strike was broken with the use of National Guard troops by the governor of Massachusetts, Calvin Coolidge.

The large industrial firms continued their security forces in one guise or another. One such large in-house security group, and its director, were the subject of increasing public attention in the late 1920s and early 1930s. These were the security forces of the Ford Motor Company under Harry Bennett. Henry Ford, who had become a well-known and controversial figure during the period because of his $5-a-day pay rate, began to attract as much attention as his product. During World War I, in addition to his factory production for war, he personally attained great notoriety with his peace pronouncements and the dispatch of his own "Peace Ship" to attempt to settle the hostilities. In the postwar era his eccentricities continued to earn space in the newspapers.

Among the eccentricities was the "purging" of many key administrators in the Ford Motor Company hierarchy. The one senior official
who was never fired by Ford, and who outlasted even his mentor in
power, was Bennett. He was recognized as his boss's closest confidant,
and was known to be the hatchet man who performed Ford's toughest
tasks. To many he was Henry Ford's chief of staff and, for a time, was
regarded as heir-apparent, with precedence over Ford's only son,
Edsel. Bennett's title was Director of Personnel and the department
he headed was called the Ford Company Service Department. It was
manned over the years, starting in World War I, with men whose
backgrounds as boxers, football players, and ex-detectives gave the
company a sense of physical security.[22] Included as members of the
department were former outstanding Federal agents like Joseph A.
Palma, from the United States Secret Service, and John S. Bugas,
from the FBI. (Bugas eventually succeeded Bennett, and later rose
to become top administrative officer of the company.) The Service
Department was assigned many tasks ranging from bodyguard duties
with the Ford grandchildren to investigations relating to the defense
of lawsuits often brought against Henry Ford individually for his
activities outside the manufacture and sale of automobiles, trucks, and
tractors.[23]

Ford's controversial philosophy, which was partly manifested in
the theory that the Great Depression of the 1930s was "wholesome,"
included very definite anti-union biases. His company had been the
target of labor organizers for 20 years, but Ford had successfully re-
sisted all encroachments, even after his major competitors, General
Motors and Chrysler, had both entered into contracts with the United
Auto Workers. Ford publicly said his company would never recognize
the United Auto Workers, or any other union. He was equally con-
demning of the National Labor Relations Act of 1935, and its possible application to his company.

The "fight on the bridge" which occurred in May, 1937, was an incident that took place during a union march alongside the Ford River
Rouge Plant. Two high union officials, one of them Walter Reuther,
attempted to use a bridge entrance into the plant as an observation
post and were ordered off. Allegedly before they could comply, they
were brutally beaten in the presence of newsmen and some photog-
raphers, who instantly captured the event on film. The same Ford
security men involved in the beating then turned on these observers,
trying to tear up their notes, smash their cameras, and destroy their

film. They were not successful, and the entire incident resulted in bad publicity for Ford and his products. It led to an eventual change in the Ford Company's outlook, recognition of and cooperation with the union, and the easing out of Harry Bennett. The incident was another in a chain that did not endear private security to union members and sympathizers.

Bennett and his security department may have represented an exaggerated, rather than a characteristic example of the use of security forces by business in the 1920s and '30s. However, the fight on the bridge at the River Rouge plant was not the only one in which there was violence between strikers and guards. It was one of the most publicized, but there were others, including the battle in 1937 in Chicago in connection with the strike at Republic Steel.

The Great Depression, ushered in by the stock market crash in October, 1929, left its marks on private security and law enforcement officials. Among the latter were the county sheriffs. Home and farm foreclosures reached 750,000 during the depression, and sheriff sales focused resentment on the officers themselves. Really representing the courts, they seemed to be taking the part of the foreclosing lenders, and as a result were blamed for what was happening by those who were dispossessed or had their belongings sold at auction. Almost all of the officers so involved were sworn officials, paid a salary, or entitled by statute for a fee for their services.

On the one hand, jobs as policemen and investigators, because of the relative security of such public employment, became much more desirable than before the depression. Better educated individuals began entering the ranks. A police department like the one in Berkeley, California, then commanded by August Vollmer, a pioneer in modern police administration and criminology, could say that each man in it was either attending college or had been graduated. The Federal Bureau of Investigation was turning away hundreds of qualified applicants at a time when their minimum requirement was either a law degree or one in accountancy. In 1938 I myself grabbed the opportunity to become an agent in the United States Secret Service at $1,800 a year, after I had been admitted to the bar of both New York State and the United States. Once enrolled, I noted the sharp cleavage between the educational backgrounds of agents recruited in the pre-depression period and those who came in afterward. This difference, in fact, was constantly rubbed in by some of the older agents who

would refer to us disparagingly as "the college boys." The phenomenon of enforcement appointments being desirable in times of economic
depression seems to be repeating itself in 1975. Suffolk County, New
York, received 16,000 applications to fill 163 vacancies in its police
department. Dade County, Florida, whose county police department
numbers 1300 at full strength, has been getting between 800 and
1400 applications a month for appointment as a policeman.[24]

The unprecedented unemployment of the depression provided
private security with a manpower pool far more qualified and capable
than that which is normally available. What influence this circumstance had on the relative stability of the rate of business loss to crime
is unknown. There are no reliable figures on crime statistics for that
period. Nationally, the gathering of criminal statistics did not begin
until 1930, with the creation of the Uniform Crime Reports. This
compilation of information was gathered by local police departments
and other agencies, though it literally took years to get them to act
with care and uniformity in collecting and reporting criminal data.

4 | The Private Security Boom: World War II to the Present

Well before Pearl Harbor the factories of the United States began to turn out the tools of war. These were destined for the countries who later became our allies, especially Great Britain. So long as America was neutral, United States laws and regulations could not restrict these places of production, and their products, from access by persons who were themselves nationals of Nazi Germany, or its allies and their sympathizers. This job had to be done by private security. The purchasing missions of the countries that were becoming more and more dependent on United States output prescribed security requirements, one of them being qualified men who could protect their armament purchases.

Very much in the mind of senior American officials was the experience of 1916, when some two million pounds of munitions in New York Harbor were detonated by German agents, resulting in the death of four, and destroying $50 million in property. Plans were made to prevent such a reoccurrence should the United States be drawn into the conflict.

Wartime security coverage became a reality on December 7, 1941, when the Japanese bombed the American fleet at Pearl Harbor. Tooling up and making war matériel for ourselves and our allies (and feeding all as well) while most young male workers were in military service, was a gigantic task. Once ready, all this matériel required delivery to where it was needed. Even the transports to move it had to be built. These shipments covered thousands of miles, to a two-front war. And the ships had to be reloaded time and time again.

Compulsory rationing to insure fair distribution of supplies available after military needs were met made security manpower a critical commodity, for the enforcement of this rationing siphoned off capable security personnel. Wartime requirements compelled local police establishments, already strapped because their young men had gone to war, to take on tasks beyond those it normally assumed. Industrial plants, drinking water and its sources, utilities and their transmission lines, and other vital services had to be guarded. Much of this was accomplished with governmental assistance, backed up by Home Guards and Auxiliary Police of one description or another. The United States Army alone committed approximately 60,000 regulars to plant protection. It also trained and administered some 200,000 Auxiliary Military Police plant guards. These auxiliaries were company employees, paid by company funds, but given this special status and responsibilities at production facilities considered essential to the war effort.[1]

Not to be overlooked in the overall security problem was the possibility that the North American mainland might become a target of actual or token enemy action. Sightings of enemy craft, both real and imagined, were reported on both the Atlantic and Pacific coasts. Additional manpower had to be deployed to patrol the beaches on foot, and naval vessels needed in combat zones diverted to coastal waters. With troops numbering in the millions embarking for overseas assignments, the need for secrecy and security was compounded.

While all of this was going on, there was within the military structure itself the growth of a supersecret, monumental enterprise: the making of an atomic bomb. Bearing the code name "Manhattan Project," it was a research effort that could not be hidden in a factory or the corner of a military reservation. Entire cities like Oak Ridge, Tennessee, and Hanford, Washington, had to be created in secrecy, as well as numerous establishments in other places. I recall visiting friends who were security officers at the boldly lettered offices of the Manhattan Project in a large office building at the foot of Wall Street without ever having any idea of what was involved, except that the project had engineering overtones. Nor did I get any inkling from relatives employed as scientists on the project when we had occasion to meet at family affairs. The security and intelligence operations involved were among the most extraordinary untold accomplishments of the war. The assignment was not merely the security of a group of installations, it included the unenviable task of hiding the very existence of the installations as well. Where the project surfaced, as it did in New York, Chicago, Berkeley, and other places, it had to be so disguised as not to be recognizable even to sophisticated observers.

Though the job of protecting the Manhattan Project was a military one, with all controls and personnel under its command, these precautionary systems were not dismembered at the end of the war. When the secret was out, the world had something else to worry about: nuclear accidents. During the project, the potential for accident was very real. The end of the war saw the Manhattan Project come from under its umbrella of military control and continue as a quasi-civilian, governmental enterprise, eventually entitled the Atomic Energy Commission (AEC). The cloak of invisibility was removed, but security requirements remained tight. Today they still extend down to the plant and personnel of each supplier, contractor, and subcontractor dealing with nuclear material. The security mission continues to be the safeguarding of military secrets, the property involved, and also the enforcement of strict regulations regarding the handling of supervolatile and dangerous substances. Security requirements covering fissionable materials extend to their use in the privately owned licensed plants operated by various utility companies.

The advent of peace in 1945 saw the gradual dismemberment of the machinery created to meet the wartime needs. Many plants discarded their elaborate security precautions and staffs. Those that continued to produce for the Department of Defense were obligated by their contracts to retain them. But a new need for special security measures came into being with the interest in rockets and interplanetary flight. Immediately on the cessation of hostilities, special Allied intelligence teams penetrated deep into Germany, seeking out key scientists with rocket experience. Those located were wooed to the countries of their interrogators. Those brought back to the United States formed a scientific nucleus within the National Aeronautics and Space Administration (NASA), whose efforts culminated in putting the first man on the moon in 1969. Because rocket propulsion is essentially a military vehicle tied into intercontinental delivery of explosive payloads the NASA program has been hedged with security requirements.

The end of the fighting did not bring instant peace. Churchill's phrase "iron curtain" put into language what was happening: a growing suspicion between the West and those countries under the domination of the Soviet Union. The Communists were aggressively seeking to expand their sphere in Greece, China, and other places. And as with the Red-hunting Palmer Raids that followed World War I, two congressional committees attracted enormous attention. In the Senate, Joseph McCarthy of Wisconsin, chairman of a Senate Subcommittee on Government Operations, held widely publicized hearings, charging many with subversion and demanding greater compulsory security clearance. In the House, the Committee on Un-American Activities also promoted inquiries along these lines in business and industry. The immediate results were the tightening of security requirements at all installations subject to government control. Industrial plants engaged in work for the Department of Defense, the Atomic Energy Commission, and the National Aeronautics and Space Administration had their security staffs review the clearance data and requirements of everyone connected with procurement, especially executives. Similar reviews extended to universities where resarch projects were operated under the sponsorship of governmental agencies. The AEC had the security clearance of some of its chief scientists, like Robert Oppenheimer, challenged. The congressional hearings dominated the news and had the effect of stimulating security requirements in places where little or none had existed before. Ongoing programs were expanded and tightened.

Some of the documentation in the hearings on both sides of the Capitol was attributed to confidential informants whose identity was concealed and who were not subject to cross-examination. This set a precedent for materials pertaining to security clearance of individuals. Anonymous tips were accepted, or, in the case of confidential informants, their identity was protected. While a person whose clearance was challenged was entitled to a hearing, and an appeal procedure was available to him, details of the charges and their sources were kept from him, and his defense had to be based on an attack of a one-sentence summary. Business often felt that access to intelligence files to determine the existence of derogatory material was urgent. Key executives and their hiring by major corporations were affected by rumors of possible clearance difficulties. Proper clearances were a *sine qua non* to obtaining government contracts.

The Korean War, where U.S. troops fought technically, under a United Nations banner, once again geared up American plants for defense purposes, and so increased the need for security staffs and personnel. The Department of Defense itself formalized its requirements for security on the part of its contractors by the establishment in 1952 of an Industrial Defense Program. Today the department issues instructions, manuals, and directives covering the 11,500 security-cleared facilities that employ 1.2 million workers. The Department of Defense maintains a staff of industrial security representatives to monitor the program and to audit the effectiveness of security at each of the contracting firms.[2]

Recently, a debate was aired in the pages of *Security Management,* a monthly publication of the American Society for Industrial Security on the department's Industrial Security Manual. One article, "Is the Industrial Security Manual an Adequate Instrument—An Industry View," by Fred W. Cary of Honeywell, Inc., made the point that the basic objective of the Department of Defense in its industrial security program is not the promulgation of uniform security practices, but rather the safeguarding of classified information. The Defense Department's program, the article maintained, is too detailed, and leaves little room for common sense. It does not provide for reasonable requirements to develop meaningful security programs at acceptable costs. In a "Rebuttal," Dr. Thomas J. O'Brien, director, Security Plans and Programs, Office of the Deputy Assistant Secretary of Defense (Security Policy), answered that it is the purpose of the Industrial Security Manual to provide information on safeguarding classified information in a uniform system. O'Brien emphasized that legally the manual is a contract and as such it must be tightly written. One can deduce that it will not be easily altered. O'Brien, in referring to a former industry representative who once explained that company budgets are based on hard facts and hard requirements, also said that unless security specifications are clearly and unequivocally spelled out, top management of the various companies might not go along in allocating the necessary funds. Implied in this argument was that strict standards are a means of compelling managements to provide for full budgets for security purposes.

But whether the primary purpose of the Department of Defense is the safeguarding of classified materials or the improvement of security practices, the sum total is that as a group these defense contractors have superior security systems against which most of the others do not compare. The costs of these systems, of course, are built into the price structure of the procurement, and the bill is paid for by the government. These costs would not be acceptable on the open commercial market.

In 1954 the Wackenhut Corporation was formed by four former FBI agents, among them George R. Wackenhut. Despite the Pinkerton

Law, this company, from its inception, specialized in supplying security for government installations under the control of such agencies as the AEC and NASA, as well as for the contractors who were supplying them and the Department of Defense.[3] Within a decade, the Wackenhut Corporation grew to become the third largest of the contract detective and rent-a-guard agencies in business in this country, after Pinkerton's and Burns.

The late 1950s were years of relative quiet. Crime figures did not escalate alarmingly and no conspicuous need manifested itself for additional law enforcement or private security. One incident, however, that did not then affect private security, but was a precursor of unrest to come, was the 1958 school integration crisis in Little Rock, Arkansas. The Supreme Court of the United States had in effect canceled its previous ruling regarding "separate but equal" educational facilities for blacks and whites. To block integration at the Little Rock Central High School, the Arkansas governor himself became involved, and President Eisenhower was forced to order regular Army troops to the city to enforce the law and keep order. The history of such use of the Army by the United States goes back to the first five years of the Republic, when, in 1794, President Washington federalized 15,000 militiamen and put them under the command of General Lighthorse Harry Lee, then also governor of Virginia, to put down the Whiskey Rebellion. Seventy years later, in 1863, Federal troops were sent from the battlefield at Gettysburg to New York City to quell the bloody draft riots.[4]

The 1960s opened with an increased use and awareness of private security in peacetime. The single employment in Arkansas of regular Army troops presaged greater use of them in the next 10 years. The rise in crime of the 1960s, as reflected by known statistics, has been detailed before. So, too, has the accelerating cost of crime to the business community. Standing by themselves, these figures do not represent the various influences that induced them, however, and the dramatic impact of crime on the business community and the general public.

In the 1960s the United States became more and more involved in another war on the far side of the Pacific Ocean. Vietnam was slowly building up to a climax of entanglement of men and matériel. Unlike any previous war in history, the draftees and their families could see what they were getting into on their television screens each night at dinnertime.

The consequent unrest was most visible on the college campus. The crew cut was out. So was the well-tailored, affluent look. They were replaced by long, disheveled hair, and dungarees and overalls became the uniform of the day. Numbers of students began to experiment with drugs—from marijuana to hallucinogens. Some even got themselves involved with cocaine and heroin. Similar drug experimentation was cropping out in diverse groups in different places, ranging from the poorest ghettos to the wealthiest suburbs. Sociologists noted the rise of various subcultures on and off the campus, with standards different from those of previous generations. Dropouts, from education and work, tended to cluster together as "hippies" and "flower children." The uneducated disadvantaged were also attracted to these new mores.

Those who had developed drug addiction now had vital need of large and steady sources of money to sustain their addictions. Many resorted to stealing and prostitution, which they did not regard as immoral or criminal. Under the curse of an immediate need, crime was accepted as normal and appropriate. Conversely, law enforcement officers engaged in narcotic investigations, and then all police who interfered with this counterculture life, were branded as "pigs." A new word, "ripoff," was coined as a synonym for "steal." Subculture authorities insisted that it connoted a Robin Hood-style of acceptable theft from those who could afford it. Shoplifting, especially at big stores and supermarkets, was an approved ripoff. Initiation into subculture groups was often marked by requirements to steal. Utility companies, particularly "Ma Bell," were marked as fair game. So were banks, and the larger the bank, the more righteous the ripoff. Manufacturers of materials used by the armed forces became choice targets.

Underground literature emanating from these subculture groups included books, magazines, and newspapers. "How-to" articles appeared, furnishing specific instructions on how to steal; how to make bombs; how to forge checks and other documents, including credit cards and travel papers. The "how-to" targets included hotels, motels, airlines, railroads, and car-rental companies. Other articles carried precise instructions on recommended behavior when approached by police, when arrested, arraigned, and tried.

Unrest on the campus over Vietnam was not the only evidence of a growing malaise in the United States of the 1960s. A large segment of the population publicly changed its stance. Instead of quietly suffering the appellation of "Negro" or "colored" it proudly commanded the term "black," and "Black Is Beautiful" became its motto. There was a potential for violence in this emergence, not only because people marched and sat for their rights, but also because others would return them to their former place. Violence was used as a weapon of subjugation from the very first appearance of blacks on this continent. In many metropolitan areas of the North, the blacks live in ghettos and make up the marginal, lowest end of the economic scale. In the South, where they were effectively disfranchised after the Civil War, movements have been under way to right the situation, with explosive results in many places. United States Regular Army troops were called out at Oxford, Mississippi, in 1962, and in Tuscaloosa-Huntsville, Alabama, in the following year. The summer of 1967 saw the peak of the unrest, if violent riots can be called "unrest." The U.S. Department of Defense noted disorders in 150 cities.[5] It furnished troops to restore order in Detroit that year. Regulars were again called out in April of 1968, following the murder of Dr. Martin Luther King, to stem disorder in Washington, Baltimore, and Chicago.

Private security played little or no part in these upheavals. Even the most efficient would have had little impact on the course of these troubles. The use of Federal troops was and remains the ultimate weapon. They are called in after local and state enforcement are no longer effective, and usually only after the National Guard has proved to be unequal to the task, or is so considered. The Department of Defense reacted to these chaotic situations in our cities' ghettos by establishing a series of operations and plans, such as "Cincstrike-Oplan 563," nicknamed "Steep Hill," and later "Garden Plot," and making seven brigades, consisting of 21,000 troops, available for riot duty. This program grew into the Civil Disturbance Planning and Operations Directorate, which eventually was called the Directorate of Military Support. Directorate plans included the training by the Defense Department of more than 100,000 persons, not members of the department, in civil disturbance control techniques in fiscal year 1971.[6]

But these riots and disorders were by no means restricted to ghettos. They were very evident on the campuses of many colleges and universities, from Columbia in New York to Kent State in Ohio to Berkeley in California. Nor were they limited to the United States.

The May, 1968, student riots in France were reminiscent of the days of the 1871 Paris Commune, as cobblestones were ripped up to form barricades in the French capital.

Stories began to appear about small fringe groups who were willing to go underground and resort to violence to obtain their goals. They were said to include Black Nationalists of various persuasions. Receiving a lion's share of attention were the left-wing Weathermen. All these cliques were reported to be studying and emulating the tactics of "Che" Guevera, who figured so prominently in the Cuban rebellion of Fidel Castro and later in other South American uprisings. Some of the underground literature attributed to them carried instructions on the manufacture of bombs and incendiaries.

These happenings alone would have shaken the boardrooms of major companies, but they were to suffer shocks even closer to home. While business was jarred by the campus and ghetto riots, during which stores were gutted and their contents looted, no individual places seemed to be the predetermined targets of mobs or radicals. Then, suddenly, banks and industrial corporations became the targets of violence. Bombs and incendiaries were planted in them or hurled at them. These bombings were not concentrated in any one city or section of the country. International Telephone and Telegraph had a bomb explode in its headquarters in New York and at some 25 of its branch locations in various parts of Europe. The Morgan Guaranty Trust Company was the object of a bomb explosion at its New York main office building in 1969. The Bank of America had its branch office in Santa Barbara attacked by fire bombs in February, 1970. In 1971 the Capital of the United States itself was the target of a bomb explosion. The heart of the New York financial district was devastated by a bomb detonated during the busy lunch hour in a private club next to one of the area's favorite restaurants, Fraunces Tavern, where Washington bade farewell to his wartime officers. This explosion, which resulted in deaths and maimings, occurred in early 1975.

Along with the bombings came thousands of false threats. At three of American Express's locations in New York City, more than 100 telephone calls were received in 1972 about a bomb on their premises. All proved false, but each case required judgment. Evacuation, with its concomitant work stoppage, is costly. Problems exist with regard to the security of valuables in and outside the vault areas. The interruption and slowdown of computer processing have ramifications of possible data loss. If the call is a hoax, evacuation emboldens the caller to repeat his threat far more than if his bluff is called. Only on two occasions in 1972 did American Express evacuate its buildings—and no bomb was found.

Federal legislation passed in 1970 broadened Federal authority in connection with explosive-related offenses.[7] In that same year, there were 43 bombings of or arson attempts on government-owned leased buildings, in addition to 421 bomb threats. In 1971, the respective figures jumped to 52 and 824.[8] The year 1971 also saw 15 people die from bomb explosions in the United States—and $10 million in public and private property destroyed.[9]

These incidents and others, led to the creation of a National Bomb Data Center, at Gaithersburg, Maryland, operated by the International Association of Chiefs of Police under a grant from the Law Enforcement Assistance Administration. A flood of instructions was issued to both law enforcement and private security personnel on the proper handling of explosive devices. Because these devices have to be brought into the premises, a large portion of the responsibility for their prevention has fallen to government and private security guards. These instances involving the planting of bombs are primarily responsible for the routine inspection of briefcases and packages in the possession of visitors to many private and official establishments.

Terror, kidnapping, and guerrilla warfare have become common in many parts of the world since the early 1960s. The ancient practice of capture for ransom has been modernized as a method of fund raising for radical causes. A single ransom of $14 million dollars was paid by one American oil company for the release of one of its executives held in Argentina. Similar cases, involving millions of dollars, have occurred in many other places.

The copycat domestic criminal has adopted this tactic for his own purposes. In the United States publicized acts of kidnapping have included a banker's wife in Wisconsin, an editor in Atlanta, a child and, six months later, a businessman on Long Island, New York. Only the full story of the solution of the Patricia Hearst case, or the publication of a full report by the FBI, will enable an outsider to determine what category that incident deserves. A special version of the classic kidnapping used both by the politically motivated terrorist and the money-hungry criminal is the holding of hostages at gunpoint. These acts have also proliferated. Major police departments have organized special squads trained to deal with such circumstances.

The wave of airplane hijackings in the sixties and seventies has also had an important impact on law enforcement and private security. Unlike piracy on the high seas, in which a ship is taken over by its crew, passengers, or outsiders, there is little enforceable international law regarding a similar act in midair. The numerous hijackings of domestic commercial flights in the United States and their diversion to Cuba raised problems not solvable by American law and law enforcement. Cuba was serving as a haven first for politically motivated hijackers and later for run-of-the-mill criminals whose sole purpose was to evade authorities.

Hijacking abroad has produced some of the unforgettable photographs of the era: the September, 1970, pictures of the exploding and burning giant airliners in the desert. Here again law enforcement was ineffective. The United Nations and Interpol found themselves powerless to combat the vetoes of the nations that had a political interest in the well-being of the instigators. They could do little but render lip service about the horrors involved.

Of the 40 attempts at hijacking in the United States in 1969, 34 were successful. A year later, there were 27 attempts, of which 18 proved successful. These figures were reduced still further in 1971: 12 successful hijackings in 27 attempts.[10] Direct United States Government intervention increased in September, 1970, with the start of the Air Marshal program, and the compulsory check of passengers and their hand luggage prior to embarkation. This latter search, performed in slow, clumsy fashion at the start of the program, has now became routinized, more efficient and faster, so as to become an acceptable part of domestic air travel. These inspections are now made by the airlines, or by contract guard services, who are employed to do the work for them. They are aided by increasingly sophisticated security devices, some that detect metal on a person, others that use X-rays to examine hand luggage without the necessity of opening it or causing damage to its contents, not even to sensitive, unexposed film.

On the local level, particularly in the large cities, the drug addict has increasingly resorted to crimes of impulse to obtain money: holdups, muggings, burglary, robbery. Some of these instances have involved brutality and violence. The outcry against these actions was echoed by politicians, who claimed that if they were elected to take care of society's ills, complete cures would result.

Sworn law enforcement stepped up its efforts, but the period coincided with Supreme Court decisions that added to the burden of proof, and required greater safeguards for those charged with crimes. The right of a defendant to counsel at each step of the arrest and trial process was spelled out. So were requirements for warrants of all types. Proper compliance consumed time. It meant that each police officer's allocation of time involved more paperwork and less street duty.

America's localities spent more for police protection—after the rise in crime had struck fear in the body politic. But like a windswept fire, crime was not to be contained by using a stopgap measure. Adding policemen on the street was not sufficient to do the job.

Nonetheless, commerce and industry, rather than the individual and his home, were the main targets of crime. Those who committed crimes gravitated to the areas where the pickings were best: the office, the factory, the bank, the railroad station, the airport, the stores and other business establishments. So business also joined in the clamor for more and more protection by the law enforcement agencies. But because they could not wait as their profits and capital eroded, they resorted in increased numbers to self-help—private security.

Evidence of such self-help is patently visible on many business streets of our inner cities. Here it exists in the form of new metal grills, blinds, or other stout shutters that cover the entire glass front of stores, and often the entrances as well. This type of metal shield has been used in the principal cities of Europe for decades, though it is not as yet being extensively used along the main streets of our smaller, less crime prone communities. Less visible, but used in increasing amounts, are improved hardware and a multitude of alarms. Less visible, too, at least to most uninitiated, has been the subtle change in store lighting. Dramatic lights focusing on window displays only tended to mask any movement in the rear of the store; lights have now been adjusted to make as great an area of the interior as visible as possible in order to aid both public and private security. In addition, the number of patrolling guards and watchmen has risen.

The increase of crime and its resulting losses impelled business executives to review their insurance coverage. Appropriate coverage was vital if profits were to continue. The casualty and surety branch of the insurance industry had been underwriting risks from inception. Fire and water damage, burglary, robbery, embezzlement, pilferage have always been among the risks they cover. In setting premium rates, there was early recognition that risks differed. For fire insurance, a building built entirely of stone was insurable at a smaller premium than another structure of the same size built of wood. In the same way, one equipped with automatic sprinklers, devices that spontaneously spray water when the temperature surrounding them reaches a predetermined level, would be charged a smaller premium than another without that protection.

In the field of insurance involving crime and criminal attack, the companies also offered premium discounts to those using certain listed devices and services. These devices included such things as tie-ins to a Central Station Protective Service, the use of full-time guards, and even the use of a watchmen's clock by the guards. The maximum use of such prescribed devices and services entitled the assured to a discount of 70 percent.

In the 1950s and early 1960s, insurance increased in importance to business as a means of covering their losses from criminal attack, fraud, and liability. In the mid-1960s, casualty and surety companies could see in their own books the rising incidence of crime and its cost to them. Losses were exceeding the limits forecast by their own experts, and they were being compelled to pay out more in claims than they were collecting as premiums. As a result, some companies stopped writing burglary and related coverage altogether. Others canceled the policies, or refused to renew those of individuals or firms they considered to be marginal risks. In addition, to increase policyholder incentive to exercise care and at the same time reduce their own loss ratio, most insurers required deductibles of increasing amounts. The deductible requires the insured to assume for his own account the first specified portion of the loss before the insurance company becomes obligated to pay out on the casualty. Insurance coverage is obtainable for the deductible amounts, but only at a prohibitive premium cost. Deductibles of $100,000 and more are common in policies now written for major business concerns.

During this same period, the premium cost for what coverage was available increased materially—especially where the insured's location and record reflected poor risk experience. Hit hardest by the tightening of the insurance market were marginal businesses and those located in ghettos. Their plight became the subject of extensive hearings in 1969 before a U.S. Senate Select Committee on Small Business.[11] The hearings resulted in legislation authorizing a program of Federal Crime Insurance "at an affordable price" in states with a critical problem of availability of crime insurance and no appropriate program of their own to solve it.

The Federal Crime Insurance Program, begun August, 1971, and administered by the Housing and Urban Development Department (HUD), has not been much of a solution either. HUD has the authority to decide if a critical problem of availability exists, but its contribution to the problems outlined in the Senate hearings have been relatively insignificant. The only coverage it offers to business is limited to burglary and larceny incident thereto, and to robbery with a limit of $15,000 per customer. None of the other lines of coverage sold to business by commercial insurance companies are available under government's program, including losses sustained from employee dishonesty, mysterious disappearance, forgery of checks and money orders, counterfeit money, breaking and entering, and robbery. It is further limited to sales in but 14 states and the District of Columbia. By August 1, 1974, three years after the program had started, only 5553 commercial policies were in effect.

The Federal Crime Insurance Program simultaneously marketed residential policies, with a limit of $10,000 each, covering burglary and robbery from the home, and including burglary from an enclosed locked storage compartment of an automobile. But here, too, the program could scarcely be termed an overwhelming success. By August 1, there were only 17,242 policies outstanding. In the first 30 months of its existence the program received 1625 claims and paid out a total of $1,522,916. Both the residential and commercial coverage have deductibles of $50 or 5 percent of the gross amount of the loss, whichever is greater.

The enabling statute that brought the Federal Crime Insurance Program into existence also provided for an advisory committee to meet with the HUD officials on a schedule spelled out in the law. It was established to assist the Secretary of HUD and his designees in the marketing of the program and in its operation. But there has been no committee—and no committee meetings—since the end of the first year of its operation.

The tightening of the availability of adequate insurance coverage was a stimulus to the expansion of the use of private security. Those who were able to get commercial insurance coverage also got the incentive in the form of premium discounts when prescribed security machinery and systems were used. A tie-in to a Central Station Protective Service system has led to the highest premium discount. Under this system as noted previously, automatic alarms are wired directly, or through leased telephone wires, to a central station. The triggering of the alarm also sounds in the central station, which in turn notifies the police; in many areas the central station also dispatches its own mobile unit to the premises involved. Such protection has been described as the Rolls-Royce of the security business.

Sales of the Central Station Protective Services assumed such sizable amounts as to prompt the Department of Justice in 1961 to bring charges of monopoly against its sponsors. The department charged the Grinnell Corporation and three of its subsidiaries— American District Telegraph Company (ADT), Holmes Electric Protective Company, and Automatic Fire Alarm Company—with violating the antitrust statutes. The U.S. District Court in November, 1964, found that such a monopoly did indeed exist and ordered divestiture.[12] The decision was upheld by the U.S. Supreme Court three years later. The courts found that the defendants did some 90 percent of all Central Station Protective business in the United States. While the antitrust litigation was pending, the business done by Central Station Protection Services doubled. It was $70.9 million in 1963, and grew to $128.8 million in 1969.[13]

Central Station Protective Services constitutes a small portion of the total industry involved in manufacturing, installing and servicing security hardware machinery and devices. The balance of the industry showed growth rates approximately the same as for Central Station Protective Services. Many new devices were adapted for security use in the sixties, and many of them have been showing dramatic increases in sales. They include closed-circuit television (CCTV) and various sensory devices based on microwaves, laser beams, and the like. Automatic dialers are another of the fast-growing protective units.

The Bank Protection Act of 1968 provides for the issuance by the Federal Deposit Insurance Corporation of regulations governing the installation, maintenance, and operation of bank security devices, and for procedures to govern their security systems. It spells out in some detail a series of minimum requirements. This law and the regulations pertaining to it stimulated sales of security devices as the banking industry began to comply.

The proliferation of security devices attracted the marketing attention of major defense suppliers. Aware of the fact that their business with the government would be phased down or out once America withdrew from Indochina, many of them, with the tools and know-how they acquired to meet their defense commitments, sought markets for security products. Some of their products are in use by official law enforcement agencies as well.

One recent phenomenon has been the increase in the manufacture and sale of alarm devices for the home. Such sales have been mostly for upper- and middle-class homes in metropolitan areas and their suburbs—homes of the type that had live-in servants until World War II. The absence of these servants has increased the vulnerability of the homes to criminal attack. Media stories of lawlessness, unsafe streets, and home and apartment burglaries have also sparked home-alarm sales. Retail outlets of such mass merchandisers as Sears and Macy's have set up separate departments for the sale of home security devices. Estimates are that this residential market has been barely penetrated. An army of fly-by-nights has been attracted to this grow-ing field. Resorting to misleading copy, and promises impossible of delivery, they and their salesmen are ringing the doorbells of prospec-tive customers, both corporate and residential.

All these devices have an overriding handicap: false alarms. Ac-cording to available statistics, more than 95 percent of all activated alarms are triggered by causes other than those for which the alarm was designed.[14] This false alarm rate applies equally to manually triggered alarms, ones that require the user to push a button or step on an activator, or in some other pre-set way operate the signal. This by no means indicates that the devices are useless. Nor does it mean that they do not accomplish much of their purpose. Their signals have resulted in many captures of intruders in the very act of robbery or burglary.

There has been no abatement of the high false alarm rate over the years. There are indications in some localities that the rate is being successfully combatted, but the burden of false alarms on police de-partments, in tying up men and vehicles, is reaching critical propor-tions. Some departments are discontinuing the previous practice of having alarms terminate in their own headquarters.

While insurance and security devices were major solutions tried in the quest for protection from losses due to crime, the greatest emphasis in business and commercial enterprises was placed on the physical presence of uniformed guards. In a majority of them, the shock reaction to crime wave accounts in the headlines usually resulted in an application of more guards. This can be seen from the figures relating to the growth of contract guard companies. Each story of the kidnapping of a businessman, of the detonation of a bomb, of a neighbor-hood holdup, or of similar happening resulted in a rash of telephone calls at their offices.

These decades since World War II have also witnessed innovations that brought with them substantial fraud losses and commensurate security problems. Credit cards grew to where there were more than 120 million in use in the United States alone. Bank credit cards suffered $420 million in fraud losses in 1973. That huge figure did not include losses incurred by those distributing travel and entertainment cards, or by the airlines, hotels, motels, department and chain stores, rent-a-car agencies, the telephone company and other issuers. Credit card fraud losses reached significant levels in the early 1960s, and zoomed for seven or eight years thereafter. Cards had become avail-able to thieves as a result of mass unsolicited mailouts by some issuers, a practice that was halted by Federal and state statutes in 1972. But credit cards were also stolen from the mails and from individual owners. To combat these losses, major changes in the operation of the card companies were needed. Stolen credit cards were first listed only at the issuer's office on index cards. Later they were printed out on hot-card lists and booklets. Now they are computerized, and a tele-phone inquiry will confirm their validity and the transaction involved in less than a minute. Thousands of such authorizations take place each day.

Recognizing the lack of precision and uniformity in the criminal laws with regard to credit cards, I made the original proposals that resulted in American Express's sponsoring intensive research by dis-tinguished law professors and their staffs.[15] From this research a model criminal statute was formulated that has, in substance, been enacted in more than 34 states. This uniformity and clarity in the law simplified enforcement and prosecution, and contributed to stopping the upward trend of the losses from stolen cards. Of major importance in placing controls on what seemed to be a runaway situation was the employment by many of the card issuers of competent investigative assistance. These security managers, with the consent of their senior management, have been meeting regularly with other managers of competing companies and law enforcement officers to exchange pertinent information and to join in efforts against common hazards.

The phonograph, an invention of Thomas A. Edison, has spawned a giant industry which in the year 1974 was to claim the loss of more than $200 million to stereo tape and disc pirates, counterfeiters, and bootleggers.[16] These are the losses due to the commercial sale of sound recordings duplicated on tape or phonograph records without the authorization of the owner of the master recording. Piracy amounts to more than one-third of the legitimate industry's annual sale of pre-recorded tapes, and more than 10 percent of the legitimate industry's total retail sale of sound recordings (including records). Here, again, existing general criminal statutes made enforcement and prosecutions difficult and confusing—to the advantage of the violator. Piracy is now being fought by the Record Industry Association of America through its New York-based Anti-Piracy Intelligence Bureau. Twenty-six states have enacted antipiracy laws, 17 of them in the last two years. Federal protection is limited to the civil sanctions of the copyright laws, and a criminal statute against counterfeiting. In the record industry, counterfeiting means the duplication of the complete package, that is, not only the recording, but also its label and packaging. The antipiracy bureau represents the alliance of an entire industry to operate a private security investigative agency for the mutual benefit of its membres. Each individual company still has its own security problems, of course, with regard to the theft of legitimately produced products by employees and outsiders.

Motion picture films are also being pirated. While this practice is said to be as old as the movie industry itself, it is suddenly causing considerable anxiety. Film piracy losses have now reached $50 million a year. This industry is also putting together an organization similar to the Anti-Piracy Intelligence Bureau.

There have been other aspects of crime against business in the sixties and seventies. The most widely used business tool of these decades, for instance, has been the computer. It, too, has been the object of criminal attention; it, too, requires security of great sophistication, a subject that will be discussed in Chapter 7. Professional criminals have also used new, post war tools against the classic defenses. Banks in Canada and the United States have had their vaults entered by gangs using antitank guns developed during World War II. Still others have used a new instrument of great efficiency called the "burning wand" to cut into vaults and safes previously regarded as invulnerable. The counterfeiting of corporate securities proliferated to a point where, in 1969, the New York Stock Exchange and the American Banker's Association had special committees sitting in emergency session to redesign stock certificate specifications.

"Law and order" has become a political issue. The great growth of crime, the attention given to crime by the media, and the actual effect of crimes on more and more individuals made it a prime topic of legislation at all levels of government. In addition to numerous omnibus bills aimed at controlling crime and the use of narcotics, a major contribution was made by the Federal government in the appropriation of about $3 billion—distributed in the last four years through the Law Enforcement Assistance Administration of the Department of Justice—for massive increases in crime reduction programs. Some of these funds were used directly by Federal organizations, some of them were allocated to state and municipal governments. They were used on projects involving the entire system of criminal justice, including the courts, law enforcement and the police, the correctional institutions, the social and psychological aspects of crime and criminals.

Only a comparatively trivial portion of these funds were allocated for use in connection with private security. One such grant, to Cedar Rapids, Iowa, for research in connection with alarms, has not been followed up, except on a local basis. The other project, a study by the Rand Corporation of the private security industry, had one of its recommendations followed: the appointment of an advisory committee to the Law Enforcement Assistance Administration. Despite numerous other recommendations in that study, nothing worthy of note has emerged from LEAA or its advisory committee in connection with their recommendations on private security.

5 | Guards

An axiom of the security field is that one can never be criticized for having too many guards.

This is a lesson I learned very early in my career as an agent in the U.S. Secret-Service. In the early summer of 1940, I was temporarily assigned to the Secret Service White House Detail. It was an election year, but it was also the period of "the phoney war" in Europe. Germany was finishing its operations in Poland, while the English and French were resting behind the "impregnable" Maginot Line. President Roosevelt had planned on traveling in the northeast to inspect some of our military installations.

One trip was to the National Guard encampments in the Watertown-Rome, New York area, and another was down along the coast from the Naval Yard at Portsmouth, New Hampshire, to the Boston Yard to recommission "Old Ironsides," the U.S.S. *Constitution,* which had been restored with the pennies of schoolchildren, and then to the Coast Guard Academy at New London, Connecticut, and the Electric Boat Company at Groton.

The head of the White House Detail of the Secret Service was Colonel Edward Starling, "Bill" Starling, who had been with every President since Wilson. Starling was a big, glinty blue-eyed, white-haired, courtly Kentuckian, whose opening "Hello, podnah" identified his place of origin. The title, "colonel," was not one resulting from service with the military; it was, like the accent, pure Kentucky—an honorary commission bestowed at that time with frequent largesse by the various governors of that state.

By its very nature, the White House Detail was a closely knit group. The responsibilities involved bred extreme but controlled tensions. These were often relieved by fraternal banter and innocent "in" games. The visit to the National Guard Camp near Watertown was a perfect background for such sport. We were there for a full day. Few, if any, civilians were around, but we were virtually surrounded by thousands of men in uniform. The Presidential train was parked on a railroad siding where there were no buildings within 500 feet. The flat horizon was punctuated by a water tower located several hundred yards down the track. To spare President Roosevelt the discomfort of his braces, or of being wheeled in his chair past strangers, it was standard procedure for him to use the parlor section of his private railroad car as his office. So there the train sat, with senior Army officers coming and going, past the cordons of military police, state troopers, and finally the inner ring of the Secret Service Agents on duty.

Two shifts of Agents were off duty at a time; we worked eight-hour shifts. The off-duty men normally would have been sightseeing, or relaxing elsewhere. Here on the plain, however, there was nothing to do; it was a beautiful day and the men gathered in knots down the track, out of the way of the official comings and goings. We were joined by many young officers assigned to the command, or who had come along as aides to senior officers attending the President.

When Colonel Starling sauntered down to join our groups, two young and naïve second lieutenants were *sotto voce* urged to get him reminiscing about his military experiences. Every ear was cocked when the first, after two or three false starts, in a most respectful voice ventured, "Colonel Starling, what outfit did you command?"

His voice was clear. Starling couldn't feign that he hadn't heard the question. He turned with a sort of intimate smile. He was going to tell all. In fact, he started with, "Well son, let me tell you . . ." He stopped with his eyes fixed on a spot 300 yards down the track. He clutched the lieutenant's shoulder, spun him around so that he, too, could see the spot, and with his arm extended, pointed. "Lieutenant," he said, "there's an unguarded path crossing the track. Can you get a squad of men and post sentries there? When that is done, check the entire perimeter. There may be other spots not covered."

After 10 minutes, when we commented on the dust the young lieutenant was raising covering the perimeter, we unleashed the second young shavetail. We thought we had the wily old rascal. He couldn't use that lack of perimeter control as an escape. We lost again. As the colonel started to explain about his career, he suddenly noted that while there were guards at the *foot* of the water tower, no one was stationed on *top* of it—a perfect post for a responsible young officer.

Colonel Starling retired a year later, and he and Thomas Segrue collaborated on a book given the title *Starling of the White House,* which was published by Simon and Schuster and was on the best-seller lists for months. I had known Jack Goodman of that firm and introduced him to Starling. As a result, on several occasions I discussed the forthcoming book with the colonel. At one of these meetings I mentioned "the game." He laughed, for of course he knew all about it and enjoyed it as much as we did. "You know, a pretty young girl might have been a winner. I was safe as long as you kept sending young officers. I could always get them to put up more guards." Then, more seriously, he continued, "Mitch, one thing you will never be criticized for is posting too many guards, especially if you keep them from getting under foot."

The guard—watchman, patrolman—is the footslogger, the infantryman of the private security army. Ninety percent of the personnel of private security agencies are in this category.[1] His functions today can be described in terms applicable to those of his predecessors centuries ago. He is assigned to a stationary post or to walk a perimeter patrol to watch and protect the grounds, buildings, floors, rooms, or cages, or access thereto, from specified hazards, including civil and criminal trespass, sabotage, and fire. He also has a long list of other things to look out for, such as burst water pipes, leaking gas, picnickers, wandering cows, drunks, noisy neighbors, and mad dogs.

In outline it is similar to the sentry function at military encampments, and identical to the duties guards perform in protecting government buildings and installations. Guards are private individuals in private employment. Their authority is limited to that granted them by their employer. This is true when they are members of an in-house department, and it remains true when they are contract guards. As mercenaries, the employer is the contract guard agency, but the authority emanates from the firm contracting for their services.

It is axiomatic that the grantor of the authority can give no greater powers than those he himself possesses. His powers are those associated with ownership or leasehold of real estate or property. Because I have the right to my land and may evict a trespasser, I can delegate that right to my agent, servant, or employee, and may even contract with an outside firm for them to use their employees in my behalf.

The converse is also true. Under normal circumstances the public police—law enforcement officers—with no knowledge of the commission of a crime, have no rights on the same private property being patrolled by me, my own in-house guards, or by the contract guards whose services I have hired.

Because my property, my plant, my mine, or my farm has value, I do not want it trespassed upon nor the valuables it contains removed. When circumstances accumulate to a point where it becomes an economic necessity to safeguard the property, I either watch the place myself or hire others to do it for me. Criminals are no respecters of the Sabbath, or of normal business hours. It is often necessary for these guards be on duty around the clock on each day of the year. Should criminal attacks become more numerous and my concern increase, I would add to the number of guards—the classic response. In most instances where costs are not a factor to be considered, the maximum use of manpower is the normal answer to problems of security.

The use of physical barriers to reduce risks and the need for manpower as guards goes back to the days of castles, stone walls, moats, and ditches. A good, high wall would allow one guard to patrol an area effectively where but for the wall five or ten might be needed. A moat, a fence, and other similar physical barriers performed the same function. They still do today. The guard on a perimeter patrol is assisted by many deterrents built into and around the area to be protected. High fences, topped by barbed wire, illuminated at night and wired so that any contact with them would sound an alarm, are now in normal use. In some places fences are now invisible. The electric eye —the photoelectric cell—has made this kind of protection possible.

Unlike guards, these physical barriers are a capital investment, take no vacations, require no pensions, are not subject to sick leave or other vagaries. But walls can be climbed, wires cut, and alarms accidently set off by a thousand causes ranging from a flaw in the installation to an earth tremor, a wandering deer, hailstones, or lightning.

An early installation of a photoelectric fence was the one used during World War II around the perimeter of the Hyde Park, New York, home of President Roosevelt. Photoelectric cells were required about every 200 feet; any breaches in the perimeter were indicated on a control board in the main security booth. During the war years, a military police battalion was stationed close by at the Vanderbilt mansion, several miles north. The MP's patrolled the outer areas, and their Jeeps, loaded with troops, would respond to all alarms.

One dark night in early autumn the control panel sounded and the indicator showed that a photoelectric cell, located down a side lane in a heavily wooded area had been interrupted. As the crow flies, it was at least a half mile from the house, by road much further away. We approached silently, using only blackout lights, two Jeeps with troops, two cars with agents and state police. The vehicles took up positions where they could block any attempt to move toward the house or back to the main road. The men then converged on the spot on foot. Closer in there was the faintly visible outline of a big, darkened car, off the dirt road, between the trees. No occupants could be seen in that light. We all had flashlights, some of the soldiers even had large ones powered by batteries that hung in a backpack. When we had surrounded the car, at a low call, all of us turned on our lights, illuminating the interior of the car and the surrounding area. The entire maneuver successfully ended an amorous adventure of a couple from a small town up river. This false alarm was more interesting than those solved by noticing deer hoof marks in the snow, or finding a heavy branch broken by a storm.

In medieval times, and probably before, guards or watchmen walking the wall or patrolling the moat had the company of a dog or two whose sense of smell, instincts, and training were counted on to give an early warning of the presence of strangers. The use of dogs for security purposes has had a recent revival, but animal assistants, then and now, have always been vulnerable to ailments, poison, a silent arrow, or a bullet. Physical barriers, mechanical and electronic machinery, trained dogs, and other aids are all vulnerable. They cannot reason. Their proper utilization is dependent on the ultimate review, judgment, and decision by the man on the scene, the guard.

The problem of perimeter patrol can become complicated by the terrain, neighbors, neighborhoods, lights, fences, traffic, and other factors. Perimeter patrols not only involve protection against encroachment from the outside, but they must also be on guard against the criminal removal of valuables from within by employees, business invitees, or interlopers who somehow have entered the protected area. If available statistics can be trusted, this latter jeopardy is one that requires greater attention.

A recent illustration in point concerns Bradbury Wilkinson, banknote and security printers, in London. This company, an affiliate of the American Banknote Company of New York, has been a major printer of American Express Travelers Cheques for some years. Their plant, near one of the superhighways on the outskirts of London, dates back to the turn of the century. Their *bona fides* is unassailable. Their other customers include many nations whose currency they print.

I can tell this story because everyone of the loopholes has been carefully closed. Some five years ago, $660,000 in printed American Express Travelers Cheques were stolen. This was accomplished in the face of a long-standing security staff, very low employee turnover, a system of inventory counts at many steps from the arrival of the paper through every process to the finished product, vaults of enormous strength, and the shipment of the end product under escort in armored cars.

It occurred at a time when a particular vault, used for packing the finished product, was being rewired for new alarms, and storing was temporarily transferred to an adjacent vault of equal strength. When the disappearance was noticed, the first conclusion was that the checks had inadvertently been placed in with the rubbish generated by the uncrating of material for the rewiring of the old vault. Porters in the employ of the company not normally in the vicinity helped in the cleanup. All rubbish was handled under security rules. It was normally segregated, and materials subject to misuse were consigned to two separate individuals for incineration or maceration on the premises. The balance was stored in large containers in a corner of the plant where at regular intervals the entire container was taken out on a special truck to a nearby dump.

Plant personnel and management refused to believe that there had been an actual theft, and clung to the theory of inadvertent destruction. Nonetheless, they notified me at American Express in New York. Within the hour, we were circulating warning notices containing the numbers of the traveler's checks involved to police, banks, money changers, and others who normally cashed these instruments worldwide.

Less than a fortnight later we had proof that the checks had not been destroyed. A young Englishman was apprehended at the money exchange bank in the Frankfort, Germany, railroad station. He had attempted to cash a $100 traveler's check listed on the warning bulletin. In a flight bag he had carried to Germany an additional $99,800 in American Express Travelers Cheques was also found. He had successfully cashed one $100 traveler's check at the Frankfort Air-

port about an hour earlier on his arrival from London by plane. He
was caught on his second pass.

The prisoner was George Haley Drummond, a young member of a
well-known Scottish banking family, distantly related to the royal
house of England. Back in England he had shared an apartment with
the actor, George Lazenby, who in one movie took the role of James
Bond. Other arrests followed in England and the matter climaxed at a
trial in Old Bailey in London in October, 1972. Haley Drummond
was defended by some of the most prestigious solicitors and barristers
in England. He was found guilty and sentenced to a four-year term.

Other recoveries of unspent loot from this same loss were made.
Instead of the case being closed, all attention was devoted to the questions of what was needed in the way of new security controls to prevent another such occurrence. It was evident that an employee had
been able to crack the outside perimeter and remove the traveler's
checks, which eventually ended up with Haley Drummond and others.

An explanation of the reforms to inner controls is privileged information and its disclosure might compromise them, so they must
remain secret. Perimeter control, however, visible from the street is a
matter that can be discussed. The plant in London consists of a series
of buildings set well back from the road. Fenced on all sides, there is
a U-shaped drive leading from one entrance gate to the front door of
the main building, and then around to another exit gate. At the two
bends of the U, roads lead straight back alongside the main building,
one past the other structures on the premises to a large employee parking lot, the other to the loading docks, the garages, and the employee's
recreation building in which the company restaurant and cafeteria is
housed.

All traffic into the grounds and buildings, foot and wheeled alike,
was funneled through the one entrance where it had to halt for inspection at the security booth inside the gate. All exiting traffic
emerged at the other gate, subject to the scrutiny of the security booth
there.

Once inside, however, with the exception of special areas in certain
buildings, little or no restriction existed. More than 100 cars daily
used the car park, as did numerous bicycles and motorcycles. Few, if
any, were inspected on departure, particularly when the occupants
were known to the guards. Delivery vans, especially those supplying
food to the commissary, made regular trips in and out of the premises.

These vans were accessible to all employees, and banter between drivers and employees was the result of years of acquaintance. The employees' recreation building was often used on Friday nights for civic and social functions by the neighborhood. Entrance for nonemployees was on foot, across the ground after being identified at the guard post.

American Express participated with American Banknote and Bradbury Wilkinson security in a survey after the theft case was closed. We were all aware that a Bradbury Wilkinson employee had been able to move the package from the vault area into the open, and then directly or by stages to a car in the car park where it was put in the trunk of the car.

Our joint recommendations, which were acted upon, improved the security without materially increasing its cost. Some of the changes resulted in the cutting down of all shrubbery growing alongside the fences, and a regular cleanup of an area at least eight feet on the inside of all fences so that the fences could be checked at a glance. Over the years these areas had become overgrown with ornamental shrubs. Also, a practice had grown up permitting the gardeners to pile grass clippings alongside the fence. Some of these piles, four feet in height, were perfect hiding places.

The area of the employee car park was fenced off from the balance of the plant, with one narrow gate installed for access to and from the buildings. The old main fence had two new openings from the back street into the car park. All employee cars were therefore segregated from the plant area. Employees removing packages to their cars would now have to pass through the guarded gate, which was double-checked by the installation of a CCTV, with a monitor set in the main control center.

The road leading to the loading area and the employee cafeteria facility was also segregated by internal fencing. Delivery personnel were limited in movement and no longer had access to the balance of the plant. Employees were segregated from the visiting delivery trucks.

There is no guarantee that these new installations will prevent the movement of an unauthorized package out of the plant. But they, and the reinforced interior controls, have changed the odds on it happening again and provide for more timely awareness of any such attempt.

The guards at the Bradbury Wilkinson plant were trying to accomplish the unobtainable. The unlimited, unobserved traffic between the buildings and the parking lot was an opportunity for concealment of stolen goods and a vehicle for its transportation at one and the same time. The new fence separating the parking lot from the plant area immediately put a single observant guard in a position to prevent a reoccurrence. The other changes increased the odds in the guards' favor.

Few other commercial or industrial installations require the intensive security that is needed by a plant that prints money. History records a case where one such plant was unlocked by shrewd confidence men who caused its management to direct the printing of a duplicate set of currency. Management was under the impression that they had a genuine order from their customer when they made delivery to the thieves. This was the 1920s case of Waterlow & Co., English banknote printers; their customer was the government of Portugal. The error led to the fall of the Portuguese government, and for Waterlow it was Waterloo. No physical security system could have prevented this gigantic fraud where management fell for the subterfuge, and initiated and supervised the operation of its own extinction.

Another currency printer, in a different country, suffered its first loss in more than a quarter century with the disappearance of uncut, printed up sheets of a foreign currency. Its plant was a multistoried building located in the heart of a city. The sheets were taken during the night shift, carried to a stairwell, and poked through an unfastened security screen so that they fell to the street below. The street was often deserted at night, and the streetlights were usually out of order, darkened by well-aimed stones thrown by young lovers who parked their cars in that quiet recess. The employee involved merely waited to the end of his shift and retrieved his booty on his way home.

The recommended reforms put into effect to prevent a reoccurrence included spot-welding all security screens. The 40-watt bulbs in the stairwells were replaced by bulbs of higher wattage sufficient to highlight anyone tampering with a window. A member of the regular guard force, using a three-wheeled motor bike would make a run around the streets surrounding the building on a frequent but irregular schedule.

Here again the simple changes tilted the odds back in favor of the guard force. Stairwells were well lighted to make any break in the window screen more visible to a guard on his rounds; patrols on the outside of the building were instituted to reveal any discards from the building, or the suspicious loitering of a potential confederate. Responsibility for the effectiveness of such changes, of course, rests as much on the guard—his training, his thoroughness, his acumen—as on the mechanical improvements.

But crime is not alone a city affair. For example, even in the most affluent suburban community in the country, construction site thefts "especially by workmen have reached epidemic proportions" which today involve millions of dollars each year.[2] Unlike a well-guarded plant, where supplies are put in protected buildings, a building site is fully exposed. Building supplies are delivered to it and stored on the open ground until ready for use. These include lumber, brass and copper pipes and fittings, frames, doors, glass, and assorted hardware. The site is vulnerable at all stages of construction until it is occupied by its tenant. Indicative of the dimension of the problem is the comment of one worker on the morals of the industry: "Everyone steals, we've seen builders bribe police and building inspectors." He made his statement after admitting stealing $50,000 worth of construction materials.[3]

Perimeter patrol requirements vary with locations. The heavy snow belt, which covers the areas of mountainside summer homes, was once considered crime free because of the difficulty of access in the winter months. This has now changed. The snowmobile has made looting of such places possible in the deepest snows. The same machine has greatly eased passage through outlying fences.

City or country, even a single post can have different security requirements, depending on the time of the day and the day of the week. The heart of most financial districts is a beehive of activity during business hours, but is a cavern of quiet at night and on weekends. With the change of just a few words, the following quotation, written in London in 1829, could apply to the metropolitan heart of most major cities of the world today:

> The City itself consists almost entirely of counting houses, offices, shops and warehouses, filled with plate, jewelry, silks, piece goods, spices, and all the choicest products of every corner of the globe: and from Saturday night till Monday morning is chiefly entrusted to office-keepers, servants, housekeepers and porters, and to the observer looks more like the 'city of the Plague' than the business mart in the universe.[4]

The modern world does not have office-keepers, housekeepers and porters live in on business premises. It entrusts its empire to its private security guards.

Protecting the property—the perimeter—is only one of the fundamental duties of a guard. Of equal importance is the protection of the product of the business. Proper performance of the guard function in connection with product protection can extend beyond the company's property. The product to be protected can include any material, from its raw state to its finished form, to which a company has legal title, on or off its premises.

The term "title" is used because it may affect security responsibility. When the United States Treasury decided it would no longer be a supplier of gold to industry, for instance, it encouraged some companies to become licensed importers and handlers of it. The number of instances of holdups, hijackings, and burglaries of this precious commodity did not make American Express anxious to engage in this venture. There could be problems of meeting shipments at airports and docks and escorting the gold by armored car to its vaults.

This reluctance was overcome through cooperative research by separate divisions of the company. The solution proffered was to accept delivery—title—at its vaultside, in its building, and to make delivery—pass title—at that same spot. Liability was thus effective only in its vault system. American Express was able to engage in a new venture in which large sums of highly salable, precious metal was involved without the need for any additional security expenditure on its part. A potential major security problem was solved by an application of law.

One modern problem inherent with the protection of products is the determination of whether or not a product has actually disappeared. And if it has, how? "Mysterious disappearance" has become an established rubric used in the insurance, accounting, and law enforcement fields. Timeliness of knowledge of the disappearance has a high correlation with the ability to control the loss. It is the basis of steps to prevent others of a similar nature.

In its *Economic Impact of Crimes Against Business,* the Department of Commerce subdivides the total loss from crime into business sectors. The single largest target of criminal attack, amounting to more than 25 percent of the total, is captioned "retailing." The department estimated that "crime costs incurred by the retail sector" were

$5.2 billion for 1973, and that they would be about $5.8 billion for 1974. Retailing constituted about 10 percent of the gross national product for 1973.[5]

In this report the department comments on the difficulty of determining the proportion of loss due to internal theft and that due to shoplifting. The definition of crimes involved in its total include only shoplifting, burglary, vandalism, bad checks, employee theft, and robbery.

The retailing industry treats this subject differently. It includes such losses under the heading of "shrinkage," which it says "represents shortages caused by clerical errors, shoplifting, and internal theft. (Losses due to burglary, holdups, arson damage and vandalism are not embraced in this definition.) It is that amount of merchandise which is unaccounted for at year-end after verifying the accuracy of the beginning inventory, markup on purchases, additional markup, sales, markdowns and the inventory on hand."[6] This shrinkage, based on the operations of department, specialty, variety, and food stores (excluding the cost of security and its systems), is currently estimated to be in excess of $3.5 billion a year, or $12 million each sale day.

The retail industry talks of such losses in percentage terms, that is, the percentage of the shrinkage in relation to total sales. While some well-managed stores claim losses as low as 1 percent, others, usually in metropolitan areas, put them as high as 5 percent. Statistics of one trade organization indicate a retail national average peaking at 2.34 percent for 1969, thereafter dropping to approximately 2% since.

Of course, shrinkage alone does not account for the total impact of crime against retail businesses. According to the United States Department of Commerce, the loss to this industry due to crime "is virtually equal to the normal profit margin in retailing."[7]

The failure of the retail industry to obtain timely, accurate figures as to each portion of its loss is a substantial contributor to its problem. Diagnosis is very difficult when the symptoms are not discovered until long after the disease has taken on virulent proportions, and then are so intermingled with other materials that specifics for the problems cannot be prescribed. As one analyst of shoplifting points out: "While there is no practical way to determine an accurate industry-wide percentage breakdown by causes of shrinkage, the likely proportions are estimated to be about one-third each for internal theft, shoplifting, and clerical errors. This mix does vary significantly, of course, for any one store or company depending on a wide variety of factors; internal theft is now often considered the greater amount."[8]

Retailing is one of the largest users of private security. It utilizes both guards and investigators, as well as large quantities of security devices and machinery. Indications are that their major problems are not on their selling floors, but in their inventory rooms and warehouses. Losses in mail-order branches, where the public never enters, lends strength to this observation.

Security staffs of the retail industry have been very effective where they have management behind them and leads to work with. They are responsible for half a million shoplifting apprehensions a year. In many jurisdictions they process their cases directly into the criminal justice system with a minimum of intervention or assistance by public law enforcement or prosecutors.

Shoplifters are often classified into two groups, "boosters" and "snitchers." Boosters, the major threat, are the commercial shoplifters who differ little from other professional thieves. Interested primarily in the monetary value of what they steal, they often have well-defined contacts with criminal subcultures. Many of them also have records for other crimes. The snitch is the pilferer, not exactly an amateur, but one who steals for his own use, real or imagined, and who seldom if ever sells or fences his loot. It is not always easy for the arresting officer or employee to determine the category of the apprehended shoplifter.

The costs of prosecuting shoplifting are great. It involves the untold loss of time spent in court on the part of the security employee who made the arrest, and on the part of sales and accounting staff to supply necessary prosecutorial data. There is also a risk involved in making such apprehensions; the potential for lawsuits for false arrest. The result is a system of private justice in which the security staff and management determine which persons of those detained should be reported to the criminal justice authorities and which should be released.

Some retail executives may disagree, but it is not easy in the retail industry to determine the full true cost of security measures. The totals spent for security staff salaries and certain security equipment, such as burglar alarms and CCTV, are ascertainable. Other measures, such as special display counters, increased lighting for certain areas, wider aisles, and, most particularly, special packaging designed to defeat easy pocketing are normally charged on different budget lines. Yet in each such case, the cost of the merchandise would have been far less but for the cost of these security measures. It is harder to palm and pocket a package of razor blades or a lipstick affixed to the center of a large, unbendable card, than it would be if that same item did not have the large backing. Whatever these protection costs may be, they should be added to the total spent to repel criminal attack. So should other measures taken by these same establishments to counter pilferage losses, such as computer control inventories that are charged as accounting costs, with no allowance of this cost, or a portion of it, as a security feature.

There are no specific statistics on retail losses due to employee pilferage. Montgomery Ward, a leading retail chain and mail-order house, reported 29,670 shoplifting apprehensions for their fiscal year covering portions of calendar 1972 and 1973. They also reported 3,165 employee apprehensions in the same period—roughly one for each 10 made for shoplifting. In one Montgomery Ward Company region thefts from company-employee pilferage amounted to $610,000, whereas those from shoplifting amounted to only $79,000.[9]

The movement of retail stores to large shopping centers has involved security in myriad new problems. They include the patrol of parking areas and the control of auto traffic on the private roads and properties of the shopping centers.

Another problem, gaining in dimension, is the operation of terrorists who plant incendiary devices. In Puerto Rico there are hardly any shops of major size that have not had to combat this problem. So have the large stores in metropolitan areas along the Atlantic Coast. Guards, as a result, now have the duty of doing a "sweep," a close search of every part of the premises once or more each day to seek out planted devices. Retail security has also gone back to using watchdogs, especially to assist in these "sweeps." In addition to their regular training, some dogs are also trained to detect certain odors, especially those associated with incendiary devices, and to halt, or bark and point, when their sense of smell indicates the presence of such an odor. I have been told of one major store that has strapped open radio transmitters on their guard dogs' harnesses. The dogs are allowed to roam on assigned floors at night and on weekends, while their guard-handlers monitor them from a central location. The guard then responds in person to the signaling growl or bark. Guard dogs are also being used extensively in warehouses and fenced exterior areas. In other locations reliance to assist the guards is put on mechanical devices, such as fire and smoke detectors, and closed-circuit television.

The retail industry is not the only one that has difficulty in determining whether and when an item has been stolen, lost, or otherwise consumed. Manufacturing is another sector of the business community that has felt the economic impact of crime. Said the Commerce Department's report on manufacturing: "The difficulty of obtaining statistics on the cost of ordinary crimes against the manufacturing sector is particularly imposing. The President's Commission concluded that there is no real information available for this sector, and this is still largely true today."[10] That statement was published in February, 1972. I know of no developments that would change this conclusion.

The manufacturing industry does not have the same problems faced by retail trade in connection with customers. In fact, most manufacturing plants do not permit non employees access. Losses therefore are generated by thieves breaking and entering, by robbers using guns or other weapon, and by light-fingered employees. The Department of Commerce estimates that losses due to crime to this segment of American business were $2.6 billion in 1973, and would reach $2.8 billion in 1974. There have been many instances of assembly-line shutdowns because of missing essential parts—ordered, paid for, and received. Expense losses and damage to profit from such shutdowns or slowdowns are not included in the dollar losses quoted above.

Missing screwdrivers or pliers, heating elements or audio tubes can be graphically apparent at certain stages of operations. The practice of overordering and overstocking has been the costly answer. The size, value, and outside marketability of these parts, of course, is a key factor in these losses.

The theft of completed products is another bugaboo of the manufacturer. Such losses range from items as small as cosmetics and pharmaceuticals to those as heavy and bulky as refrigerators or colored television sets. Losses are particularly severe in cases of brand merchandise, especially items not marked with individual serial numbers—soap, breakfast cereals, cake mixes, pots and pans. Some of these "shrinkages" have reached such proportions that the stolen merchandise competes in the marketplace.

The Department of Commerce commented in its findings that "defense industries suffer less from employee theft" because of their practice of employee screening and plant security [11] These are required by government contract, basically to combat possible foreign espionage and sabotage, and not as a method of crime control.

Service industries are among those businesses that find it difficult to assess their losses to criminal attack. "Again, there is no satisfactory estimate available for service industries as a whole or for most service trades."[12] One of its sections, that pertaining to restaurants, hotels, and hospitals, has been estimated to have lost more than $3 billion due to ordinary crimes in 1973.[13]

In its February, 1972, report, the Department of Commerce indicated that most of these losses were due to internal employee pilferaging of cutlery, food, liquor, silver, linen, and other similar articles. In commenting on the same problem two and a half years later in July, 1974, it added a statement attributed to a *New York Times* survey to the effect that "one out of every three hotel and motel guests steals something during his stay."[14]

Management perpetuates a futile feeling on the part of security personnel, which is usually very privately expressed by competent, trained security directors. They feel that their efforts are like holding an oar against the incoming tide. Their jurisdiction and involvement within the company are limited. They are compelled to assign manpower and machinery on a hit-and-miss basis because there has been no effort or willingness on the operational levels to make such changes as might be necessary to delineate the areas and time of loss. Unfortunately, the antagonism by operations divisions to security is never a hidden company secret. The feeling of futility is echoed down the line, and results in the inept type of individual often selected and employed as a guard.

There are areas where the security forces are faced with still another dimension of responsibility. In addition to safeguarding the property and products of their employer, they also are answerable for the person and property of the customer. The innkeeper and the restaurateur for many generations have had the advantage of special legislation and industry custom to help limit this liability. Signs like "Not Responsible for Coats Unless Checked" were once on large placques on the wall. Now they can be found in small print on the backs of menus. Few hotels fail to post the notice of their limited liability under a local statute, and the advice that a strong box or other similar security depository is available to each guest through the front desk or assistant manager. These signs are usually on the back of the room door or inside a closet.

While their liability may be limited by law, hostelries are always on their mettle to avoid bad publicity. Criminal attacks on guests or their valuables can lead to a loss in business, even if restitution is not involved.

High on the list of hotel and motel problems are room keys. In a busy, commercial establishment the same room and the same key may be held by as many as 200 different individuals each year. In practice room keys are often so available that thieves can easily obtain them. I witnessed an arrest in Honolulu where the prisoner carried a bag containing 190 local hotel keys, each complete with the hotel name and room number. Included with the bag were a dozen employee passkeys, giving access to an entire floor.

Hospital security has also become a deepening concern—and a more complex problem. Narcotics and other medical items have become the object of more and more criminal forays. Internal pilferage has reached the point where even the professionals—the doctors and nurses—are participants. A senior professor at one of the great metropolitan teaching hospitals told me that he delayed the introduction of an important new device for several months until after the first of July —the date old staff members leave and the new interns and residents arrive. He was advised that an earlier introduction would mean replacing the devices in July, since the departing staff would each probably take one.

When a university teaching hospital has been unable to indoctrinate its professional staff to a greater degree of responsibility than is illustrated by this account, how can it hope for better controls among its nonprofessional employees? The introduction of non-reusable, throwaway materials such as thermometers, hypodermic syringes, and patient hygienic supplies made of plastic instead of stainless steel was dictated as much by the high loss of the more expensive permanent items as it was by the needs of modern sanitation. Property of patients, both alive and dead, have become problems to hospital administrators and their security aides alike. Radios, wristwatches, jewelry, and other valuables frequently disappear from patient's rooms while they are out taking tests, or even while they are in the room under sedation or asleep. The press has related stories of hospital employees, morgue employees, and employees of funeral homes being arrested while cashing winning parimutual tickets known to have been on the person of a patient brought to a hospital and listed DOA (dead on arrival.)

The transportation industry is another whose loss figures are a jumble defying analysis and making the application of meaningful security measures difficult. In February, 1970, the United States Department of Transportation concluded: "The economic significance of loss and damage must be sensed through contact with people working in the field of shipping and traffic rather than through analysis of statistical data. Any intelligent perception of the problem would indicate that it is a large problem but its size cannot be readily grasped with the tools at hand."[15]

Total cargo theft was estimated to be around $1.5 billion in 1972. Available Department of Commerce figures show no variation since. Recognition is being given by the industry to the fact that each handling of a package is an exposure, with resulting losses at each point. A major breakthrough in avoiding such losses has come about through the use of containers for over-the-road and sea shipments. These large containers, loaded and sealed at the place of origin, are hoisted onto a flat-bed truck, and when bolted together the result looks like a truck-trailer. They are hauled by truck tractors to their destination. When sea trips are involved, the container is picked up by a special hoist and loaded into the hold, or bolted onto the deck.

Thus, the containers have their seals intact until they are broken at the very final destination. Sometimes these containers are secured with special locks. Still others are welded closed. The security inherent in this type of delivery is dissipated, of course, if it becomes necessary to open a container for additions or deletions en route.

There have been a few attacks on full container loads. But most attempts to steal their contents have been through subterfuge, by the use of switched documents. One container load so diverted was almost immediately abandoned after its successful theft. The bill of lading was in German; the contents of the container were empty boxes for Swiss watches.

The loss of cargo in and around airports increased more rapidly than the business of the airlines involved. Stories about such thefts have come out of airports located around the world. While I was in charge of security at American Express, we had major losses of blank traveler's checks at Kennedy Airport in New York, at Heathrow Airport in London, England, and at the airport in Nairobi, Kenya. We even had a loss from an airplane in flight, one operated by the United States government in connection with servicing American troops in Vietnam. There, of course, members of the crew were involved. In all the other cases the responsible parties were either ground personnel employed by the airlines or by the peripheral services. Other shippers had far, far greater losses of cargo, ranging from cash, bullion and jewels to expensive furs and machinery. These losses are being combatted by the direct action of the security staffs of the various airports. In some key areas they have been backed up by special task forces whose expenses are a joint contribution of shippers and carriers alike. Upgrading of guards, retraining, and more professional deployment of security men, supplemented by new, enforced operational changes and the use of more effective security mechanisms seem to have checked the increasing rate of loss, and given rise to the hope that the drop in the loss ratio can be made more permanent.

The various components that make up the shipping industry, air, marine, rail, and trucking, are all aware that there is an element of employee involvement in their losses. In some local areas segments of the industry have had control commissions established to assist in preventing such losses; the New York Waterfront Commission is one such example. Other segments have banded together and established mutual help organizations like the Airport Security Council which covers the airports of Greater New York. But these are few. The Department of Justice in Washington has directed 16 U.S. Attorneys in major metropolitan areas to hold meetings with shipping interests in their jurisdictions to foster greater security cooperation. To date these combined efforts have yielded little more than some local improvement. Shippers of cargo have been compelled to fall back on insurance on their merchandise to combat these losses, thereby increasing the cost of each movement—a cost that is added to the consumer's price. The practice of insuring all cargo, which requires extra charges and higher rates for the movement of insured merchandise, detracts from the attention given by shippers and their employees to the handling and security of shipments of uninsured materials. The extra cost of such broadly insured shipments, which correlates with criminal attack, has not been included in most estimates of losses due to crime.

The theft of airline tickets and the use of stolen credit cards to obtain tickets is still a growing puzzle whose size is not fully realized by the very lines affected. To some airlines, it is not regarded as a cash loss, but computed as an empty seat in making up load percentages. Professional thieves have found it so enticing a caper that they have used front men to purchase travel agencies for small down payments. Their real purpose was to obtain the blank airline ticket stock. Once this was marketed, they would abandon the business. Others have gone into the counterfeiting of airline tickets.

There is as yet no effective way of checking ticket numbers at airline counters. The various hot lists of stolen tickets are cumbersome to review during the rush of loading an aircraft. Machine-readable magnetic-stripe tickets have been designed, but are not as yet authorized for use.

A major user of uniformed private guards is the banking industry. Those licensed as national banks, and the many more who have their deposits covered by the Federal Deposit Insurance Corporation, have an additional protection in that any criminal attack is a Federal crime, subject to the investigative jurisdiction of the Federal Bureau of Investigation. As a licensed industry, banks are individually audited by bank examiners who report to the comptroller of the currency or state banking commissions. Federal legislation sets up mandatory security requirements.

Where figures are available, results indicate that the application of law enforcement and private security, in the form of men and machinery, has yielded good results. In 1973 there were 2974 instances of violations of bank robbery statutes, that is, robberies, burglaries and other larcenies, a drop from 3,354 such instances in fiscal 1971.[16]

Internal bank crime, however, has been propelled upward. Losses, as reported by the Department of Commerce, have tripled in a decade, rising from $14.1 million in fiscal 1963, to $135.6 million in fiscal 1973.[17] These represented reported losses. Banks have been notoriously unwilling to announce such embezzlements and pilferage because of their effect on their standing in the community. In many cases they have been willing to accept full or partial restitution and thus avoid making the report.

In the mix of remedies and preventatives applied by both public and private security to the problems of criminal attack on business, the private security guard occupies a giant share. Comment has already been made that private guards make up more than 90 percent of those employed by contract guard agencies. In the discussion to this point most of the guards were employed on a full-time basis. In the rapidly expanding sphere of activities involving places of public assembly like theaters, sports arenas, stadiums, and festivals the use of part-time security guards is a keystone of the operation. Here a skeleton security staff needed when the scene of action is quiet and no events are scheduled must be greatly expanded to handle the safety and security aspects of crowds.

The charges for these guards to the arena operators by private contract security firms vary widely. These charges do not necessarily reflect the labor cost of the men or persons involved. In some places where the arena management uses the services of unionized stagehands, electricians, ticket takers and other service categories it feels obligated to require that the security employees be members of an affiliated union. In such cases the minimum hourly rates paid by the potential suppliers of security services are fixed by union contract. Yet even in such instances the rent-a-guard agencies quote figures out of all proportion to their costs. In one such arena where only unionized guards were acceptable at a base wage of $3.25 per hour, the prices quoted by some 15 guard firms ranged from $4.40 to $6.35 per hour. With some 50,000 man-hours per year of projected use, the difference in cost is considerable. Where no union or similar consideration is involved, payments for part-time contract guards are at the minimum rate set by law, or a few cents more. A portion of the labor force in such instances is often made up of students recruited from local colleges and high schools.

At the other extreme of costs for such services are the localities where moonlighting local police in full official uniform are hired. Such hiring, starting as the result of political pressure or a desire to achieve maximum results, often becomes habit: "we always did it this way." These police officers are usually paid at the same rate they earn when on official business, and more recently at time and a half, since it is construed by some to be overtime.

These part-timers at places of assembly are thus paid at rates per hour that range from $2. to $8. and even $10. The cost is eventually added to the admission price paid by the attending public. It is worthy of note that many of these arenas are operated by municipalities and other public agencies.

The variation in hourly rates for contract guards is not limited to guards supplied to public agencies or authorities. I can testify to being quoted hourly rates for contract guard services in 1973 by different companies with a range of more than 100 percent between the lowest and highest. These guards were offered by firms, including some of the largest in the field, at prices as low as $2.85 an hour and as high as $6 an hour. While these highest bidders talked glibly about better men, better training, and better supervision, they at the same time all agreed that they were recruiting from the same labor pool. None of them were willing to change their rates when told that we used our own in-house supervisors. These lower figures were clearly less than American Express would have had to pay had it used in-house guards.

The choice of whether to use contract guards rather than an in-house security force is usually a dollars-and-cents decision, and as such is made by senior management. It is the contention of the contract guard industry that it can supply guard services at savings estimated at 20 percent of the cost of similar services on an in-house basis.[18] The argument marshals the following factors: the contract agency hourly rate includes the cost of uniforms and their upkeep, liability insurance, fringe benefits, and shift differentials. As a total, this rate is usually lower than the total payment to the lowest in-house factory category of regular employee who is also entitled to fringe benefits, vacations, and compensation during sickness. Using a contract agency also eliminates procurement and other personnel costs, as well as training expenditures. Coverage during vacations or unavoidable absences for illness or other reasons is the responsibility of the contract guard agency. Often hiring contract guards eliminates the need for supervisors, even for an in-house security expert. Another argument advanced is that contract guards are usually more impartial in enforcing company rules than are in-house employees, who develop attachments or loyalties that influence objective judgment. The essential factor, however, is that contract guards can cost less.

Proponents of in-house staffs admit that their personnel are more expensive computed on an hourly basis with uniforms, fringe benefits, vacation costs, training and procurement factored into the charge. They point out, however, that the quality of the individual on the in-house staff is better—and that he is better trained. Furthermore, they contend, the lower in-house turnover results in greater individual experience and therefore greater effectiveness. There is also the psy-chological argument that the in-house guard has an undivided loyalty to the firm he is protecting, while the contract guard is a mercenary, with a loyalty divided between his employer, his agency, and his temporary assignment. In any showdown his loyalty would probably rest with his agency, where the worst result of any misjudgment would be a transfer to another job, not dismissal.

6 | Security Personnel Practices

Guards make up 90 percent of all the persons who earn their liveli-hood in private security. Seventy percent are employees of in-house departments, and the balance are employed by contract, rent-a-guard agencies. According to the 1971 Rand Corporation study, a typical guard is an aging white male, poorly educated and poorly paid. This conclusion was arrived at after considering various information, rang-ing from 1950 and 1960 census studies to more current interviews with security executives, recent surveys done by the American So-ciety for Industrial Security, and an in-depth survey of 275 security workers.[1]

Rand found the average guard to be between 40 and 55 years old, with little education beyond the ninth grade, earning a marginal wage of between $1.60 and $2.25 an hour, with many working be-tween 48 and 56 hours a week. Annual turnover rates were found to range "from less than 10% in some in-house" groups to "200% and more in some contract firms."[2]

The hundreds of pages of testimony, taken in late 1973 and early 1974, by a Select Committee of the Pennsylvania House of Repre-sentatives bear out these Rand findings.[3] The testimony, taken two to three years after the Rand material was collected, showed that many guards were still paid at a rate of $1.60 or $1.65 an hour, with a majority seeming to receive less than $2.50 an hour. The testimony challenges the Rand finding that the typical guard is white, however. It indicates a major use of non-whites in the metropolitan areas of Pennsylvania.

The words of some of the witnesses at these hearings are dramatic illustrations of how the guard is paid and used. Here, for example, is part of the testimony of John A. Kruzinski, a private security guard who had long before passed the tests for entry into the Philadelphia Police Department, but did not accept appointment when it was offered; before becoming a security guard, he had served five years in the U.S. Marine Corps, retiring after 20 years as a steam fitter. In the security field he rose to become an assistant manager of a contract agency employing 250 men. On October 26, 1973, he testified:

Today, gentlemen, the hiring practices of many of the security agencies in the City of Philadelphia are a joke. They only ask you to be 21 years of age, no police record, have a home phone, and an automobile. You go into this agency and get an application; they will fingerprint you; and on the application it states, 'Do you have a police record?' You put 'No,' you could go to work that night. You are hired and you are ready for a uniform. You get a shirt, a hat, a jacket, a pair of trousers, along with two badges of the security company. You are given a location to work. And all you know when you leave the agency is that you are to report to such and such a location. . . .

I went on such a location, told the man who I was. I was in uniform. He handed me a .38 pistol, one of the old jobs, with a 6-inch barrel, and told me I was to stand on the platform of the place and just watch for troublemakers.

I was new at this thing. I didn't know what this guy meant by 'troublemakers.' Boy, this is bad! He has given me a gun, and what am I supposed to do with it? I know what a gun is; I know what a gun can do; my training in the Marine Corps taught me this.

. . . It might be interesting to note that 90%, maybe more, of your security members in this City [Philadelphia] do this kind of work as a second job, as a pension, and because some of them, many of them, I would say, cannot do physical labor, cannot do intelligent labor, so they go into the security field, in order to make a living wage. If these guys are only doing this, they work some terrific number of hours, for $1.75 to $2.00 an hour, you'll find men working sixty, seventy or eighty hours weekly to take home some kind of decent pay. No one stops to think that after 40 hours a week, this guy—or after nine or 10 hours a day—this guy is not effective as a security guard, which he should be.[4]

Kruzinski's statement touches on many points, including the arming of guards. According to the Rand findings, about 50 percent of all guards are armed. A more intensive review of this aspect of private security is made later in this chapter.

Leonard Elliot, then 66 years old, another guard who had spent most of his adult life in the U.S. Marines, testified that same day. He had been a private security guard, working for four different contract agencies, for about four years. He said that for two and a half months immediately prior to his appearance before the committee he was involved in attempting to unionize private security guards in the Philadelphia area. He stated:

Now, 90% of the security system in Pennsylvania, or let's say, in Philadelphia, mainly is black. And the reason I say that is because these guys who don't have what you call a good education, these are the only types of jobs they could get.

You have good guards, and you have some that are not qualified, let's put it that way. Every guard is not a thief. Every guard is a man who is trying to do a job, does the job. The guard that's not being treated—you know, an employee of an agency who has the Canine Union, they think more of their dogs than human beings, and I resent that, you know. They take a contract for a dog for $7. for $9. an hour, and pay a man $1.65 an hour. It's not right. . . .

I went as far as the Sixth Grade. And I got a job as a guard. And a lot of the guards—you know, this is all you have to do; they can't do nothing else. What I'm saying is that you have some that can't read. You have some that can't really help themselves.[5]

Two weeks earlier, on October 12, at the hearing in Pittsburgh, Richard Durstein, president of the Fidelity Security Systems of Pittsburgh, had testified that his company, a contract guard agency, had 100 employees, all male and 50 percent black, with an average age of 50. They were paid at a rate of $1.80 an hour. Their educational level, he said, was about the seventh or eighth grade. About 40 percent of his employees, said Durstein, came through referrals from the Pennsylvania Unemployment Commission.

James Gregg, treasurer of the Union Security Services and of the Attorneys Investigative Services of Pittsburgh, two agencies with more than 300 employees, was also questioned that same day. In answer to an inquiry about the hiring standards and qualifications of his company, Gregg said:

> As far as educational requirements, there are none whatsoever. A man has to be able to read or write or communicate; he must be a citizen, of course, with no criminal record. Now, when I say "criminal record," there will be men in my employ for a month, and I go back and get a "rap" sheet on them, and they are terminated.[6]

Both the Rand study and testimony taken in the Pennsylvania hearings make the point that many guards are part-time workers with their security assignments supplementing income from another source. These part-timers are used most often on the second or third shifts, and on weekends and holidays. Both the study and the testimony mention the use of teachers and students as part-time guards too—and their inclusion in any statistical base would tend to raise the education and literacy levels of the group.

It is fair to conclude that prevailing employment practices have no physical or mental minimum requirements or standards; no minimum educational or literacy standard, and no age standard, except for a minimum age restriction as required by local law. Citizenship is required in some areas. It is also fair to conclude that the private security guard, especially the contract agency guard, is among the lowest paid of any workers in the United States. This guard, whose assignment is the protection of the assets of the business of America, is at the very bottom rung of the employment hierarchy. He rates below that of common pick-and-shovel laborer, and would often not have the qualifications, either physical or mental, to qualify for a common labor job.

None of the foregoing is intended to demean the background, physical and mental ability, or educational qualification of many guards. I have had personal experience with hundreds of competent guards, and, as in any other line of work, there are wide differences among them and between private security agencies. I have had occasions to write letters of commendation to contract guard agencies, whose guards we were using, detailing acts performed by their men beyond what was normally to be expected, and of material value to our over-all security. One of my own supervisors tried to dissuade me from such practice, because, he complained, the guard so praised would be moved to another location where the contract agency was trying to make a good impression, leaving him to start all over again in training a new man.

There is a consensus that private security guards should be of good moral background, and have clean records. Questions as to the existence of a criminal record are part of most employment applications. Usually the applicant is fingerprinted at the same time. The prevailing practice is to hire an acceptable applicant who answers "No" to the question about a previous conviction without waiting for the fingerprints to be checked. In many areas fingerprint checks are made against local police records only. The checking of fingerprints of applicants for jobs against the central fingerprint files of the FBI in Washington is controlled by law, and in most cases does not allow for guard prints. One proprietor of a rent-a-guard agency told the Pennsylvania legislators that he was forced to dismiss about 10 percent of all of the guards he hired because they turned out to have former records with local police departments. This fact was usually revealed about 30 or more days after he had put the men to work, because it took that long to process the prints. Even the Board of Education of the City of New York was rudely shaken when some of its security guards were picked up in the act of committing crimes, and turned out to have long prison records.

Operating with workers of concededly marginal abilities, the private security business generally does little to train them. Individual training programs vary considerably in quality. Most of the programs are inadequate, or do not exist except as on-the-job training by another equally untrained person, or poorly qualified supervisor. In its summary, the Rand investigators point out that "private security personnel receive almost no initial or in-service training."[7]

Durstein in his testimony before the Pennsylvania committee said that guards in his company's employ were sometimes assigned to jobs without any training whatsoever. James Gregg, of Union Security Services, in referring to guard agency proprietors, had the following to say on training:

They're not going to pass up a job because they don't have trained men; they're not going to do it. They're going to use these men, and give them the basic requirements, if they give them that. . . .

The type of training we use on some jobs—I am saying "some jobs," because on some jobs I have men with no formal training than what I told them in the office, prior to taking this job, actually, how to fill out truck sheets, and so forth, because, like I may put them in a metal factory, and their main job is checking orders, etc., and the training is mostly a "JT," and I can't train a man in that. . . .

In the guard service business, they hire men, put a gun on them and send them out.[8]

Ian B. MacLennon, president of Security Bureau, Inc., of Pittsburgh, and for 10 years in charge of the FBI's Pittsburgh office, on April 18 urged the Pennsylvania legislators to require mandatory training for private security guards. At the same time, he undertook to remind the committee that there was no mandatory state training requirements for public police officers. Police officers in the larger cities were trained by local direction, said MacLennon, but there were rural areas that had no such program. In discussing the need for mandatory training for private security men, even if it involved greater charges for such service, MacLennon argued that "we get back to the theory that you get what you pay for and right now there are many, many companies that are paying for guard service that aren't getting guard service. They are getting bodies, B-O-D-I-E-S."[9]

Along with most other security directors, I can testify to my own experience with guards who are but bodies. A recent case is the one recently reported where a jewelry establishment was rifled by thieves who broke through a wall from an adjacent office. The operation was accomplished while the security guard on duty had deserted his post and had gone to a nearby movie. Spot checks by our in-house supervisors of contract guards have indicated that guards will leave their posts hours before they are due to be relieved, but their time sheets show they worked the entire shift. Such misrepresentation requires the tacit knowledge and consent of other guards on the same tour. The cots in the company infirmary, and in one of the lounges for women employees, would on occasion reveal that a contract agency employee had been sleeping while his clock was being walked by another guard.

Paul Schmitt, manager of Globe Security Systems, of Philadelphia, said at the hearing on October 26, 1973 that his company grossed some $15 million a year, 90 percent of it from contract guards. His men, numbering between 2000 and 2500, were not high-school graduates and were almost always assigned to jobs without training. They were then given on-the-job training by another guard. The following colloquy reveals his opinion:

Q. . . . To my way of thinking, these companies are going to be willing to pay considerably more, as much as $6.00, $7.00, or $8.00 an hour to have this function performed by a person who is properly trained in all aspects of the job?

A. This is an assumption that most people would make. However, the fact of the matter is that the larger the corporation, the less they are going to pay. We do work for one of the giants in the country, and I mean, one of the top ones. They are the lowest paying client that we have. It is virtually impossible to even get two or three cents an hour additional out of them. They have the muscle because they have the people. They have the number of guard hours that they require, and this, of course, is what forces the wages down. . . .
. . . our product is a service; it is a manpower product. And if we can't sell it, then we cannot remain in business. So, the only way that is feasible, practical, to do this would that it be incumbent and required of agencies in this business to do the same thing. I was trying to get across the idea that we agree that wages are substandard. We would like to see them higher. We will support anything that will make it mandatory to get it to this position, but unilaterally we cannot do it.[10]

The same general question has been raised before. Would increasing the rate of payment to some of the contract guard agencies result in a better-trained, better-qualified staff? Unfortunately, the record can only suggest a "maybe." I once reviewed a contract guard detail in a building for which the hiring concern had been induced to pay a special rate because the guards were supposedly better trained. The rate was almost 75 percent higher than it normally paid for similar guards at other buildings. These other buildings were manned by guards of a different agency. After some intense study, I found that there was no difference. They were both uniformly untrained, without any real sense of loyalty to the ownership of the property they patrolled, or any real desire to accomplish anything beyond passing time and collecting their paycheck. Close questioning disclosed that the guards at both places were being paid at identical hourly rates. The entire difference in the payment for the so-called superior, better-trained men, touted off at the higher rate, was going into the coffer of the contract guard agency. When this was taken up with the agency officials, they answered that they normally supplied closer and more qualified supervision on the costlier job, but in this instance unfortunately their supervisor had quit some months before, and they were having trouble finding a replacement.

The position of many contract guard agencies on the issue of training was voiced at the Pennsylvania hearings by Robert Raphall, attorney for more than 15 years for Allied Security Services. Allied has more than 2000 guards working for it in Pennsylvania. On April 19, 1974 Raphall told the legislators:

> Going on, on the matter of training personnel, I know from reading previous statements—I read that. House Bill 2079 requires at least three days of training in the field and others have suggested that this is not enough. Let's take a realistic look at the matter. Based on my own experience with Allied, I would venture to guess that more than 90% of the uniformed guards carry no weapons except perhaps for chemical mace. How much training do you really need to walk and look which is basically all that most guards do? Sure, there are a few rules to follow for handling, let us say, things, but let us not magnify the duties of the uniformed guard. My client, Allied, uses training films as well as lectures to teach their employees. I strongly suggest an intense quality program of one day is more than enough for the unarmed guard. . . . Overtraining makes no sense and only adds additional expense to the guard.[11]

The Wackenhut Corporation took a different approach. It was represented at the hearings by the head of its Philadelphia office, William Allen, who testified on April 4, 1974 and emphasized that training should be an inherent part of the economics of the contract guard agency business. Said Allen: "I wouldn't care if I had to charge a client $10 an hour to insure training requirements put out by the State as long as everybody else had to do the same thing."[12]

It is difficult to disagree with the conclusions of the Rand survey that while private security training programs vary considerably in quality, most training is either nonexistent or clearly inadequate.[13] Only two states, Ohio and Vermont, have mandatory training requirements for guards or investigators. Rand did a survey of 11 firms utilizing security forces in areas where training was not legally obligatory. Thus, any variation between their training practices would be based on voluntary management programs. Training schedules in each of these firms were self-imposed as business decisions. Rand's findings were that the training standards varied from a total of 166 hours for the in-house staff of a private research firm down to 4½ hours for the temporary staff of a large contract guard firm. Only 4 of the 11 firms provided more than 25 hours of training; three of them were in-house employers, and one a contract firm.[14]

Representing a company engaged in the processing of nuclear fuel, and therefore subject to the licensing and regulations of the Atomic Energy Commission, David Blumenstein was called as a witness on April 19, 1974. He told the Select Committee that his firm employs 24 armed guards, a number of them women. Each guard is required to have clearance by the government, which entails a background check. As to their training, Blumenstein said:

> We are required by the federal regulations of the Atomic Energy Commission to give a course of instruction to our guards which in this case included us having one of the professors from the Duquesne University Law School at the recommendation of Dean Davenport to come out to our plant and give a course of instruction to the guards and in addition to which, of course, they are instructed in the use of firearms.[15]

Joining the Atomic Energy Commission, both the National Aeronautical and Space Agency and the Department of Defense have security requirements that include minimum standards of selection and training, as well as strict clearance regulations. It is no surprise that the Department of Commerce in its report on *The Cost of Crimes Against Business* mentions that concerns doing business with these agencies seem to have smaller losses to crime.

The practice of arming guards is widespread, though no exact figures exist as to the number armed. While the Rand study estimated
that about half of all guards carry guns, the Pennsylvania hearings had
conflicting testimony on the point. New York's strict gun control laws
undoubtedly temper any national statistics. In New York gun permits
must be obtained by each individual, as an individual, and there is no
provision for blanket covering of an industry, or firm, or occupation.
Individual permits are difficult to obtain. Applicants are both fingerprinted and interviewed, and then are subject to police investigation.
The result is that armed guards are not as prevalent in New York as
they are in other areas. Where they exist, a large proportion of them
are retired police officers.

This is not true in most other states, however, where firearms are
obtainable with little or no preliminary screening or training, especially when private guards are the intended users. Evidence of this
absence of restrictions was included in some of the Pennsylvania testimony. When arms are easily available, the results can be frightening,
as was aptly summarized on October 25, 1973 by the testimony of the
clerk of the Court of Quarter Sessions of Philadelphia, Edward Lee.
Lee's jurisdiction also includes the licensing of private detective agencies. In referring to private security guards, Lee told the committee:

> These guards are armed with revolvers, mace, tear gas, knives,
> blackjacks, attack dogs, billy clubs, and occasionally 12-gauge
> shotguns.
>
> They are paid minimal wages to take verbal and physical
> abuse, expel troublemakers, catch bullets during a robbery, out-
> smart shoplifters, protect valuables and save store personnel from
> the clutches of roving gangs. These are Herculean tasks en-
> trusted to people who are, for the most part, undereducated,
> untrained, and poorly supervised.
>
> They lack the authority to arrest, but they have the power of
> life or death on their hips. *It is a fact that security guards in this
> area shot 13 people.* This is an alarming statistic because it
> seems to indicate any guard with a gun on his hip is inclined to
> use it [emphasis added].[16]

However, Lee concluded his testimony with the following statement:

I recognize the fact that security guards are just as vital as city police in the day to day operations of many local retail businesses, factories and schools. Properly regulated and supervised, they can be a highly specialized force in the security field. They can fill in the gap as police surrogates and may well be a short-term answer to urban crime.

I recall the worrying predicament of an acquaintance, a senior official of a major corporation in charge of a multistory branch office, who was authorized to install armed guards on his premises. He obtained the services of a reputable contract agency, which, after a survey, recommended armed guards on a 24-hour, seven-day a week basis at an estimated charge of $120,000 a year. He told me that it was some weeks later, after the guards had been installed, that he struck up a conversation with one who looked in on his office when he was working late one night. In the course of that conversation he casually asked the make of the gun the guard was carrying. The guard replied that he did not know, he had never looked; in fact, he had never held the gun or any other gun in his life. My acquaintance said he returned to his office at 7:30 the next morning, a half-hour before the third shift was due to leave and the first shift was to report for duty. He called each guard from both shifts individually into his office. By questioning, he determined that not one of them had ever had any training or experience in the handling of their weapons. He, himself, a wartime aviator, had a thorough knowledge of hand weapons. He persuaded each guard in turn to permit him to reach into each holster, remove the gun, and extract all of its ammunition. At 9 o'clock, with a drawer full of bullets, he sent for the security company's manager. There is a new guard service in the building. Each guard now carries a two-way radio instead of a gun.

The Pennsylvania legislative hearings also disclosed the use of subterfuge by some contract guard firms that I believe is highly dangerous. Schmitt was the first to mention it in his testimony. At the hearing of October 26, 1974 he was asked by the chairman of the committee, Representative James B. Kelly:

Q. Mr. Schmitt, you've said that you have approximately 1,000 guards in this area and 30 or 35 of them are carrying firearms at a given time. Half of these firearms that you described as being inoperative, what does that mean?

A. Due to the fact that the man is carrying a gun will discourage people from coming in here and trying to hold us up. And we want him to have something that looks like a gun. And we want him to have this. You don't have to put bullets in it if you don't want to, but we want a gun on the guard. So the lack of bullets, obviously isn't going to deter anything. What we do in that case is to use an inoperative gun, because bullets, of course, are obtained too easily. So we put a gun on the location strictly for show, and it is an inoperative weapon.

Q. It's a weapon that could not fire?

A. That is correct.[17]

This practice turned out not to be unique with Globe Security. Later that same day, William F. Robinson, J. C. Buford, and Jimmy Reed, who did business as the B & R Detective Agency of Philadelphia, gave testimony that they employ 60 men, all of whom carry guns. Of these, only six are operative weapons. The other 54 are dummies.

A nervous criminal, stimulated by alcohol or a narcotic, under high tension in the course of a holdup, would probably not be able to determine whether the weapon in the hand or holster of a guard was inoperative. Rather than risk capture or being shot in the back as he ran, he might very likely shoot first. Conversely, amateur teenage thieves could wrongly assume that all guards wear dummy guns and ignore a command to halt. Guards with dummy guns are clay pigeons, targets at an average wage of $1.90 an hour. There is no reliable information on how widespread this practice has become.

Years ago, as an Agent in the Secret Service, I was paired with a United States postal inspector in upstate New York, where we both had jurisdiction, on a long investigation involving the theft from the mails and forgery of government checks. Finding ourselves in a small community with several hours to wait for the return of a witness we needed to interview, I accompanied the inspector to the nearby village post office so that he could do his annual inspection. I was re-reading the file at a desk next to the open safe while the postmaster and the inspector were going over the checklist. They had come to the office gun. To speed up their work, the inspector asked me to look into the safe to see if the gun was there. The postmaster said I would find it in a big, old, tan leather cavalry holster. I saw it at once. But instead of merely acknowledging its presence, I reached in and took out what was supposed to be the holstered piece. I found an umbrella handle tucked in where the gun should have been. The postmaster eventually produced a rusted, useless old World War I army automatic from a locked tin box in the furthest reaches of the safe. It had been there for years. The postmaster was afraid of guns, and his umbrella handle had passed many a previous inspection. Fortunately for him, his technical deception did not place him in the same jeopardy as the wooden gun in the exposed holster of a uniformed security guard.

Mace, billy clubs, nightsticks, even handcuffs are tools whose use must be controlled and limited to trained personnel. In the hands of the untutored they can become boomerangs that can injure both sides. These are not the only tools entrusted to guards. With increasing frequency they are using sophisticated two-way radios, closed-circuit television, and a growing list of alarm devices, each representing considerable capital investment. Failure to train persons in their proper use endangers the investment and severely limits the returns expected by proper handling.

The fact that this training deficiency has not been corrected by business itself must be attributed to the lack of knowledge and understanding of this problem by senior managers. While training minimums are dictated to business for their security by contracts with the Department of Defense, the Atomic Energy Commission, and the National Aeronautics and Space Administration, all other users will eventually be forced to institute minimum training standards by legislation. There seems to be general agreement in the security industry that such legislation is inevitable. The presently existing proposals for Model Statutes do little more than suggest a bottom standard of training. Many concerns will try to do little more than the absolute minimum, so as to conserve what they regard as their competitive position. Voluntary upgrading, a more effective method, can only come from senior management's realization that it can improve business, reduce losses, and present a more positive corporate image. At the present time none of the business schools connected with universities give more than a cursory nod to the private security area. Risk managers, whose advice is heeded by the boardrooms, lump loss figures of various types and look for ways to reduce the company's overall cost of risk control. They pay little attention and have little understanding of the analysis of operations and its interplay with security where appropriate modifications might increase control costs for a temporary period but reduce losses over a longer time span. Business schools have devoted considerable attention to the management of risks. These studies have placed emphasis on the definition of risk areas. Even so, little has been accomplished in clarifying the boundaries of business losses to crime. But as I have noted before, "the most serious difficulty associated with analyzing the impact of crimes against business continues to be the sparseness and sporadic nature of the data available."[18] Identification, measurement and specificity of place, time, and amount of losses are essential elements in instituting programs for control.

With an occasional exception, most senior business managers have had little or no training, or even exposure, to the problems and opportunities of private security on an academic or on-the-job basis. The literature of this field consists primarily of security manuals addressed to "how to install and control a security system" rather than to "why." Reviewing a security-cost budget is not training in how to appraise the various alternatives in the quest for an economical, viable security program. While such organizations as the American Management Association, the National Retail Merchants Association, and others have sponsored day-long and even two- and three-day symposia on private security, attendance has been primarily by security directors, not senior managers charged with the overall problem.

Directors of security, whatever their title might be, perform two major functions. Theoretically, they advise their employer on the security exposure of the company and what should be done about it. They also administer the company plan for security, literal or understood, set down by management. When a contract guard agency is employed, it acts for the company in a more or less similar capacity through its representatives who service customers.

The average security director was described by the Rand study as being about 45 years old, college educated just short of a degree, with about 11 years of experience in industrial security.[19] Twenty-seven percent of them employed by companies with more than 500 workers had business administration backgrounds. Only 3.4 percent of them had experience as Federal investigators with such investigational services as the FBI, Secret Service, Bureau of Narcotics, or the Postal

Inspection Service. Local police experience was the background of some 22 percent. Those who only had a college education were limited to 7 percent of the total. The figures varied for firms with between 100 and 500 employees, but they were not materially different.

Security executives have relatively little in the way of literature to increase their understanding of their field. Academic programs aimed at this level are limited to seminars, if any information is offered at all. Seminars covering the wide spectrum of security are sponsored by the American Society of Industrial Security and the American Management Association, among other organizations, including one that publishes a magazine, *Security World*. Attempting to get the largest attendance possible, these meetings cram in information about management, law (both civil and criminal), alarm systems, schedules, kidnapping, retail security, fraud, informants, fire prevention, and a host of other subjects. The result is that several sessions are held simultaneously in different rooms with those attending compelled to make a choice. Both as a speaker-instructor, and as a participant-attendee at several such sessions, I left with the feeling that though I might have caught a glimpse of a problem, any real understanding of it was impossible because of the lack of time and opportunity for discussion. Some people attending such meetings, where fees of up to $300 are charged, have been antagonized because advertised speakers failed to appear and because in some cases the information furnished was a rehash of what was well-known. Despite the attendance fee, many of the seminars are limited in that speakers are selected from persons willing to contribute their time and services without compensation or honorarium. In some instances speakers are expected to provide their own transportation and assume their own expenses for food and lodging.

In theory, 50 percent of in-house directors of security of large concerns report to the president, a vice-president or one of the three top officials of their company. Such reporting increases to 75 percent in the case of smaller concerns.[20] But in practice, many companies now give their security chiefs the title of vice-president. A review of organizational charts will disclose that those reporting directly and regularly to one of the three top officials of major concerns constitute a very small percentage of security directors.

The key to the success of any organization is the acumen, training, and integrity of its supervisory personnel. They have been found to be the essential ingredient in stimulating production. They are the business world's noncommissioned officers. Supervisors, their problems, their role in management, their selection, their training, and other facets of their use have been the subject of studies by both business and social research departments of many universities. It is therefore doubly unfortunate that so little attention has been paid to the selection and training of supervisory personnel in the security portion of industry.

The security supervisor, in addition to his supervisory function, is called on to train new employees, persons often of low perception and education. These people require training to operate in situations where the use of discretion and judgment may be necessary. The new guard, for example, may be carrying a gun for the first time in his life. This training must compensate for handicaps of age, physical or mental infirmity, dubious literacy, and minimum wages while at the same time successfully instructing in how to use a gun; what to do in the event of fire, holdup, and bombing; who to permit access to the premises; and what to do in the event of accident—or catastrophe.

Here again there is no existing academic base for such training. Some of the institutions offering degrees in the criminal justice field include a course or two in "security problems" or in "methods of security" under the myriad requirements in police science. But few graduates in criminal justice take jobs in private security. I have heard of only one. Most of them are already in the public employ when they take these studies, or look for public employment once they have their degree. What training for supervisory security personnel does exist is conducted by employers. One contract guard firm is reported to have a three-week course.[21]

By comparison, industrial plant safety, hygiene, and the administration of adequate first-aid programs have been the subject of academic interest and study for many years. Degrees are awarded in these fields, and few big companies entrust their departments handling these matters to persons without recognized academic qualifications and appropriate experience.

The Guards and Investigation Sub-Committee of the National Security Advisory Council of the Law Enforcement Assistance Administration proposed a model private security licensing and regulatory statute in January, 1975. If adopted by the LEAA, it would be recommended to the various states. It proposes a mandatory eight-hour training program for contract guards prior to assigning them to a job. These eight hours would be subdivided as follows: two hours for "orientation," two for "legal powers and limitations of a security officer," two for "handling emergencies," and the last two for "general duties." Each guard would be required to receive an additional 32 hours of "in-service" training within 120 days of his hiring. The proposed statute makes no stipulations about eligibility for in-service training. Guards who are to be armed would be required to have an additional three hours of pre-issue weapon instructions on the "legal limitations on the use of weapons," the handling of a weapon, and the safety and maintenance of the weapon. Thereafter guards would have to meet minimum marksmanship requirements. Training, which would be conducted by a qualified officer or his appointee, could, in his discretion, be a "combination of personal instruction, audio and/or visual training aids." The proposed statute does not spell out requirements that the guard pass any minimum test; exposure to instruction seems to fill the training requisite. The subcommittee did not make it clear whether these minimum training requirements would apply to in-house staffs. Industrial security management personnel were excluded from the training requirements, however, as were "in-house industrial security personnel who supervise guard operations unless they actually perform security guard functions as part of their principal duties." Discussion of the other facets of this model statute is continued in Chapter 10 on Law, Legislation, and Regulation.

These recommendations of the *LEAA* subgroup for training private security guards should be judged against the hours needed to prepare and train individuals in other occupations. For example, the minimum requirement for physicians is 11,000 hours; it is 5000 hours for embalmers, 4000 hours for barbers, 1200 hours for beauticians, and somewhat less than 200 hours for policemen.[22] These figures were assembled in 1969. Police training has improved markedly since then. Many police departments have enlarged their initial training periods considerably. They have introduced "paired" field experience in the training schedule. Retraining on a regular basis is also becoming standard procedure. More than 200 colleges and universities have adopted programs toward the granting of degrees in the field of criminal justice. In addition to bachelor's degrees, some of these schools of higher learning are offering master's degrees and doctorates. Tuition aid has become available in the form of grants emanating from the LEAA. This has resulted in a concerted movement by the more ambitious young police officer, eager for promotion, to take these courses on his own time while still holding down his police job. Some of these colleges have arranged for specific courses to be given by the same instructor during both day and evening sessions for the convenience of the working police officer who is subject to a changing job schedule. The number of young policemen seeking degrees beyond the B.S. is worthy of note. Promotion opportunities within many police departments are now geared to the advancement of the better-educated and better-trained person.

The selection and training of private security personnel should follow suit, not to fulfill minimum standards imposed by law, but as a matter of opportunity for improvement and for the purpose of preventing incidents and reducing loss. Greater emphasis should be placed on the education and training of private security supervisors, mid-management, and senior security directors.

7 | Fraud Investigation

In background and experience, investigators contribute a giant share to the probity and standing of private security in the American business community. They have served as the catalyst for the broadening of the base of private security. The three largest contract guard concerns had their roots in investigations. Pinkerton and his firm had decades of experience as investigators before they began to furnish guards in any number. The Burns Agency was originally formed as an investigation business. Wackenhut blazons the FBI experience of its founder and other corporate executives. Many of those who created the thousands of other agencies have similar backgrounds. Today, investigators constitute about 10 percent of the personnel in the private security world.[1]

Large numbers of security managers and private investigators are recruited from the ranks of law enforcement. The FBI has long served as a reservoir for such manpower, especially when younger men were sought. Unlike most other Federal investigative agencies, FBI agents are not covered by Civil Service which has resulted in a larger turnover of FBI agents than persons serving in similar capacities in other Federal agencies. Within the last 10 years, veteran agents who have elected to retire after 20 years of service, and having reached the age of 50, are entering the ranks of private security personnel in increasing number. Many local and state police have similar retirement plans, and detectives from these departments form a prime source of investigators for private employ.

Private investigators are normally used after a loss has occurred, or the claim has been filed. The investigator's essential task is to ascertain all pertinent facts. There are exceptions to this rule, especially in the retail trade. Theoretically, their reports serve as a basis for action by their employers, and are designed to show how a recurrence of a particular kind of loss can be prevented. They often have the responsibility of trying to make recovery as well, in which cases they work with law enforcement officers and effect prosecution.

Many of these veterans are assigned to complex investigations where they use their former contacts to obtain information. Similarly, sworn officers, searching for information, will seek out these retirees when the tables are reversed and it is the official agency that needs assistance. Common training has given both groups a similar set of standards and a homogeneous technical language. The intimacy of these interchanges has been the subject of criticism both here and abroad. Supporters of it argue, however, that both groups are engaged in a battle with a common enemy, the professional criminal, who is not hampered by any rules of conduct or ethics, and who profits by all restrictions imposed by the rule makers.

One type of criminal for which the talents of investigators are widely used is the "bum check" artist. The prey of "paperhangers" include banks, hotels, and retail stores—or just any business or individual who can be induced to play the sucker. Some "penmen" who commit these acts rub it in with wry humor; they have been known to draw checks on the "East Bank of the Mississippi" and sign them "U.R. Stuck." Bad checks are not limited to the retail industry. Spurious checks drawn by the City of Los Angeles, in amounts of just under $1 million each, were the subject of news stories in December, 1974. The intended victims were not retail stores but banks. The checks were designed to end up in a bank as a deposit, with the account cleaned out before anything out of line became evident. The scheme was spoiled by an informant.

One instance of paperhanging landed at my own desk at American Express not long ago. A telephone call from an irate banker, calling from a city in central Ohio, was switched over to me. He was fuming because American Express, alerted by its field agents, had returned unpaid through the banking system a $100 item. I had the file on that case which contained a photostat of the returned item. It was a purported check or promissory note drawn on the "Travelers Security Company." It was printed in black ink on white paper. In the upper lefthand corner in small print were the words "Ninety (90) Days After Date." It bore two lines for signature and countersignature, and for this reason only might be assumed to be an American Express Travelers Checque. On its face the instrument said it was payable at the "Security National Bank," but no address, city, or state was designated for the bank. Counters in all four corners showed the figure of $100. The caller was so certain that the lines for signature and countersignature were an indication of a genuine item that it took some time for him to calm down enough to see reason. By no stretch of the imagination was our company responsible.

Any banker can regale you with stories of checks put through for credit, or for cash, without date or signature. Carelessness at the point of cashing makes this fraud possible. Each forgery case is, of course, a crime. When used in interstate commerce, subject to certain restrictions, bad checks come under the investigative jurisdiction of the FBI. Almost all large police departments have forgery squads and forgery specialists. Yet because of the sheer volume of this crime, it is a major area of private investigative work. Outside of the banking business, where checks are handled for known customers, the honoring of checks for merchandise, or cashing them as a service to customers, is a management decision, clearly hazardous, but not actually indispensable in the conduct of the business.

In the supermarket business in the United States the words "Will you cash a check?" are regarded among the most costly in the English language. In 1969 they were said to have cost these supermarkets more than $600 million. American business as a whole that year lost about $1.5 billion in bad checks. Management's choice to cash checks relates to the profits from the additional volume of business generated by offering this service. Existing safeguards in the handling of these practices are well known, and if instructions are followed, losses can be held to a minimum. The failure of staff to adhere to the rules is the great loophole.

As a young Agent in the Secret Service, my partner and I had an unusual experience in point. After closely following a suspect for more than an hour, and literally watching him break into mailboxes in lobbies of three apartment houses, we took him into custody. When we searched him we found some 30 stolen government checks jammed into his pockets. Many complaints had been received concerning stolen checks in that area, and investigation showed that many of them were being cashed at a certain department store. The volume was such that we suspected collusion between the thief and store personnel.

Faced with the evidence of the checks found on his person and the obvious testimony that two federal agents observed him in the act of stealing mail, our prisoner elected to cooperate. He was bargaining for leniency at the time of sentencing. Handwriting samples proved to our satisfaction that our prisoner was the man who did most of the fraudulent cashing at the department store. He denied collusion or special arrangements with anyone there. He kept to his story even when we showed him that the same set of authorizing initials appeared on almost all of the checks he cashed there. At a lineup he was viewed by the store personnel. None of these employees recognized him.

When informed that he had not been identified by store personnel, our prisoner was nonplussed. Fearing that consideration of leniency was in question, he begged to be taken to the store. He would identify the man who had approved the cashing. With the consent of the U.S. attorney on the case, we took him back. Within minutes of our arrival, he spotted his man, the manager of the ground floor rear. Walking up to him, he asked, "Do you remember me? You cashed my check the other day."

The answer was a puzzled negative. The thief did a doubletake. He then tried for recognition again, after turning up his collar, rumpling his hair, hunching his shoulders, and saying in a wheeze, "Mac, this is my WPA check. Your salesgirl won't cash it without your John Hancock." The manager's face turned red. He remembered.

We all ended up in the credit manager's office. In the floor manager's presence, the thief showed us how he obtained over 40 approvals from this one victim. His disguises consisted of the simple expedient of putting his collar up or down, wearing a tie or having his shirt open, putting glasses on, or taking off his jacket. The store had a rule that identification should be shown to the approving manager before he initialed the check. This manager claimed he was too busy to follow that rule. The dollar loss involved was sizable. A forged check is charged back. The thief couldn't make it good. It was the store's loss. The floor manager's gullibility was almost as costly to the store as if he had been in a conspiracy with the thief.

Every investigator has a favorite case of a cunning forger. Mine can be safely told because it goes way back. Penmen of this type and skill still ply their trade, however.

Let's call him Sam, the butcher. We could just as easily call him Sam, the painter, or the baker, or the candystore man. He would have answered to the name of Sam Brown or Sam Bloom, or Louis or White. He was known to have used at least 50 aliases. His specialty was swindling—more particularly, in passing forged checks.

When my partner in the U.S. Secret Service and I had his file assigned to us in late 1940, he was wanted by the police of a dozen cities for the forgery of commercial checks, and by the Secret Service and the postal authorities for the theft and forgery of countless government checks. We read all of the files available. They showed him to be a man in his late forties, who had twice been arrested and convicted of check forgery. Since his last discharge from prison some three years earlier, he had been active, according to the evidence, in metropolitan areas from Boston to Miami. Informants indicated that he was known to buy stolen government checks from fences.

Sam could go through a locale with a pocketful of forged checks and cash between $1,000 and $1,500 worth in a single day. He seldom remained in the same place for more than two or three weeks.

There was no evidence that he had ever been a butcher. We got to calling him Sam, the butcher, after running down a particular group of checks in which his *modus operandi* was to appear in a store wearing the blood-spattered apron and smock of a butcher. He would open his conversation with a version of the following: "Hello, I'm Sam, the butcher. You know my boy, Herbie. The little fellow who's been hanging around looking at that bicycle," pointing to the most classic bicycle on display. "He said you wanted $35 for it. It's Herbie's birthday tomorrow. I'm just a butcher, can you give me a break on the price?"

In rapid asides Sam implied that he and his family lived two blocks away, that he had to get back to work in a butchershop in a nearby neighborhood, since his boss would need the truck. With a buildup like that, a bargain was soon struck. Sam would produce a check for at least $100, often for more. Sam would leave with the bicycle, and between $70 and $80 in cash. There was, indeed, a truck, a rented one, usually parked a block or two away. No one ever got its plate number. When sometime later a known fence was arrested for dealing in stolen bicycles, he told of a man bringing them in brand new, a half dozen at a time. The description was of Sam.

Before his first arrest, according to our files, Sam was married and had two daughters. We started by trying to find his wife. She had moved. School records eventually led us to one of his daughters. This young woman had completed college and was now a teacher. She did not want her mother questioned. Her parents had separated and eventually divorced more than 10 years before. She agreed to help us on condition that we would not bother her mother. She had accidentally run into a friend from the old neighborhood who had news of her father. She understood he was now living with another woman, and had a little daughter about three years old. She gave us the friend's name and address. She also told us that her father's principal interest and indulgence was betting on the horses.

We called on the friend. Some discreet questioning soon disclosed that this friend's elder sister was the woman living with Sam. We implied we knew all about it, and the child. An involuntary eye movement to the picture of a child on the mantel which followed our statement brought an admission that this cherub was indeed Sam's daughter. The photograph was of an unforgettably beautiful, blond, curly-haired child. Both my partner and I studied the picture very carefully. We were given no further information.

We had picked up our lead. The back of the photograph showed it to be a product of the photograph studio located in the Bloomingdale department store. We had both memorized the number and the date imprinted on the back, showing that it was taken about 45 days before. The department store was able to provide us with a record that it was paid for through a charge account of one Sam Browder. The charge account was past due, with a balance owing of $295. The home address listed was Gun Hill Road in the Bronx. The credit application showed him to be a dealer in chemical supplies with offices on 29th Street, and a bank account at the Amalgamated Bank. Two business references were also listed. The office turned out to be that of a public stenographer who for a fee allowed customers to use her address as theirs. She later identified Sam from a group of photographs, but said she had not seen him in months. The bank reported that the account, which had been opened with a deposit of $300, was not only depleted, but somehow overdrawn by almost $200.

We hotfooted it to the Gun Hill Road address. It turned out to be a furnished flat. The resident landlord said that the Browder family had left early that morning for a few weeks' vacation. In fact, Mr. Browder had cashed a large check with him, using part of its proceeds to pay his rent in advance. He showed us the check. It was on the Amalgamated account we had checked an hour before. After the landlord spoke to the bank and found that he had been victimized, he used his own passkey into the apartment, inviting us in with him. Inside, it was obvious that the bird had flown. Everything had been removed. There was no evidence of intent to return. Empty boxes from assorted department stores were all over the place. Later investigation showed that Sam had defrauded each of these stores in the same manner.

We had to start our search anew. Our current information was that we were seeking a well-dressed family of three, a middle-aged father and mother, and a strikingly beautiful, blond, three-year-old child. That afternoon we again reviewed our files and noted one other factor. Sam's movements seemed to coordinate with racetrack openings. The racetracks in Maryland were due to open early the next week. On a hunch, we thought we would check out places—hotels—between New York and Maryland where Sam might stay and "work" on his way to the tracks.

Bright and early the next morning we were at the offices of the New Jersey Hotelmen's Association at the Robert Treat Hotel in Newark. Their director was cordial, but rejected out of hand any suggestion that Sam could be either in Lakewood or Atlantic City where the association had representatives—and where Sam had previously victimized hotels. He was well aware of Sam's activities. He showed us circulars issued by his organization which covered warrants obtained for Sam's arrest for swindling Lakewood and Atlantic City hotels—and others in Newark, Asbury Park, and Cape May. He was reluctantly persuaded to telephone his Lakewood and Atlantic City representatives.

The Lakewood Hotelmen's Association was under the leadership of the manager of the Clarendon Hotel there, and he was called first. From his side of the conversation it was obvious that the Lakewood man was positive that Sam would never venture back into that resort again. Rather than to be by-passed in such routine fashion, I asked permission to lift the bridge telephone. Before I could even say "Hello," Lakewood was assuring me that there was no way that Sam could operate there, where he had taken almost every hotel two years before. When I was finally able to get a word in, I suggested that there might be a new angle in locating him. I asked him to concentrate on getting word to every hotel to watch for a middle-aged couple with a doll-like blond child of three. I emphasized the child's golden curls and dainty appearance. His end of the phone was quiet so I started to repeat.

Suddenly the line became heated with his profanity. Sam was right there at his hotel. He had played cards with him the night before. The moustache fooled him. The Lakewood manager was anxious to conclude our conversation. Anticipating his action, I cautioned him under no circumstances to move in on Sam unless he attempted to check out. My partner and I were on our way to Lakewood, and would be there in 90 minutes.

When we arrived we found that our instructions had been ignored. The local police had been called in and the commotion gave Sam time to lock himself in his room. By the time the door was forced, a lot of paper had been flushed down the drain.

Sam could have saved himself the trouble he went through in trying to destroy evidence. He was wanted in so many places that one more charge would have made little difference. The dismantled trap of the toilet disgorged evidence of many recent check thefts.

The manager of the hotel was really shaken. He had personally approved a bum check for Sam two years before. He failed to recognize Sam, and was taken in completely by his role of proud father. "He was on the phone for an hour this morning calling his brokers to buy some stock to put away for her college education," he said, gesturing to a pay phone. We had the telephone company representative open it, and found it full of slugs. They matched those that we found in Sam's valise. Sam always used them to place his daily bets on the horses with his bookies.

Confidence artists operate today with as great or greater imagination than did Sam, and investigators for law enforcement and private security have their hands full with such exploits. Bad check losses are estimated to be costing $2 billion a year, of which $600 million are losses to the banking industry.[2]

Educational and training efforts to prevent these losses are constantly being aimed at the clerks and other employees who cash checks. In many localities special reliance is placed on verification by way of an automobile driver's license. This document has taken on almost the same aura as did a passport when used in European countries a decade ago. A part of the bad check problem rests on just this over-reliance. Blank driver's licenses are easily available and fictitious ones are not difficult to create. Since licenses are usually found in most wallets and purses, stolen ones, together with companion documents, are available for a price from a fence, and wherever pickpockets congregate.

In many instances the acceptor of a driver's license as identification is so busy making notation of the number that he fails to check the obvious—age, sex, height and weight, and other identifying marks. Clever cashiers who receive rewards for noticing discrepancies are apt to come up with cases like the 20-year-old man who offered a license for identification made out to a woman born in 1915. Or the blue-eyed man of five-foot-six with a license showing it was issued for a six-footer with brown eyes. Counterfeit licenses made to order are much harder to spot.

Many business establishments now use cameras which simultaneously photograph the person asking to have his check cashed, and through the use of a prism put a copy of the check on the same photographic frame. There have been many ventures into the potential use of fingerprints for this purpose. When I was with American Express many inventors brought their identification devices to me. While I, too, am an optimist with the hope that somewhere down the line a mechanical or electrical device will be perfected that will defeat the forger, the use of a fingerprint is impractical currently; much of the problem lies in the inability to have these prints classified and to make a successful search for a match in the criminal files.

One inventor who left his equipment with my secretary inadvertently did me a favor. She had locked it in a cabinet. During the night an attempt was made to force the cabinet open, and the fingerprint powder spilled. While it discolored the rug, it also must have gotten on the culprit's hands, because there were smudges indicating clumsy attempts to remove the powder. Nothing was taken. Obviously the fingerprint powder all over his hands had frightened the intruder away without accomplishing his purpose.

The credit card was designed as a new instrument of payment by the consumer; its acceptance by the retail trade, however, was in part due to its difficulties in safely cashing personal checks. The credit card evolved from the department store system of extending credit to its better customers. The stores grew larger and to insure the clerks' recognition of the charge customers they issued identifying tokens. Individual store accounts are still two-party affairs, involving only the firm extending credit and the person receiving it. The three-party card was an outgrowth of the problem of enabling long-distance drivers of company-owned vehicles to purchase gas and oil for the company's account, and have the bill rendered directly to the company. The modern credit card involves three parties: the issuer of the card, his customer, and the service establishment that honors it. Thus, Bank A is the issuer of the card to John Doe, who uses the card at the XYZ store. XYZ receives payment from Bank A, who in turn bills John Doe. More than 100 million people now use cards and a sales volume in excess of $30 billion a year is transacted in the United States alone.

The credit card now in use is a piece of plastic on which a machine has pressed out a name, number, and other symbols by the application of heat and pressure. When used, its face is covered with a piece of carbon paper and a roller transfers the raised lettering through the carbon onto a piece of paper, the bill. In short, it is a printing template. Newer cards also include a magnetic stripe imbedded on the reverse side of the plastic. These magnetic stripes carry a message which can be read by appropriate equipment and can be transmitted over wires to distant computers.

During its period of growth, notably in the second half of the 1960s, the credit card was subject to many criminal abuses. Part of its vulnerability lay in the practices of certain issuers. To correct some of these abuses, legislation has been enacted, both by the Congress and by many state governments, forbidding the unsolicited mailing out of credit cards. Other legislation limits liability of a credit card owner when his card is stolen and he fails to notify the company involved.

Obviously, the vulnerability of credit card issuers starts with the very creation of the card. To become familiar with the manufacturing process, and to stimulate ideas for anticounterfeiting, I arranged to visit the plant supplying American Express cards. Because they also were unfamiliar with the process, I took five of my key men with me on that first inspection. On the way there I suggested that we quietly observe the plant's security as well. As befitting representatives of a major customer, we were met and escorted by the plant manager, and as we proceeded through the various stages of manufacture, by the section managers and supervisory personnel. We all quickly and silently noted the appalling lack of security. I became aware of my associates' reactions when I noted one surreptitiously pocketing American Express cards improperly lying about. Closer observation indicated that every one of my party was entering into this exercise.

At the end of the tour in answer to the general manager's confident question as to our satisfaction with the manufacturer's methods, I turned to one of my men and held out my hand. He brought finished and unfinished cards out of a variety of his pockets. As each group of cards came out from a separate pocket, he identified the exact section in which he had found them and the breach of security involved. When he finished, each of the other men in turn went through the same process. None of our hosts had noted a thing.

The result of our inspection was a new security design. We set forth minimum requirements for them to meet if they were to retain our business. We later learned that they solicited business from other customers on the basis of their security system "approved by American Express." Some of our competitors were not that lucky, and large losses have occurred in the industry traceable to the manufacturing process.

It was some eight months later, in mid-1967, that we became aware of the use of a counterfeit American Express credit card. It was the only instance of counterfeiting we had to combat during my eight-year tenure with the company. Early warning of fake cards came when the computer, processing records of charge, noted that card numbers involved were invalid. Genuine card numbers had built-in check digits. This discovery sparked an investigation that took us to all parts of the North American continent and Europe. More than 60 arrests resulted, as did the recovery of 300 counterfeits. The cost to American Express through the counterfeit was some $160,000. The last one was used five months after we first became aware of its existence. Most of the persons arrested were professional criminals, some with long records. Our investigations, and those of the local and Federal authorities, led us to believe that the counterfeiting was an operation of, or was approved by, one of the so-called organized crime "families," the Patriarca family in Providence, Rhode Island. The counterfeiting plant itself was dismantled before we could get to it.

The result of this $160,000 caper was an intensive study into the design of the card to make it as security proof as possible. Some of these modifications are visible to the naked eye, others are not. An attorney I had known while in a previous post represented some of the godfathers of organized crime in New York. He called me once on behalf of one of those clients who operated a bar. His client, he said, was willing to sell American Express an infallible way of detecting genuine cards. His client had inadvertently stumbled on a safety feature we designed into the card and figured he had made a great discovery. He was using this attorney to try and sell it to us. It took me a while to stop laughing. American Express will undoubtedly continue to redesign both the obvious and invisible security features of its card.

In the past, the chief criminal involvement affecting credit card companies came about through the theft and misuse of cards. Some of these thefts were by credit card company employees. Many, many more were the results of thefts from the mails. Still others were stolen from or lost by customers. These cards were falling into the hands of organized groups.

Though the misuse of a card was (and still is) clearly a crime, the specific crime involved depended upon local statutes and interpretations. Strict construction governs interpretations, and ambiguities are resolved in favor of the criminal. Possession of a dozen stolen credit cards is a crime, but the value of the dozen cards is merely the actual value of the printed plastic, a matter of pennies each, rather than the representative value, which, depending upon the card, could be several thousand dollars each. Federal jurisdiction, when it applied, came under the mail fraud statutes, enacted back in the 1880s.

By 1966 the number of card thefts and misuses had increased to the point of becoming a sizable problem to card issuers, card holders, the business community, and law enforcement. The Postal Inspection Service had 10 percent of its entire budget allotted to combatting all mail frauds; of this amount, 10 percent was assigned to credit card investigations. The clerical problem alone of merely documenting credit card losses would have strapped the resources of the Inspection Service.

A quick review of state statutes indicated that some had none at all and those that did were of doubtful value. The oil industry, then the largest issuer of credit cards, had a committee which conducted a cursory study of existing statutes and then recommended passage of statutes similar to the one in existence in Hawaii. At that time the Hawaiian law had not been tested in a single court, or used in a single prosecution. While many other card companies reacted favorably to my suggestion for a research project into the criminal law, with a model state statute as its end product, it was clear that it would be difficult to get them to make the necessary financial commitment. American Express decided to proceed alone. A research team of more than 25 was headed by Jack B. Weinstein, then a professor at Columbia Law School and now a U.S. District Court judge, and Tom Farer, then also a professor of law at the same school and now at Rutgers

University. Every known reported credit card court decision was researched and analyzed. By the end of 1967 their report containing the summary and the draft of a model statute for state enactment was issued.[3]

The proposed model criminal statute won unanimous endorsement from the industry. A number of other companies then made voluntary contributions to the cost of the research. That model, adapted into the legal framework of the various states, has been enacted into law by 35 of them, including all of the more populous ones. Recognizing the representative worth of a credit card simplifies prosecutions. One of the first states to enact the model law was Hawaii. Its previous statute was superseded without ever having been used.

An important defense against the misuse of stolen cards is immediate notification of its disappearance to all service establishments. Under their contract with the card issuer, establishments that accept a card after receiving notice of its loss do so at their own peril. When stolen cards first became a problem, mimeograph lists were mailed periodically to the establishments. These grew into booklets called cancellation lists, now known as "hot lists." At optimum efficiency, there still was a delay of from 10 days to several weeks from the time an individual notice of loss was received until it was included in a printed up hot list and mailed out across the country and around the world. This time lag represented the free time thieves had to use the stolen card with impunity.

To cut down on this time lag, telephone authorization was introduced. High-volume establishments were instructed to call for authority when cards were offered in payment beyond a predetermined amount. "Look-ups" in a manual card system were slow and inefficient. And for a time, thieves, aware the authorization offices were closed on Sunday from 6 P.M. until Monday morning at 9 A.M., made that particular period a prime time for the misuse of credit cards.

The present authorization systems allow direct input into computers, which can look up a record and respond in a fraction of a second. Computers operate 24 hours a day, every day of the year, and are updated the instant a report of a stolen card is received. Some companies, with telephone operators available at all times, permit toll-free notification of a stolen card.

By 1971 investigators employed by the big card issuers had organized themselves, both nationally and locally. In large metropolitan areas credit card investigators, together with enforcement officials, both Federal and local, began meeting on a scheduled basis to exchange information on credit card gang operations. The result has been that credit card fraud losses stopped their upward spiral in 1972, leveled off, and then, compared with the increase in business, started a downward trend. The investigators were backed up by the operational changes and by the passage of appropriate legislation.

Through the filings of false claims insurance companies are directly involved in private security. They are also victimized by the connivance of their own employees, where settlements of false or exaggerated claims are arranged and approved. This connivance is a form of embezzlement or employee pilferage—and it has become a matter of considerable concern to insurance companies. Party to this private kickback scheme are adjusters, doctors, and attorneys. According to one report, some 10 percent of all claims filed with certain insurers are false. These spurious claims cost the industry $1.5 billion a year. On average, this amount may be responsible for some 15 percent of all insurance premiums.[4]

Like the rest of the business world, the insurance industry is fighting back against fraud. Its weapons include the Index System of the American Insurance Association by which files are maintained on all individuals who file casualty claims against subscriber companies. This file is cross-indexed by the names of attorneys, physicians, and adjusters involved in the claim.

Another intercompany defense agency is the Insurance Crime Prevention Institute (ICPI), successor since 1969 to the Casualty Insurance Fraud Association. The ICPI claims the support of more than 250 insurance companies. It has a staff of well-trained, competent investigators, many of them veterans of public law enforcement, headed up by former chief of police of New Haven, Connecticut, James F. Ahern. It investigates casualty insurance claims of all kinds on a referral basis, except those pertaining to accident and health insurance and workmen's compensation. ICPI advertises that it "will not take a case where a company just wants restitution and then will drop prosecution. That isn't the way to stop fraud."[5] ICPI has proven its efficiency and ability by indictments and convictions of fake accident rings, their claimants and hangers-on, as well as the ambulance chaser, the doctor and the lawyer involved with the claims. But ICPI's caseload is limited by the size of its staff. At most, ICPI handles several thousand claims a year, while its contributing sponsors have to handle millions.

Workmen's compensation is a form of insurance whose purchase by employers is mandatory in the United States. It covers workers in the event of accident or death connected with their employment. In 18 states special state funds have been created to underwrite such policies, though in only six are the policies issued exclusively by the state funds themselves. Private insurers currently make more than 60 percent of workmen's compensation payments.[6] Workmen's compensation coverage is more closely experience rated than most other insurance—that is, the amount required to be paid out by the insurer is usually reflected in the new premium. With thousands of cases processed in each jurisdiction, it is not surprising that stories of fraud and exaggerated claims have been rampant for many years. It is also not surprising that with thousands of claims the private investigator has been frequently called in by the insurer. Because the essence of a compensation claim is the inability of the worker-claimant to return to his job, a key tool of investigators in this field has been the motion picture camera, loaded with fast film, and equipped with long, telephoto lenses. These cameras are used for the purpose of capturing the claimant on film performing acts that would belie his argument that he is totally or partially disabled. Health and accident policies purchased by individuals are prone to excesses similar to those filed under workmen's compensation: the filing of false claims of disability in order to collect damages under the policy.

As an industry, insurance companies are one of the principal employers of private investigators. Though the title assigned an investigator may be different—it is usually that of an adjuster—an analysis of the job descriptions of an insurance adjuster would equate it with that of an investigator. Many of them are in-house employees. Others are employees of contract agencies which, because they handle insurance matters, are usually called "adjustment services." Others are free-lance "adjusters."

The special accounting requirements of the insurance industry make it difficult to achieve a full understanding of their investigation costs. Upon notification of a potential claim, an insurance company first confirms coverage. It creates a file, sets up a reserve (it adjusts its books to reflect the maximum anticipated outlay, sometimes referred to as "the amount on the file"), and assigns an investigator to look into the claim. All payments, including the cost of outside assistance—whether investigative, medical, or legal—are posted to the individual file as a charge against the reserve. The result is that a high percentage of autonomy is given to field offices in retaining locally enlisted investigators to check on claims. There is a dearth of statistics on indusrty-wide investigative costs, or on such costs on a casualty-category base.

Despite the ICPI manifesto that prosecution, not restitution, is the only way to stop fraud, the insurance industry is a major practitioner of private justice. The financial rewards of the ransoming of stolen property are still a motivating force in cases where the casualty loss involves valuable items.

The insurance industry is involved in private security in still another way. In setting premiums for the policies it sells, it assesses the potential loss and endeavors, naturally enough, to collect through premiums more than it will pay out. A reduction in the crime rate, therefore, would have a direct effect on their underwriting experience. In other words, smaller losses and prevented crimes would be reflected in the company profits.

All risks are not equal, and this fact is a recognized basis in setting rates. A concrete building is not as great a fire hazard as one of similar size made of wood. One hundred thousand dollars stored in a guarded steel vault is not subject to the same risk of burglary as a similar amount maintained in a tin box or a file cabinet. These factors and experience charts, as well as its analysis of the market, and its own cost factors, are used by insurance companies to set premiums.

For a decade or more casualty companies have systematically weeded out and refused to renew policies for customers they regarded as unprofitable. As a group they have added to the list of items they will not insure, or for which they will charge a much higher rate. Many companies have discontinued their efforts in certain casualty fields entirely.[7]

The insurance companies involved in casualty and surety claims are not only inexorably connected with private security as it now exists, but with the future of the private security industry. It is difficult to consider the insurance companies as one group, because they differ among themselves in types of ownership, marketing practices, and viewpoint. This is apparent in the different contributions they make to upgrading a customer's ability to resist and deal with fraud and attack. Many don't try. Many approach losses of this type in almost exactly the way they do damages from a tornado or a hurricane. They equate fraud and other crimes with tornados and other storms—something as natural as it is inevitable. Their attitude is that nothing can be done to temper their frequency or intensity. Thus, the insurance companies move to the next step: reduce losses by co-insurance, which is a combination of the large deductible, making the insured a partner in the loss, and the participation in the coverage by other insurance companies.

The existing system of premium discounts for the use and maintenance by an insured of certain security precautions by way of construction, machinery and equipment, and service, is antiquated. I can see no more scientific basis in their discounts than did the principal investigators responsible for the Rand study.[8] By operating on the present system, these insurance companies condone the lack of reliable, comprehensive statistics in the field of fraud and white-collar crime. There is a system of private justice, under which victims of a crime fail to report its occurrence. This is done in consideration of full or partial reimbursement. Sometimes prosecution is not attempted for reasons of cost in time and employee involvement. This often can be traced to insurance company tacit approval. The indulgence of some insurance companies in "educational" crime-prevention campaigns, addressed primarily to their own customers or used as a public-relations gimmick to attract new ones, have had the effect of hitting the rising rates of fraud loss with a bag of feathers. This same industry, years back, took far-reaching steps in connection with automobile accidents, traffic, and traffic control. It financed the Traffic Institute at Northwestern University in Evanston, Illinois, the National Safety Foundation, and many similar safety groups. Some of their funds have helped the traffic court program of the American Bar Association. In connection with its automobile coverage, the insurance industry also contributed to the formation and support of the National Automobile Theft Bureau. Many insurance companies also have been generous in making grants and furnishing other aids to law enforcement. But in the area of private security, where improvement can profit them most directly, they have done little or nothing.

Embezzlement is specifically excluded by the Department of Commerce in its calculation of the cost of crimes against business. The U.S. Chamber of Commerce in its estimate of losses places the loss from embezzlement at $3 billion a year, and the loss from employee pilferage at $4 billion a year,[9] suggesting that the total loss due to criminal activities of regularly engaged employees is a staggering total of $7 billion. Embezzlement stands alone as the single largest avenue of criminal attack.

While a carefully instructed uniformed security guard may serve as a deterrent to pilferage, there is little, if anything, that he can do to detect or prevent embezzlement. Basic sources of detection include complaints from victims, such as the customer who insists that he has paid his bill, which has been pocketed by the cashier operating a kiting scheme. Kiting is a practice of taking payment from A, and later, when B pays his bill, crediting B's payment to A's account, and so on. Usually, sooner or later, a customer asked for a payment the second time will squawk. Such a protest should sound a clear call for an audit, and not the statement that "our records are never wrong." A large percentage of embezzlements are kiting operations, with the embezzler moving the figures while money keeps dropping into his lap.

Embezzlers are often exposed by tips from informants. Sometimes these tips emanate from the person at the next desk sending anonymous notes, or from the lady across the street who can't understand how people on $12,000 a year can afford three big, gas-eating cars. Obviously, the earlier the victimized business learns of its exposure to embezzlement, the better opportunity it has to limit the size of its loss. Notices from the outside are often late. When, in 1970, a New York savings bank received a call from New York City detectives about one of its officials, its losses had already reached gigantic proportions. A bookmaker, turned informant, had told the detectives that one of his customers, an official in the bank, had been betting as much as $30,000 a day on the ponies. His kiting scheme was not too difficult to solve, once the finger had been pointed. On other occasions the information from police sources is more direct: the police have come across substantive evidence of misappropriation. Employee pilferage is small-scale embezzlement, though the dollar amount involved in the removal of two or three watches a week from a jewelry section can soon mount up.

Once a loss through embezzlement or pilferage is established, the role of the investigator becomes crucial. He is often indispensable in determining the method used to defraud, in assisting auditors to assess its size, in finding out if anyone else was involved, and in locating assets left in their original form or converted, which could be attachable to mitigate damages. He is also frequently charged with preparing proof-of-loss statements when insurance is available for indemnification.

Simply waiting around for an informant or regularly constituted law enforcement officers to tell a company that it has internal problems, is not good business. Most firms operate under set rules, laid out in great elaboration in company manuals, or by simple orders issued orally. They are designed to facilitate operations, increase turnover and profit, and prevent defalcation. In almost every case of embezzlement or major pilferage, the loss was made possible by a breakdown in executing existing company rules. In few cases has it been the result of a lack of rules.

It is entirely possible for company auditors to conduct performance audits in addition to reviewing financial documentation. These performance audits often flush out minor instances of pilferage before they assume serious proportions. More important, they serve to keep supervisors and middle management on their toes, knowing that they will be checked on their adherence to company rules and the correctness of their financial data.

Not only is embezzlement marked by the failure to follow company rules, it is also marked, all too often, by a willingness on the part of company management to sweep the whole matter under the rug. Many business firms and their managers feel that it is to their advantage to conceal as much information as possible about fraud losses. Some believe that public knowledge opens them up to censure as poor managers. Others worry that it will affect their company's credit, and in the case of public companies, stimulate embarrassing questions at stockholders' meetings. That a company's practices and procedures would be the subject of court scrutiny and news stories has been the deciding factor in more than one instance of a decision to "forget it." Similar conclusions have been reached on the basis that prosecution might require attendance at court of members of senior management. The great overriding reason for such concealment is the fact, or hope, that the loss, or a substantial part of it, will be eventually repaid. Professor Jerome Hall summarized this attitude in *Theft, Law and Society* as:

Perhaps the most important of all factors influencing the employers' conduct is restitution. The practice of foregoing prosecution where restitution is made or arranged for is so frequent and widespread that it tends to reduce embezzlement to a merely private transaction, the defalcation being viewed as damage that can be fully repaired by the payment of a certain sum of money —like a breach of contract. Restitution pervades and defines the entire meaning of embezzlement.[10]

There are many instances where embezzlers, learning that they were in imminent danger of exposure, steal further large sums to use for bargaining purposes. In one documented case, a defense attorney advised a client worried about his jeopardy to "take $125,000 more." After that was accomplished, the attorney dickered with the bank involved to the point where it accepted a return of $100,000 in full satisfaction of the client's liability—and the attorney got $25,000 as his fee.

The most salient feature of the entire embezzlement situation is the widespread practice of private justice—private individuals deciding who shall be prosecuted, who condoned, and what, if any, sanctions shall be applied.[11]

This is Hall's summation.

The private investigator is deeply involved in this practice of private justice. He often combines the function of investigator with that of prosecutor, while his business colleagues sit in judgment. The operation of these private, kangaroo "courts," of course, means that the crimes they are dealing with are unreported and that justice has become a private affair. In this area the function of the private investigator represents a challenging and disturbing problem in criminology.

In their anxiety to reduce losses, check on employee productivity, on supervisors, and on labor relations and the mood of workers, many managers make use of the services offered by special contract investigative agencies. These firms supply undercover agents. The undercover agent is put on the payroll as an ordinary employee. He is paid his full salary for the job he has been hired to do, and the agency, from the fee paid to it by management, pays him an additional sum. Most such undercover agents of both sexes are used in relatively unskilled positions: in shipping rooms, stockrooms, at mail desks, and similar posts. Their job is to infiltrate into the existing cliques and social strata of the company. Some of the techniques used can be said to border on entrapment, or the actions of an *agent provocateur.*

Many make it known that they are interested in "making a fast buck," placing a bet, obtaining marijuana or more potent drugs, joining the union—whatever it is that their assignment encompasses. Their reports, usually transcribed from tape recordings, often make interesting reading for management.

A number of specialty agencies contract with the company hiring them to follow up on the material ferreted out by the undercover agents. They have investigators who will question those "fingered," and obtain confessions and restitution. Cases developed in this manner are seldom referred to the criminal justice system. In many firms there is no connection between these activities and those of its security department. It is justified as a method of obtaining early warning in instances of embezzlement and pilferage. This technique is often a one-shot approach with the expensive specialty contract agency moving its undercover staff along to its next job.

One activity prominently portrayed in the Sunday supplement is sometimes connected with private security investigations: espionage. American businesses have been known aggressively to seek knowledge about what a particular competitor is doing, or about the market generally. The actions involved are offensive, rather than defensive. By its very nature the existence of offensive industrial-business espionage is a secret endeavor, not recorded in company annals and never admitted, whether true or not. No statistics exist on it. Few, if any, of those involved will admit their connection with or even the existence of corporate spying. Optimum results, when achieved, are concealed lest lawsuits result or future espionage is compromised.

Tangible lawsuits and evidence adduced in them are proof that such espionage does exist. No responsible inquiry has been made to determine if such activities occupy a measurable portion of the private security effort. There is no doubt that a defense against such improper incursions by a competitor constitutes a legitimate, appropriate use of private security.

Espionage is not industry's only secret weapon; wiretapping and the planting of hidden microphones are also used by business organizations. The stories involving agents for Investigators, Inc., a private contract agency, illustrate the point. Investigators, Inc., was retained by Robert Maheu and assigned the job of locating Howard Hughes. Maheu, Hughes' former general manager was involved in a lawsuit with his former employer. In the course of its investigations, a number of Investigators took up temporary residence in the Bahamas. There, they reported that their hotel rooms were bugged, their telephones tapped, and their mail opened. These measures were said to have been performed by agents acting for Intertel, another private contract firm, in the employ of Howard Hughes. In recounting the story, the Investigators' spokesman said that these actions were not totally unfair "because we had electronic spying devices in use ourselves."[12]

The rise in the sale of such surveillance devices and equipment from $27 million in 1958 to $83 million in 1968 is a small measure of their use by business. A number of witnesses representing contract guard agencies admitted to the Pennsylvania Select Committee on security guards that they owned such equipment. Samuel Dash, Counsel to the Senate Watergate Committee, in his book on wiretapping said:

> Modern business has no reluctance to eavesdrop, especially on its own personnel. Usually an employer first learns of the practicability of a hidden microphone and a wiretap when he seeks help from an attorney or private detective to solve a security leak or a serious problem of pilfering. Many businessmen today are "tap conscious" after reading magazine articles on the subject and discussing it with fellow businessmen. After one try at it, the employer usually becomes a confirmed eavesdropper and is ready to set up listening posts throughout his plant or place of business.[13]

This quotation, written 10 years before the Senate staff unearthed the recording of conversations by hidden microphones in the President's office, indicates that the Senate Committee investigators were probably instructed to seek such evidence on a routine basis. The substance of the quotation represents an attitude that would account for the lack of surprise by many that such a recording practice was in effect in the White House.

Industrial espionage is not necessarily a matter entrusted by those firms who engage in it to their security departments. "Headhunting is the most legitimate form of direct industrial espionage."[14] In an era when lateral movement in management has become commonplace, trade secrets have often accompanied the moving officer. The gobbling up of some companies through merger has had the same effect. Neither of these approaches involve the company security staff.

Accurate, timely information is a keystone to decision-making. Data of all sorts is now processed by new, electronic machinery. Because it potentially exposes business to enormous security risks, the computer, today's business phenomenon, is at once a great plus and a great puzzle. Possibly because of their complex nature, criminal cases involving the misuse of computers have received relatively little publicity. There is at least one instance where a lawsuit was dismissed because the court found it too complex to understand.[15]

There have been many cases involving criminal manipulation of computers, and documented individual losses have ranged into the millions. Computers have also been the victims of vandalism and sabotage from internal and external sources. However the computer's greatest enemy is the well-intentioned error of its operators and planners. These matters do not come within the purview of private security.

From a private security point of view, the computer is a unique business machine in that it possesses the technical capability to safeguard its own information. It can be programmed not to reveal its secrets unless first unlocked by a predetermined word or code. It can also be set to limit its revelations on a selected, escalating scale. It can be instructed to maintain automatically records of each use and user. Yet computers are vulnerable. Even their largest manufacturer, IBM, concludes in its new manuals on computer security that "there is no such thing as perfect security . . . the objective of a data security program is to cut the risk and probability of loss to the lowest affordable level and also be able to implement a full recovery program if a loss occurs."[16]

In the delicate environment of computer location and operation the need for classic private security guards, investigators, and security equipment is essential. To these needs for overall computer security should be added trained computer auditors and systems executives. The failure of plan or performance by any of these key security elements can be disastrous.

Classic computer frauds include the case in Mansfield, California, where a firm's chief accountant embezzled $1 million in six years. He used the company computer to print out projections of accounts receivable and accounts payable. He then manipulated these two essentials of the company's well-being by kiting with such finesse that he failed to arouse suspicion or upset general company financial goals. For quite a while, that is.[17] Across the Atlantic, in France, finesse was also apparent in the case of the supervisor authorized to adjust the company's payroll program to round off all salary payments to two decimals. He went just one unauthorized step further, however. He instructed the computer to credit his own salary with all excesses thus removed.

Computers have also been victimized by persons serving out their time after receiving notice of their dismissal. These individuals have been known to commit sly and costly acts of sabotage. One, a tape librarian in the computer installation of a large insurance company, replaced all tapes in the vault with new blank tapes during her 30-day-notice period. Direct cost in retrieving the information and replacing the tapes, and the indirect costs attributable to their erasure totaled some $10 million.[18] There were destructions of data files in a pharmaceutical house, erasures of purchasing data in a U.S. Army file, and several instances of deliberately mislabeled tape reels.

There have also been verified instances of thefts of blank tapes and other supplies. American Express had a practice for a time of selling worn tapes after they were completely erased. A supervisor charged with selling them began to include some new tapes too, personally pocketing the proceeds. He became bold enough to have his deliveries made by a trucking company, charging this cost to American Express. After his arrest, the trucking firm's records laid out the trail to the buyers, who were persuaded to return the tapes, if still unused, or to pay the true owners. In other companies entire minicomputers have been dismantled and removed. Two of these instances involved university students, one in Illinois, and another in Boston.[19] Computer programs, computer time, printouts, and tapes containing data have all been subject of employee theft. The materials were not just limited to proprietary information unavailable at any price through normal business channels. Mailing lists maintained on tapes have been subject of such larcenies. Many computers can now be queried for confidential corporate information over telephone lines vocally or by way of data sets. They are protected by having code words, or machine readable indexes, made part of the entry procedure. Even so, there have been cases where they have been made accessible to outsiders through the connivance of insiders.

Computers have also been the targets of violence and terrorism, as well as mob action in connection with protests and demonstrations. These incidents were more prevalent during the student demonstrations at the height of the protests against the United States participation in the Vietnam War. Each bombing represents a failure of private security. At the University of Wisconsin, an Army Data Center was bombed. The detonation, in addition to killing a researcher, did $1.5 million in damages, and caused the loss of 20 years' of accumulated data.[20] Other computer installations at colleges and universities that were targets during this period included Boston University, where damage was done by acid and wire cutting; the University of Kansas, where the Data Center was bombed; Fresno State College in California, where the damage was inflicted by fire bombs and came to $1 million; at the Sir George Williams University in Montreal, where the installation was totally destroyed, as was the case in Toulouse, France. At New York University, an Atomic Energy Commission computer was held by sit-in students for $100,000 in ransom, and planted incendiary devices were defused just before they were due to go off.[21] Computers at the University of Massachusetts were also held for a time by demonstrators. Computers other than those on campus have also been attacked by individuals. Shots from revolvers were fired at computers in the unemployment offices of the State of Washington and at a privately owned computer in Johannesburg, South Africa.

Computers have come under criminal attack by more than just individuals. The Equity Funding Life Insurance Company misused computer technology in the early 1970s to create fake evidence of some 56,000 insurance policies. It was not a situation that could have been guarded against by an internal security program, no matter how elaborate. The fraud was designed by management to accomplish criminal ends. Company officials were not about to promote the discovery of their own machinations. Through the cooperation of a company's operational management and its security staff, computers have been harnessed to promote the overall security of a business and its products. Properly programmed, the computer can furnish accurate and current statistical data on losses, their amount, the time of their occurrence, and the points where the company is vulnerable to losses. They are of great value to the investigator, and of even greater value as indicators for preventional measures.

By design and instruction of its most senior officers, computers at the American Express Card Division, for example, were programmed to furnish clues for its security investigators. Printouts of fraud were not confined to seriatim listing and totals. These same figures were reworked so that the data also showed fraud by state, by city, or metropolitan area, and within each geographical area by service establishment, the place where each fraudulent card had been honored. This computer process was like getting an up-to-date map of the activities of thieves misusing American Express cards. When frauds were indicated in a single establishment in a city, and no other frauds were shown to have occurred in an area of hundreds of miles around it, it was a beckoning finger to the investigator, saying that the thief was in all probability connected with the ownership or operation of that particular place. The investigators were highly successful in such cases. That same printout might indicate an inordinately high number of frauds at another place on Fridays, Saturdays, Sundays, and holidays. In a number of such instances, our investigators were able to concentrate on the extra waiters and part-timers put on for the rush periods. Printouts of the same frauds by types of businesses furnished still other clues. The use of computer-generated material was constantly refined and updated with inputs from American Express's security, marketing, and operations divisions, all under the close eye of senior managers. The result was a tight rein on fraud.

Investigators, going back into history, have been aware of the importance in the overall scheme of theft of the receiver of stolen goods: the fence. His existence and activities are indispensable to the operation of almost all professional thievery involving items other than cash. Removing the fence, or limiting or hampering his operations will ultimately reduce the theft of merchandise. Translating this fact into business terms, the fence makes the market for stolen goods; kill the market and you do irreparable damage to the business of the producer, the thief.

The staff report prepared for the U.S. Senate's Select Committee on Small Business, entitled *An Analysis of Criminal Redistribution Systems and Their Economic Impact on Small Business,* dated October 26, 1972, reprints in full a paper dealing with the history of Jonathon Wild, the great fence of the early eighteenth century, whose activities were touched upon earlier in this volume. A point made in this excellent report is that now, 250 years later, so little has been done that the President's Commission on Law Enforcement and the Administration of Justice had remarked on the failure of research on fencing operations in its report of 1967. The Senate Select Committee held hearings on these operations in May, 1973, with much of the testimony and exhibits pertaining to the loss of cargo from all modes of transportation—air, rail, ship, and truck. The committee developed evidence of fencing in these transportation areas.[22] By clear implication, losses of similar merchandise from the premises of manufacturers, warehouses, distributors, jobbers, and retailers go into the same hands. The total amounts involved make distribution by these fences big business by itself. The size of the business alone indicates that these fencing operations must use the same transportation systems to move their ill-gotten gains to the hands of their ultimate retailers.

Not sufficiently covered in those hearings, or in much of the works on this subject, are the duties and opportunities for legitimate business in this area. The Senate Select Committee recommendations after its hearings involve changes in the criminal law to make prosecution of fences less difficult. It is no secret that the identity of many fences are known to law enforcement and to private investigators, both of whom are powerless to act upon their knowledge because of the lack of admissible evidence. Frustration has led many a police investigator into a relationship with these fences as a source of information about other criminals. In many cases these fences do act as informants on a limited basis, thereby adding to their position of impregnability by having curried the favor of the enforcement authorities. They turn in those thieves they regard as dangerous to their own position, especially those who have no standing, who are unable to find out the identity of the informant, and who cannot seek retribution—operating, in other words, in exactly the same manner that Jonathon Wild did. One of the most difficult tasks of a competent private investigator is to explain to his employer that he knows the culprit, but is powerless under the law to take any further action. This impasse, at times, has led to negotiations for ransom, repeating the steps along a well-worn path.

There are ample laws that make it a crime *knowingly* to receive, retain, conceal, possess, purchase, barter, sell, or dispose of stolen property. More recent statutes and rulings provide legal shadings under which possession under certain circumstances can be interpreted as being within "knowledge." "Knowledge" is the key word in much of the problem. It is extremely difficult to provide a legal answer to the question of the person in possession of stolen goods, "How should

I know it was stolen?" There is an additional problem, too, of course: how does the true owner prove his ownership of standard merchandise. These problems permit stolen goods to compete blatantly with their legitimate twins in outlets on the same street, to the detriment of the legitimate producer and retailer. When merchandise stolen from a manufacturer is sold in this manner, the manufacturer loses twice— first in the value of the goods stolen and his potential profit on it, and second his legitimate merchandise tries to compete with the stolen items.

It is unfortunate that the sales departments and security staffs of many organizations fail to recognize that they can be of value to each other and to their mutual employer. Very often the sales staff is aware of outlets for stolen items similar to those to which they are trying to sell. Despite the present difficulty in making cases against these outlets, that information in the hands of security investigators and law enforcement officials might assist in providing leads and eventual results.

Police departments across America have launched "Operation Identification" of many types. They have even supplied equipment, usually a burning or engraving tool, that can place indelible identification marks or names on items ranging from bicycles to television sets. Participants are urged to place these identifying marks at locations where they cannot be removed or be obliterated by paint. Business now uses its computers to keep track of millions of items in its changing inventories. Some firms use the same computers to record customer warranties, and update them promptly. Still others invest in enforcing retail sales prices which they have placed under the protection of the "fair trade" laws. Such existing records could be combined with a copy of the bill of lading, or shipping document, to keep track of each manufactured item from its creation to its eventual place on the shelf of a retail outlet. Using any one of many random access modes, the machinery to look up a computer record, this same program can be accessed to determine the last recorded name and address of true consignee or destination. Free inbound telephone calls to the manufacturer would answer the question, "How should I know it was stolen?" So would an obliterated identification number, or replaced part without a number. While the application of such a program is expensive, it might be less so than the losses are today. It would certainly serve as an aid to investigators, both private and public, who would then be able to follow leads indicated by properly designed printouts of reported losses by date, by shipper, by city, and perhaps even by place of eventual sale when the guarantee card arrives in the mail.

Although transportation is among America's most regulated industries, its losses of cargo are so extensive that they affect a rate of inflation. In 1972 more than 85 percent of this cargo loss was reported as "shortage," as reflected by the Quarterly Loss and Damage Reports submitted to the Interstate Commerce Commission by Class I motor carriers. Less than 15 percent of the loss was reported as due to hijacking, theft, or pilferage. In short, transportation companies are saying they do not know when or how the cargo was lost and that they have no reportable idea of who might be responsible. How does one prosecute a person found in possession of "lost" items when the one charged with their last legitimate control cannot account for the goods as missing, often is unable to identify the items, or name the employee last responsible for them?

This situation has not gone unnoticed by law enforcement authorities. Former Attorney General William Saxbe, with the cooperation of the United States Department of Transportation, asked 16 United States Attorneys to convene local working groups consisting of representatives of the cargo carriers and enforcement representatives from both Federal and local agencies. Formation of these committees is a far-reaching move, designed to place law enforcement and prosecutorial agencies in a position of close relationship with this industry in order to improve the probabilities of the prevention of loss and the apprehension and conviction of those involved when a loss does occur.

Industry's response was odd. It assigned various kinds of representatives, almost none of them with operational responsibility. The railroads sent mostly attorneys, and in a few instances, officers of state railroad associations. The trucking industry uniformly named directors of state trucking associations. None of the maritime interests were represented by the shipping companies or steamship lines; instead, officials of differing qualifications ranging from an employee-relations officer to a manager were assigned by port commissions and authorities. The airline industry selected its senior security executives; it assigned specific representatives to cover specific cities. In so doing, Los Angeles was represented by a senior official whose home office and home was in New York; New Orleans was represented by an official based in Atlanta; Boston was covered from New York; Detroit and Seattle were both spoken for by Chicago.

I know and respect many of these men. I sympathize with their assignments. As a group, they are an agglomeration of representatives from different corporate levels, so that in each case their recommendations have to be processed along the different corporate paths, with many intervening companies and hierarchies along the way. Many of these security executives have long been aware of the problems of "shortage." They were hired for the purpose of combatting them. They have made recommendations to their operating divisions and to their seniors that have been ignored, denied, or overridden, or put on a back burner for later review. The prospect of this new Department of Justice project generating effective action would be greatly enhanced if each representative of private business who attended were required to bring a senior operating manager with him to the committee sessions.

8 | Security Equipment

In their evolution from their common ancestry military forces have far outdistanced their relatives, public and private security men. The military forces were adapted to the protection of the nation and its rulers from foreign attack. They have also been used by these same masters to attack. Public and private security evolved less broadly— for the protection of the individual, his property and his rights. In some situations they have operated to repress these very rights at the behest of their leaders.

There is an enormous imbalance between the resources assigned these two groups—the military and the security. Military needs and available budgets have generated scientific inventions and improvements of revolutionary impact. But little attention has been paid by the world of science to the needs of the security services. Almost all of their advances have been in transportation and communication, and many of these have been adapted from the military. There have been few improvements and inventions designed specifically for security use.

Compare a soldier and his equipment at the turn of the century— an American on his way to fight in Cuba or an English trooper en route to the battlefields of South Africa—with his modern counterpart. The most dramatic difference discernible is in basic firepower. A single soldier today bears with him the firepower of a squad of his forebears. His basic tools have been the subject of intensive research and modernization.

Not so the policeman or private security guard whose basic tools remain almost the same as they were. They carry the same baton, nightstick, billy club, and, where armed, the same revolver. The great argument in 1974 concerning law enforcement equipment was over a proposed change from revolvers firing .38 caliber ammunition to those carrying magnum loads.

This lack of scientific imagination and attention to the vexing questions of security exists in other areas. For example, today's money, checks, stocks and bonds, and other security documents could have been produced on existing machinery by most firms engaged in their manufacture on January 1, 1900. No improvement in the end product has been introduced in the last 75 years. The experts still point to the fine lines produced by hand engraving as the best way to distinguish between the genuine and the counterfeit.

Another typical example is the reliance placed by both private security services and the discount-offering insurance companies on the archaic "watchman's clock." Coupling a clock mechanism with a paper tape, it will record the time and the number of a key inserted into it. These keys are attached at various places in the guarded area. The clock is designed to check up on the watchman and his adherence to his schedule. His rounds, however, could easily be made for him by his 10-year-old son or his 80-year-old mother. In most establishments the tapes are seldom checked by security supervisors except after a break-in or other preventable attack has occurred.

As a high school student, I once found myself locked out of my own home. It was a small, private house, identical to every other one on the block. All the houses had a common builder. I could have entered the house easily enough through a window, but that would have involved damaging a screen recently installed for the summer. Or I could have waited for one of the other family members to come home. A third approach was simpler. I went to the hardware store in the neighborhood and bought a skeleton key for 10 cents. That key fit our backdoor, and probably every backdoor on the block. It fits doors across the city and country and is still in use extensively today.

Along with the staff, the bow and arrow, and the slingshot, the lock is among the oldest of security devices. In the United States its manufacture and installation makes up about one-third of the "builders hardware industry," which employs 30,000 people and has annual sales of $800 million. The December, 1972, marketing analysis attached to the manufacturing subcommittee's report to the Justice Department's Law Enforcement Assistance Administration said:

It is significant that locks are *not usually* purchased by the ultimate user. Rather they are specified in the architect's office, purchased for speculative housing developments by the general contractor or purchased for replacement where the original selection usually governs [emphasis in original].[1]

The ease, simplicity, and economy of installation undoubtedly plays a greater part in the selection of the locking device to be used than does its ability to withstand attack. The old and overworked adage of the chain being as strong as its weakest link has literal application here.

This was the case when a close relative telephoned me early one evening. She had returned to her apartment to find it ransacked. I got the details from the investigating police officers who were willing to talk with me over the phone. Entry had been made through the door. Evidence showed that it had been forced by a screwdriver or a crowbar. A good lock gave way because it was installed into the door frame with one-inch screws. I suggested that the lock be reinstalled with four-inch screws that would reach into a bearing stud. While she continued to live there, by actual count of added door scars four more attempts were made to jimmy the door. The lock and screws held.

The manufacture, sale, and servicing of security equipment is the major component of private security. Annual expenditures for security devices are greater than those for guard services and armored car services combined.[2] The equipment is often subdivided by the industry itself into deterrents, monitoring and detection, and fire-control systems.

Builders hardware is but one element in the deterrent group. Others designed to deter entrance or penetration include fences, gates, doors, safes, vaults, and special lighting. Alarms of all sorts are included in the monitor and detection group, as are the warning signals some of them activate, sent over wires to central stations, by automatic dialers over the telephone to answering services or the police, or by sounding gongs, blowing sirens, and flashing lights. Closed-circuit television is also included in this group. Fire-control systems range from the chemical extinguisher that hangs on the wall to the complex automatic sprinkler system that goes into action and sounds simultaneous alarms elsewhere, including fire stations.

There is no publicly available cost-effective analysis of security equipment. Within recent years this field has become so crowded that a full listing of all such devices has been undertaken by the National Bureau of Standards for LEAA. No evaluation is included in the project. Underwriters' Laboratories, Inc., tests machinery and materials used in connection with fire and casualty hazards. Products that meet its requirements are "listed" and the "listing mark" is affixed to the product itself. Their approval does not include any cost-effective evaluation. Competing devices of different manufacturers often bear the same approval stamp.

With so many establishments still using locking devices that require little or no effort to open without a key—by picking or by force—or which can be bypassed entirely, it is nonetheless important to note the efforts that are being made to produce more effective equipment. Mortised, dead-bolt locks, with case-hardened strikers, are now being made with key-operated tumbler locks on both sides, instead of knob operation on the inside. While such a lock may be inconvenient for the user, it can foil entrance where a glass panel, in the door, or in an adjacent wall, can be smashed and an arm inserted to unlock the door.

In hotels an interesting use is being made of keyed card inserts that can be used instead of an ordinary metal key. The keying can be set from the hotel desk at the time a guest registers, the card keys punched, and furnished simultaneously. At the time the room is re-let, a new setting is made, and a new card key issued. This may avoid the collection of room keys that is so often the hallmark of a hotel room burglar. It does not solve the problem of passkey access by chambermaids and other hotel help, however. Other changes include keys not capable of being copied by the key machines available at hardware stores and locksmith shops.

Significant for its size and importance in the deterrent group is the manufacture and installation of vaults and safes. They range from fire retardant file cabinets with plunger locks to vaults built into bedrock below buildings that are veritable fortresses, as indeed are the installations at Fort Knox and at the Federal Reserve Bank in New York City. Used to house gold bullion and untold sums of money, they are made primarily of steel and reinforced concrete. Access is by way of vault doors operated by machinery and controlled by pre-set time locks and dial settings usually held in strictest confidence by two different persons, both of whom are jointly needed to manipulate the settings.

These deterrent constructions are buttressed by monitoring and detection equipment, a fire-control system, and a complement of guards and investigators. Here reliance is placed on all the many elements of security available. The monitoring group includes alarm signals triggered by pressure, magnetics, vibrations (including ultrasonic), microwaves, and laser beams, as well as alarm signals set off by photoelectric cells, heat, and other indicators. In addition to guards, the installations are monitored at a distance by closed-circuit television.

Such installations are not limited to major gold vaults. Many others exist on smaller scales, but are manned with equal sophistication. Vaults are used by manufacturers where the items involved are of great value and marketability, such as furs, precious stones and metals, jewelry, and even fabricated assemblies.

Monitoring and detection equipment, coupled with devices to prevent further entry, are not new. Adaptations of traps used for the capture or killing of large animals have been in use for centuries. The leaf-and-twig-covered pit, or the noose from a bent sapling releasable by pressure, were made man-size long ago. So were spring-activated traps, and their more dangerous successor, the spring gun. This latter device was usually a shotgun, activated by a series of springs and cords when any weight entered into the triggered area. Spring guns were once used so extensively in the United States and abroad that the wholesale carnage of friend and foe, both human and animal, of all ages and sex, finally resulted in legislation forbidding their use even on private property. Now, as then, however, the lines strung low along the ground that sound an alarm when stepped on, are still being used.

Some of these devices have taken on sophisticated shapes and disguises. To illustrate, let us say that a building housing a safe in a second floor office is part of a factory complex but separate from the main factory. This building is not used except on weekdays from 8 A.M. to 6 P.M. Round-the-clock guards patrol the main building and grounds and their main guard post is equipped with an alarm console and closed-circuit television. All normal and emergency accesses in the separate building could be wired with magnetic contacts, leaf contacts, or plunger contacts (or a combination of these) which would be connected to the main factory security console. Any break in these contacts by the opening of a door would activate an alarm on the console. By simple additional wiring, the alarm could also activate a siren, a gong, bells, flashing lights, and if desired, forward a signal to a central station or police headquarters. All windows would also be wired with magnetic or leaf switches that would operate as would the doors in the event they were opened. The glass of each window-pane could have thin strips of foil pasted on the windows that would have contact with the other wiring. Breaking a glass would tear the foil and cause an alarm to sound.

Entrances and window areas can also be protected by invisible security systems such as a photoelectric device. This device transmits an invisible beam to a receiver positioned between 3 and 75 feet away. Many such installations now have the receiver and transmitter in the same instrument, and the aimed beam is focused on a positioned re-flector. Interrupting the beam causes the alarm mechanisms to be activated. For interior use photoelectric systems are now designed to resemble two- or four-plug electric wall socket receptacles. For ex-terior use, special systems have now been developed that can span distances of up to 1000 feet. These longer distance installations use pulsed beams rather than steady beams to avoid triggering by wind-blown leaves or other small debris. Other improvements include trans-missions in fencelike patterns to avoid penetration by slipping under or climbing above the beam.

Security equipment also includes mats sensitive to pressure. These are often installed in hallways, entrance foyers, on steps, and on the floors in the vicinity of safes. They can only be installed on hard sur-faces. They are usually covered by rugs, carpets, or other mats. They, too, are wired.

An additional security device is one attuned to vibration. Vibration detectors are mounted on the surface to be protected, such as a wall, ceiling, safe, or cabinet. Vibrations of sufficient force on the protected surface activate the trigger mechanism. When installed, these detectors need to be tuned and tested. They are sold mainly as protection from intrusion through common walls or ceilings.

Another device that can be added on is an ultrasonic motion de-tector. This usually comes in a case measuring about 10 inches long, 5 inches wide, and 2 inches high. In operation, it transmits inaudible sound waves in patterns, some covering areas 25 feet long and 12 feet wide. These waves bounce off existing obstacles and accept a stable, constant return. The introduction of a new object or movement causes a change in this wave pattern, and an alarm is activated. The ultrasonic detector, the vibration detector, and the others, all can cause the full alarm system to be put into action.

The safe, itself, in our sample building, can also be wired, so that even touching it will sound an alarm. There are a variety of safe alarms that are in effect proximity devices. These turn the safe into an electrical field that reacts to a new mass coming close to it.

Nor has the old-fashioned line stretched between two posts and from there to a tin can or the watchman's big toe been abandoned. Many catalogs of alarm systems and supplies include a modern adaptation, usually listed as a "trap." Lines stretched in this updated device will cause a signal or alarm to be given if the tension on the cord is increased, as when it is kicked by an intruder. The catalogs recommend it for use in connection with duct openings, air-conditioning grills, skylights, overhead doorways, and internal aisleways.

Of course, with a safe, holdup alarms are recommended for use when the safe is open. These alarms range from finger-activated buttons to foot-activated rails or treadles to special money clips in the cash drawer or register that will send a signal if the bills kept within it for the alarm purpose are removed. The signals can be wired to react in various places, and set off lights and noisemakers, but they are often kept "silent." Thus, they are wired to a central station of a police station with the primary purpose of summoning help.

All these alarms, and many others activated by such different stimuli as acoustical waves, laser beams, and temperature changes, can be supplemented by putting the sample building, or areas within it, under survcillance by remotely monitored closed circuit-television cameras (CCTV). In our example this monitoring would be done at the security panel or console in the main factory building. It would permit the guard on duty to view on one or more screens the action taking place in the areas covered by the CCTV lenses. Automatic rotation of the viewing area, remote manual override, and zoom lens capabilities are available. Monitors coupled with TV-tape machines enable recordings of what is on the screen to be made automatically, or on manual command. Any one of the intrusion devices can be wired to activate a tape machine so as to preserve a record of what caused the alarm signal.

Some CCTV devices themselves are adaptable to note movement and send a signal. A particularly intriguing advance in this technology, not yet marketed at the time of this writing but whose prototypes show promise, is the use of computer technology to digitalize the entire scene viewed by a CCTV camera. A monitor screen receiving the picture is divided into 1600 dot segments. Each of these dots is assigned a numerical value, from No. 1 black to No. 15 white, with the numbers in between ranging in shade from black to white. The process is completed in far less time than the one-thirtieth of a second it takes for each television frame. The entire scene is reduced to a series of digits, and is retained in the memory of the device. This scene is matched with each succeeding frame. Any change in it triggers an alarm, starts the tape machine, and commands whatever else is designed to be done with the signal. The exciting prospect of this device is that the area of the screen can easily be subdivided so that movement in one part of the scene can be accommodated without affecting the alarm potential of movement in the remaining frame. For example, a CCTV device equipped with such a machine could monitor a busy museum, permit the unrestricted movement of attendees, keep all under observation, yet react and signal an alarm only when any object came within a predetermined distance of a painting, a picture, statue, cabinet case, or other object of value.

Vital in the use of these many devices is proper construction, installation, and service. Equally vital is the need for the user to be properly instructed in its use and care. In almost all cases these instruments are dependent on wires for their power to operate and transmit their signals. Standard supplies include batteries and other sources of standby power. Despite their sophistication, these devices still suffer from the problems of the man-trap and the spring gun: they find it difficult to distinguish between the "good guy" and the "bad guy."

These alarm devices are a far cry from the twentieth century's military inventions—air power, rockets, hand-held bazookas, intercontinental ballistic carriers, napalm, deadly chemicals, atom bombs, nuclear-propelled ships and submarines. By comparison, the innovations in security devices have been puny.

There are, to be sure, examples of successful crimes where no amount of security equipment would have changed the outcome. I previously mentioned the experience involved in breaching the security of the Bradbury Wilkinson check printing plant in London. During my tenure at American Express, I was responsible for the investigation of two other similar losses from equally well-guarded vaults. In each case American Express Travelers Checques in the face amount of

$100,000 disappeared, one from the main vault in the headquarters building in New York, the other from a distribution vault in San Francisco. In neither case was a physical breach involved. In neither case was a single security device on the scene at fault. As investigation after the fact was to prove, the thief in each case was present at the scene of the crime with the knowledge and implied consent—though not for the purpose of theft—of the staffs involved. In each instance the rules promulgated for the operation of the installation were ignored.

In New York, the packaging material used in connection with the mailing of traveler's checks to banks was stored in the caged area adjacent to the vault. This violated the rule barring from the area all materials other than those requiring vaulting. A porter not permitted by regulation to be in the vicinity was allowed regular entry into the cage with a dolly to pick up the packaging supplies. After his presence under these circumstances became routine, it was no trick for him to ride out some traveler's checks. Substantial recoveries were made but at considerable expense in investigative time and cost.

In San Francisco, the loss was first reported as "mysterious disappearance." It happened in the course of vaulting a shipment delivered by armored car. A work crew repairing the alarm wiring system was given authorization to continue its operation within the restricted area while the valuables were being uncrated, recorded, and put into the vault. Debris from their work and from the unpacking and handling the traveler's checks was permitted to be removed from the area before the vaulting was completed. Both the presence of a work crew during the arrival of a shipment and the removal of trash at the time of such operation were listed as taboos in the manual of procedure. I was assured by the supervisors involved, as well as by my own investigators, that this loss was one of paper only in that the missing checks were buried under tons of debris and trash that they had traced to landfill operations. Nonetheless, we included the numbers in our stolen list. Well over a year later, these checks began to appear, being cashed up and down the Pacific Coast. No increase in security equipment or guards would have prevented either of these two losses.

An increasing attack on such vault installations, especially those under single control, has come in the form of kidnapping of the manager of such installations, along with members of his family. The family is held hostage while he is compelled to return and open the vault. One such case, occurring in the early 1970s, involved the kidnapping of the manager of a branch office of a bank located in the vicinity of Fort Hamilton, in Brooklyn, New York. He was taken from his home at gunpoint. Part of the gang was left to guard his wife and children. Under that pressure, he bypassed the security devices and manipulated the safe's dials to give the thieves access to the cash and other valuables. Among the items stolen were American Express Travelers Cheques whose numbers later assisted the FBI in apprehending the culprits.

Planned use of light is often overlooked as a security deterrent. The lack of statistical data on the success of lighting security makes a cost-effective judgment difficult. Statistics show, nonetheless, that increases in street lighting have resulted in marked reductions in crime. Lighting designed by a shop manager is often not as effective a device to prevent loss as the same wattage focused by a trained security expert. A change of angle can be a positive deterrent. As we have noted previously light focused on a window display may serve to shield the presence of an intruder in the shop interior. Window wiring that permits the flick of a single switch to darken an entire area with no emergency backup light is also a hazard.

Many industries and businesses, in an attempt to keep out undesirables, institute identification systems. Usually this security device is an ID card with a picture.

I, myself lost faith in the effect of a photograph on an identification card early in my career. As an Agent in the United States Secret Service, I was issued a badge and a commission book—a leather folder, postcard size, containing my laminated photograph (full face), my signature, and the engraved legend identifying me as an Agent. Regulations required that we introduce ourselves by holding open the commission book to show the photograph. On one occasion a man to whom I showed mine studied it intensely. He then looked up, handed me the book, and said in all seriousness, "Sorry, I can't help you. I've never seen that man before. But he is a tough-looking guy. I hope you have luck finding him." While my partner nearly choked with suppressed laughter, we developed the fact that he was truly referring to my photograph. Nor was that the only incident. On two other occasions my commission book was returned to me with the comment that I did not look like the man on the photograph, and did I have other identification. In both cases, they accepted my badge as proof.

Uniforms and badges issued to expedite recognition of those who belong to an organization or company have given way to colored photographs in laminated carriers with color-coded backgrounds and names clearly visible. These are worn by all employees. The background color-coding is often designed to indicate area limitations for the wearer. Recently, these identification cards have been given another dimension by way of machine-readable edges, punches, and magnetic encoding, so that the cards can be used to operate locked gates and barriers, and, in more sophisticated systems, make a record of each use and the time thereof. An early prototype of the card as a machine-readable gate pass was used at the Democratic National Convention in Chicago in 1968, although we heard that American Express credit cards were also successful in activating the entry machinery.

When I visited Singapore some years ago, senior police officials there shared a problem with me. Every citizen was issued an identity card with his photograph encased in laminated plastic. Regular visitors from neighboring Malaysia were issued similar cards of different color. The authorities were plagued by altered identifications. Cards were often split open, a new photo inserted, and then resealed so that it was difficult to tell that they had been the subject of tampering. In the United States I have seen identification cards with a new picture pasted on top of the laminate go unchallenged. I have also seen the new picture pasted on the surface and the entire surface covered with a new laminate, resulting in a slightly thicker card.

I have had occasion to note, especially when visiting plants engaged in Department of Defense work, that all employees and all visitors wear identification that includes their names in large letters. The only persons on the scene not identifiable by a name tag or by a conspicuous number have been the security guards.

Surveillance is an age-old method of noting infractions of law and regulation. It is done openly when a uniformed officer is stationed where he can watch, report, and react. The theory of "the halo" of enforcement that rides with the recognizable police car on the highway applies to private security as well. It becomes most apparent in museums, zoos, parks, and other places of assembly, where the appearance of a uniformed guard usually results in improved decorum. Surreptitious surveillance also has its roots in history. The hidden passages and listening posts of ancient castles were models for the observation posts built into many large post offices. Specially constructed slits permitted postal inspectors to spy on working employees.

Gambling casinos make lavish use of one-way mirrors for the same purpose. It is a basis for checking on croupiers, dealers, and other employees, as well as on cheating gamblers. Similar fixtures are used in fitting and try-on rooms of many stores. This is the area of the store of greatest exposure. The use of infra-red sensitized film for surreptitious photography in darkened places was known to law enforcement decades ago. Military inventions perfected in the last decade included those in which light is intensified (as sound is amplified), and permits observations in almost total darkness, have been adapted to law enforcement and private security purposes.

The tools now most used for surreptitious surveillance are audio equipment and closed-circuit television. Sound, conversations, can be overheard through increasingly sophisticated technology that has utilized miniaturization effectively. "Bugs," microphones, are now small enough to be easily hidden and fitted into inconspicuous crevices. Used alone, they have to be wired to the point of reception. They have been supplemented by transmitters that have also been miniaturized. Even batteries to power the transmitter are now inconspicuous enough to be easily hidden. Used together, they eliminate the need for wiring, and the sound picked up at the point of surveillance can be transmitted to a receiver anywhere within radius of a block or two where it can be monitored or recorded, or both. Microphones have also been improved; long-range ones can be aimed like a rifle to pick up sounds from a distant target area. CCTV has been the subject of intensive interest and use in the last decade. Several cameras can be monitored at one time by a single guard. Most give clear pictures in black and white in ordinary light, and can be equipped with both zoom lenses and swivels for remote operation. Coupled with a television tape machine, viewed action can be selectively preserved as evidence for later replay, or for other use.

Surreptitious may no longer be a proper description of CCTV. Its use has become as commonplace and well known to the professional thief as it has to the employee. As a result, dummy cameras, simulated exteriors that look like the real thing, are hung in very obvious places to act as deterrents. The general public is fooled into believing they are being watched. It can be said that the horizon of scarecrows has broadened.

As we noted earlier, at the time the Grinnell Corporation was ordered in 1964 to divest itself of some of its subsidiaries because it was in violation of the antitrust laws, it controlled some 90 percent of all Central Station Protective Services (CSPS). These monitored central stations are connected to hazard-detecting devices on the subscriber's premises over wires usually leased from a local telephone company.

In their defense the attorneys for the Central Station businesses contended that the Central Station business should not be judged by itself, where the defendant companies dominated, but rather be judged as a portion of the over-all private security business which includes private guards and all other alarms and security machinery. As a part of that larger total, CSPS and their domination were far from a monopoly. The Court, in deciding against this argument and ordering the dissolution, said:

> Quite plainly, non-automatic systems differ not merely in technology but in utility, efficiency, reliability, responsiveness, and continuity from all automatic arrangements. The difference between watchmen and watchdogs, at one end of the spectrum, and electrical systems at the other lies at the very heart of what is meant by such phrases as "the industrial revolution," "the machine age," "technological advance" and the "era of automation." Antitrust judges in their employment, no less than unskilled workers in their unemployment, recognize that markets for services rendered without tools and without education in the handling of them differ *toto mundo* from markets related to machine.[3]

Proprietary alarm systems can use sensoring equipment identical with those systems connected to a central system. These sensitive devices are activated by a number of selective stimuli. Their energy sources are either batteries or the normal electrical current available. They are sufficient to send a signal indicating their activation. Major differences lie in what happens to the signal. In the case of CSPS, it goes over a leased wire to the manned central station which in turn reacts by summoning police, sending its own guards to the scene, notifying the fire department, or taking other action as directed. Proprietary systems usually are set to respond by activating bells, gongs, sirens, lights, and in more complex systems, illuminating an indicator board on the security panel at a local control point. It is the lack of trust in the response to these signals that causes the proprietary systems to be less prestigious than those connected to central stations.

In some localities high security risks like banks have their proprietary systems wired directly into a local police station. This privilege was extended in some areas to include the alarm systems installed in private homes. The tremendous expansion of private home systems, however, has caused many police departments to refuse further tie-ins, and in some cases to discontinue the service entirely.

Intrusion detectors are becoming more sophisticated. New automatic sensors react to both visible and invisible stimuli and are being adapted to utilize the most esoteric new inventions and discoveries. Manual alarms still react to a push button, a foot pedal, an elbow treadle, (an alarm button to be activated by elbow pressure), or mousetrap configurations set off by the opening of a drawer, or the removal of papers or of money from a particular clip in a particular compartment.

Few people can say that they have never heard the sound of a proprietary alarm. Unfortunately, very few ever react and notify the police. To many it is a normal sound associated with the opening or the closing of a shop. In New York City, the Chemical Bank is now engaged in a new project in which special signs are installed outside high above each of its branches. Tied in with their holdup central station alarm, it will light up and in flashing red announce a holdup in progress. Its stated purpose is to discourage customers from entering while a hold-up is in progress, and alert passing law enforcement personnel that the alarm has been transmitted and help is on the way. No result of its effectiveness has yet been announced.

The weakest point of the alarm industry is the false alarm rate. Nationwide, more than 95 percent of all alarms prove to be false.[4] Both the CSPS and the proprietary systems have the same problem. Manually triggered holdup alarms have similar false alarm rates.

Inadvertent activation of the wrong button is a common occurrence. My own experience along this line was embarrassing and deflating, because it took place on the night of my first assignment to the White House Detail of the Secret Service. While a young Agent assigned to the New York office, I was temporarily transferred to Hyde Park where President Roosevelt was to spend a long weekend. I reported to the ad hoc Secret Service office maintained at the Hotel Campbell in Poughkeepsie, where the Agents also stayed. Each shift would meet there, receive its briefing, and proceed to Hyde Park, usually in one of the big escort Cadillacs.

I was assigned to the midnight-to-8-A.M. shift, and at about 11:30 that night, after the briefing, we emerged in front of the hotel. It was a lovely evening and the escort car, then a 16-cylinder armored, convertible Cadillac, of a size that earned it the nickname "Queen Mary," was waiting with its top down. The shift leader signaled for us to enter the car. I was unaware of the customary seating arrangements based on strict seniority; shift leader in the seat alongside the driver, senior Agents on the back seat, juniors on the jump, or folding, seats. In my gung-ho enthusiasm, I jumped into the front seat. Rather than go through an explanation for the 10-minute ride, the shift leader waved me over so that three of us could ride in front. I moved, and my big foot landed on the siren button. The sleeping city was rudely awakened by the wailing sound and flashing lights. Not knowing that I was the cause of it all, I did not respond to "Get off that button!" I did not know I was on it. When the chauffeur finally kicked me, I moved. I still blush when I remember it, especially when I recall the explanation to the police who rushed to the scene.

This embarrassment was not relieved when I later learned that even the President could inadvertently sound an alarm. I recall several occasions later on when President Roosevelt accidentally triggered an elbow treadle that required all Agents to rush into the Oval Office with guns drawn. On one occasion, the look on Secretary of War Stimson's face had the President, and later the secretary, convulsed in laughter.

Not all false alarms are due to user problems, but a recent study in Seattle placed responsibility for half of all false alarms on user error. The police there responded to 7775 burglary and robbery alarms in 1972. Only 230 of them proved to have resulted from criminal activity. Seattle's false alarm rate, including user errors, is computed as 97 percent. A breakdown of the figures showed that 75 percent of the false alarms came from business establishments, 15 percent from banks and other financial establishments, and 10 percent from private homes.[5] Major factors that enter into the false alarm rate, in addition to the human one, include the use of the alarm for purposes other than those intended, poor installation, and defective equipment.[6] The Rand study, in discussing certain security equipment and alarms, reported:

Ultrasonic devices are well suited to protecting isolated areas but not large open-space areas. Magnetic detection devices can be circumvented fairly easily. Photoelectric devices can be circumvented easily if intruders wear special lenses that can pick out the beam. Magnetic foil is circumvented by simply cutting a hole in the window or door without disturbing the system, which is usually placed around the edges. Resonance devices have a serious weakness in that they often trigger false alarms on the basis of sounds that are simply part of the environment.[7]

In short, alarms are vulnerable and often detect a door being opened, or a window being broken, but not what caused it. It could be that the door was not latched, or was jarred by the passing of a heavily loaded truck. Ultrasonic devices are prone to being triggered by such stimuli. Some alarms can be set off by a vigorous knock at the door. CSPS alarms have been set off by telephone linemen checking for open circuits. Many of the difficulties are traceable to the poor quality of an individual alarm, and in other cases to the poor quality of the installation.

I have spent some time with senior officers of major manufacturers of alarm machinery. I learned that those with full lines of products manufacture some of them themselves, assemble others, and market imported devices under their own label. Often, they make products for others for distribution under labels other than their own. They all agreed that business has been growing and one proudly pointed to a 35 percent annual increase in business for each of the last 10 years.

As a group they conceded that the false alarm rate was well over 95 percent in the United States. Though they attributed most of the fault to the user, they acknowledged that at times improper installation was to blame. They made the point that inept installation would tend to make the equipment inoperable rather than prompt a false alarm. They had no answer to the observation that poor installation leaves the user unprotected.

Equipment manufacturers normally sell their products to local alarm installation companies. These local firms sell, install, and service the machinery. According to the manufacturers, there is a scarcity of competent local agencies. Competent installers and servicemen are also in short supply. Backgrounds in electrical, hi-fi, and telephone installation are considered ideal for such installers. Only one manufacturer operates training facilities for local alarm personnel. The courses offered include: (1) residential wiring—one day; (2) burglar alarm business—two days; (3) Underwriters' Laboratories approved installation procedures—one day; (4) new mechanics—three days (devoted to alarm installation and troubleshooting); and (5) new products—an informal evening meeting for sales and installation people. There are no prerequisites for any of these courses other than the payment of the fees involved. Those who attend are not screened in any way.[8]

In reply to my comment that these seminars might be training classes for thieves, I was told that anyone with rudimentary experience in electrical installation could acquire the knowledge needed to defeat an alarm from any one of a dozen books available on alarm installation. A paperback book now being distributed by a major mail-order house was pointed out as being particularly useful for that purpose.

The alarm industry associations have come out with their own sets of statistics. They state that on average the CSPS works more than 99 percent of the time, and that each year 40 and more known captures are made for each 1000 systems in use. But for these systems, they argue, public enforcement costs would be far higher. None of their material directly refutes the high false alarm rate.

Most technicians engaged in rendering public services are required to submit themselves for examination by an appointed board before being granted permission, by way of a license, to ply their trade. Barbers, beauticians, morticians, plumbers, electricians, surveyors, and with increasing frequency, television and auto mechanics all have to prove their proficiency. No such technical qualification is required of alarm company personnel or executives. Existing and proposed legislation on the licensing of alarm companies and their staffs covers only review and clearance as to character and lack of criminal record. As far as I can determine, none of them have any prerequisite of technical competence. Several proposed statutes, however, are now calling for the licensing of all installations and provide that do-it-yourself installations be inspected, approved, and certified by a licensee.

Relatively little money is spent on research and development by this industry, according to one senior executive. Much of what the industry does is to try to perfect existing products. By way of example, he pointed to the problem of passing airplanes that put snow on a television screen for a few seconds. That same interference can set off a sensitive alarm. Once it is triggered it requires inspection and manual resetting. None of the major alarm companies employ, or even use as consultants, persons of professional law enforcement or private security backgrounds. Most of their outside input comes from inventors trying to market their inspirations and in most cases both new products and the ongoing perfection of "the line" is the responsibility of the engineering department.

The Cedar Rapids Project, a unique approach to alarm operations, has caused a struggle involving portions of the industry and law enforcement. Back in 1965, the Cedar Rapids Police Department formulated a plan calling for the installation of a network of simple burglar alarm devices to be wired directly into their headquarters. For each installation a matching business not to be so serviced was selected. The resulting statistics were to be used for comparison purposes. A grant from the U.S. Department of Justice, through LEAA, was made to assist in the financing of the program. Published findings indicated that the alarms were most effective. The department also indicated that false alarm rates "can be reduced to an acceptable figure."[9]

The LEAA-financed portion of the project covered a two-year period. With the completion of the project, LEAA consented to the sale of the equipment to the Cedar Rapids Police Department, which thereupon went into the central station business itself, using its own personnel to install and service the equipment. National and local alarm business associations promptly condemned it as being in "direct competition with private alarm companies," and as "not . . . [a] governmental function." It also "tend[ed] toward monopoly, and [was] generally anti-competitive," and "thereby [threatened] the termination of the contribution to crime prevention made by private industry."[10] They conceded that the Cedar Rapids Project false alarm rates "would normally be much lower than the industry average, since all equipment was new and of the simplest design."[11] They also pointed to the fact that every accidental or careless customer-caused false alarm was investigated by a uniformed policeman who re-explained proper customer operation, something they could not duplicate, and they also acknowledged that "the commercial alarm industry cannot users and the Cedar Rapids Police Department permitted the removal of a system from customers "causing excessive false alarms." And they also acknowledged that "the commercial alarm industry cannot call upon these techniques, and is expected to maintain more complex and sophisticated systems."[12] Still, they strongly objected to a public police department being in the CSPS business. In support of its position, the Cedar Rapids Police Department says that 65 other departments are now in the alarm business.[13]

The advent of the dial telephone has led to the relatively recent but rapidly expanding use of automatic dialers as security equipment. These dialers are listed in one product catalog as a "dependable, highly sophisticated device that silently dials and transmits emergency messages to pre-programmed destinations." They can be wired to the bell or silent terminal of most burglary or fire control instruments, and to manual holdup buttons as well. When activated, they dial a preset telephone, and when answered, repeat a pretaped message through the use of an endless tape cartridge.

I received a post-graduate course in mule skinner profanity listening to the complaints of a suburban police director. His area had been the target of a team of salesmen from a newly organized alarm firm selling home alarms systems, complete with automatic dialers. The salesmen were setting the dialers to the police emergency telephone number as part of their sales pitch. No prior notice was given to the department, and no permission received. Further, I was led to understand that the equipment was poorly constructed and the customers given a minimum of instruction. The result was a rash of false alarms, each one tying up the emergency switchboard for the four minutes of the recorded message and causing a dispatch of two police cars. The added burden of the rash of home-alarm systems was over and above the problem the police were having with the high false alarm rate from commercial CSPS input. Nor was the problem alleviated when the automatic dialers were set to a telephone answering service that in turn called the police. That police director finally asked his local government to ban all automatic dialers; similar legislation has been introduced on a statewide basis. I have been told that the alarm company involved moved its operations to another, nearby suburban area, but only after vigorous protests had been made by the company's attorney, a prominent local politician.

Local ordinances in various parts of the country levy fines for false alarms. For St. Petersburg, the local law provides a $10 fine for the first conviction, $25 for the second, and $50 for the third, within a one-year period. Denver, punishes false robbery alarms with a $50 fine. A $5 service charge is assessed for each false alarm by Virginia Beach. A graduated scale is used in Scarsdale, New York, with no fine for the first false alarm, a $10 fine for the second, $25 for the third and fourth, and $50 for each one in excess of four in the course of a year. In Seattle, $25 fines for each false alarm resulted in the collection of $10,900 for the last 10 months of 1973. A suggested model ordinance, originated by the International Association of Chiefs of Police, recommends the use of graduated fines on an annual basis.

Innovative legislation has recently been adopted by San Jose, California. It provides for a service charge of $10 for each alarm signaled by user equipment to which the police respond, valid or false. The ordinance was adopted because it is easy to administer in that it eliminates not only the need to keep records of the number of alarms per year, but the usual reviews and hassles over whether an alarm was valid or false. San Jose also has an ordinance making the activation of a police alarm system without reasonable cause a criminal violation, a misdemeanor; conviction provides for a sentence of up to six months in jail or a fine of up to $500.[14]

Some of the major contract guard companies are also in the alarm business. Walter Kidde & Company, Inc., whose subsidiary Globe Security Systems, Inc. is one of the five largest contract guard agencies, has other subsidiaries that make vaults, safes, locks, intrusion- and fire-detection devices, fire-control systems, and lighting equipment. The Wackenhut Corporation is an operator of central station protective services, and also sells surveillance devices. The William J. Burns group distributes security devices manufactured by others. It operates some 21 central stations, some of which were acquired as the result of the divestiture provisions of the Grinnell antitrust case. Baker Industries, which owns Wells Fargo Guards Services, also acquired and operates central station facilities. It also operates armored car services and manufactures both smoke- and fire-detection equipment and chemicals for use in fire extinguishers. Pinkerton's manufactures some security devices, including watchmen's clocks. One is not surprised, then, when the contract guard agency, completing a security survey, just happens to recommend equipment manufactured or distributed by one of its affiliates.

> But something, we are persuaded, might be invented for rendering both houses and warehouses more secure, and it is really a reproach to this mechanical age, that nothing in the construction of locks, doors and windows, and even in the protection of walls,

and in the mode of giving alarms, can be devised, that shall frustrate any nocturnal efforts of the midnight plunderer.[15]

Written over 150 years ago, that plea has yet to be adequately answered. The improvements thus far made have not frustrated the efforts of thieves. No impartial source as yet exists to evaluate successful inventions of security equipment and disseminate the information for the mutual benefit of business and the public.

9 | Armored Car Services

A few years ago a Wells Fargo armored car was held up in Queens, New York. Several million dollars were involved because the car had made pickups at several banks and at the Aqueduct Race Track and was on its way back in with its load. Nearly a year before the holdup, American Express had sold its Wells Fargo Armored Car Service subsidiary. According to an apocryphal story, the president of American Express was watching the late news, heard the details of the holdup, and remarked that because American Express had sold the subsidiary the loss was no longer his concern. He would get a good night's sleep. He awakened during the night with a start, however. He suddenly recalled that another subsidiary of American Express, Fireman's Fund, a San Francisco-based insurance company, might be the insurer for that multimillion-dollar loss. It was only after the opening of the offices in San Francisco the next day that he received assurances that Fireman's Fund was not so involved.

Few companies anywhere operate their own armored cars. Armored car service is almost entirely a contract business, and the key to any understanding of it is that the cash, bullion, and other valuables transported in those cars is fully insured. This insurance is purchased by the armored car companies. Salesmen of armored car services stress this insurance feature in making their pitch to selling potential customers. No one who uses their service, they point out, ever loses. The cost of the carrier's insurance is factored into the charge for its service. Most service is provided under annual contracts, and the value of each shipment forms the base for the service charge. Companies purchasing armored car services take into consideration the fact that they will be reimbursed for any loss. They also take into consideration that such loss will not reflect on their own insurance profile.

Because of this insurance feature, commercial customers do not often become involved in the operational methods of the armored carriers. In fact, customers are not disturbed when on occasion a station wagon is used by a carrier instead of the usual armored car. Insurance coverage is the main reason why this industry is able to say of itself that it transports all valuables to and from 99 percent of all the commercial banks in all the cities of more than 75,000 in the United States, Canada, and a number of foreign nations.[1] Despite the rapidly increasing cost of these services, it is difficult to imagine armored car companies losing the business from commercial banks as the result of economy measures. In its October, 1972, report to the Law Enforcement Assistance Administration, the Private Security Advisory Council, the Armored Car Sub-Committee said: "Because of the increase in attacks by criminal elements upon the armored car industry, the cost of insurance has increased as much as 1700% during the past five years."[2]

Another factor contributing to the increased cost of armored car hire is rising labor costs. Receipts of the armored car services grew from $67.3 million in 1962, to $90.6 million in 1967, an increase of 35 percent. In this same period the number of industry employees rose by 12 percent; payroll costs during that same time, however, shot up by 40 percent—from $36.9 million, to $52 million. A greater percentage of employees of the armored car services are members of trade unions than are employees in any other area of private security. The Teamsters Union is predominant in this field.[3]

The growth in the crime rate has been an important factor in the growth of the industry. Businessmen have become increasingly anxious to have accumulated cash receipts safely removed from their premises as often as possible to lessen the danger of loss through holdup or other larceny. Insurance company efforts to raise the deductibles for such insurance coverage has increased this anxiety, because the customer is solely liable for the losses in the deductible range.

Like other interstate transportation, the interstate operations of armored car services are subject to the regulations of the Interstate Commerce Commission. In this respect it is the only portion of the private security industry subject to direct Federal regulation. Little can be said about the efforts or the influence of this regulatory body to reduce losses to cargo in transit from carriers subject to their regulation. Much of the commission's enforcement activities are devoted to policing the regulations it has set forth. There is no uniformity in state or local laws with regard to the licensing or other regulation of armored car companies, and in most jurisdictions they are relatively unregulated.

In the United States the entire armored car industry encompasses fewer than 70 companies. Seventy, however, is probably sufficient; as one financial analyst has suggested, new companies seeking to enter the field would have difficulty in "proving need" because armored car carriers have already acquired such operating licenses and permissions as are needed for the conduct of their business.[4] Looming above them all is Brink's, Inc., which does more than half of the total business of the country. In 1969 it had about 1100 armored vehicles. Three years later the entire industry was operating 4000 armored cars. The other large concerns are Loomis, Inc., Wells Fargo (Baker Industries), and Purolator. Together with Brink's, these companies are reported as being responsible for more than 75 percent of the total volume of business done in the United States; the balance is divided among the remaining 60-plus small firms.[5]

One portion of the business done by the car service branch of the security industry is referred to as "courier service." This service provides for the transfer of items that have little or no intrinsic value by courier or by special handling. Examples of such items are bank paper, like cashed checks, payroll checks, and other non-negotiable items; radio isotopes; and blood plasma. The American Courier Company, a division of Purolator, is one of the larger suppliers of this service.

Less is known of the armored car business than of the other branches of the security industry. Though it is mentioned in several places in the 1971 Rand study, no employees of an armored car company participated in the Rand survey, nor was any armored-car company among the groups of firms interviewed in depth. Police officials have mixed feelings about armored cars. To many they are nuisances to be tolerated. They often block the movement of traffic. Their guards are a constant danger, walking in and out of banks and other institutions with guns in their hands. Armored car personnel are at times prone to strong language, even when addressing police. Armored car companies often call upon the police for surveillance assistance when a truck breaks down, or other trouble develops, a call that is difficult to turn down in view of the amounts of money involved.

When an armored car is robbed, the crime becomes a sizable police problem taking up many man-hours of investigation efforts. These efforts have an element of exasperation about them for the investigating officers. The basic reason for their impatience was aptly described by the LEAA Armored Car Subcommittee in its report mentioned above: "Each time we experience a loss, we usually find that the employees involved have failed to follow established procedures which in most cases could have prevented the loss had the procedures been followed."[6]

The subcommittee report also revealed what this industry feels are its prime problems, and the avenues of solution they suggest. In line with its problem on employee failures, the industry suggested the development of psychological tests for potential employees in order to predetermine those with a "natural inclination" to follow procedures. It proposed that this research be financed by LEAA. Later, learning that LEAA was considering the funding of similar projects relative to the psychological testing of prospective police officers, the armored car industry requested that the results of the findings be made available to it.

The industry's second recommendation was in two parts. First, LEAA should promote a better relationship between the FBI and members of the industry so that they could submit names and fingerprints of prospective employees directly to the bureau for analysis. Second, LEAA should intervene on the industry's behalf with the legislatures of certain states, specifically Massachusetts, California, and New Jersey, where laws bar the use of polygraph (lie detector) screening in pre-employment situations. The industry feels such screening is vitally important to it, and that these states should exempt armored car companies from restrictions on the use of polygraphs.

The funding by LEAA of research into the development of better equipment for preventing armored car robberies was the industry's third recommendation. This research should be directed at the creation of "lighter, stronger, more bullet-resistant materials." Other reseach should focus on improving bullet-resistant glass. In this connection the industry suggested LEAA intervene to have the plastic-type materials used in military aircraft made available to the civilian market. Other areas of research suggested for government funding included the development of alarms to be used in money bags or other containers; explosive devices for use in similar receptacles; dye and smoke markers; homing devices, radio signals which can be followed by triangulation; "on-person alarm-radio signal devices"; and carts with electrical fields controlled by the accompanying messenger.

The report also requested assistance to help establish closer relationships between the industry and the Law Enforcement Standards Laboratories, so that it would be able to obtain current information on many subjects from weapons to communications and electronics. The report urgently asked LEAA's help in communicating the problems or the armored car industry to law enforcement agencies in order to obtain the "complete cooperation" of local police. The areas in which the industry particularly wants this cooperation to be manifested are in impressing upon the police the necessity for the armored car industry's "gun-in-hand policy" and its need to park as close as possible to their delivery points.

The subcommittee further sought intervention with the Federal Communication Commission for the assignment to the armored car industry of at least one radio frequency on the police band, so that its crews would be able to communicate directly with the police in the event of a robbery. Closely allied with this request was another that industry trucks be included, along with police cars, in the newly developing Vehicle Locator Systems. These systems have police cars emit pulsed, nonvoice signals at regular intervals. Using these signals, receivers located in widely different areas compute each car's position by triangulation, and transfer their findings in the form of a light, stationary or moving, to an enlarged map. Because this nonvoice signal can be modulated to indicate if the police car is on a call, and thus change the color of the indicator light, a police radio dispatcher can tell at a glance the exact position of each car, as well as those available for assignment. The armored car industry suggested that its trucks be included in this monitoring and, by implication, a special modulation in the silent signals be devised to indicate an ongoing holdup. This same report made the point that in the 20 months preceding October, 1972, 12 armored car employees were killed while on their jobs protecting their trucks and their contents. It emphasized that a number of these instances involved ambush type shootings, without verbal or other warning.

Great Britain still leads the world in the dubious honor of being the victim of the largest single cash robbery, the $7.6 million train robbery of 1963. Runner-up and holder of the title in the United States is the armored express division of Purolator Security, Inc., an armored car service located in Chicago. On the weekend of October 19–20, 1974, more than $3,930,000 was stolen from its own vault. The vault was used to store receipts picked up after the close of banking hours on Friday and held for delivery Monday. The elaborate alarm system guarding the vault and the building was succesfully de-activated without any signal sounding or going through to a central alarm system or other points. After breaching the vault and removing all but a small sum of money, plastic bags filled with gasoline were left in place of the stolen funds. Ignition was to be by a delayed-action fuse. It was hoped by the perpetrators that the resulting fire would burn the cash that was left and confuse the authorities as to the amount of the theft and the amount destroyed by fire. Ignition failed because of the lack of oxygen. The small amount of smoke that did result, however, triggered an alarm, and that was the first notice of the break-in. One newspaper account of the police search of the home of a suspect reported that it yielded "sophisticated electronic equipment, burglary tools, devices for dismantling different security systems and dozens of manuals on the installation of burglar alarms."[7] One of those eventually charged with the crime was a former guard who had been employed by Purolator.

Armored car company vaults always seem to be a favorite target for so-called master criminals. Another example was the Brink's hold-up in Boston in 1950; the loot amounted to $1.5 million. A weekend in October, 1965, was marked by the burglarization of a Brink's storage vault in Syracuse, New York, when some $415,000 in cash and checks was stolen. This was a landmark in criminal innovation. The men involved, mostly French-Canadians, had arranged to purchase two surplus 20-millimeter, armor-piercing cannons and a supply of shells in Alexandria, Virginia. Using fictitious names, they had the cannons sent to themselves in care of the Railway Express office at Plattsburgh, New York. Instead of calling for their packages at the counter, however, they burglarized the office at night and removed their artillery. One of the cannons went to Quebec for an attempt to lay siege to a bank vault there, but before the job was completed the aspiring thieves were scared off.

In Syracuse, things went differently. A truck with the artillery aboard was driven into a garage having a common wall with the

Brink's establishment. The truck also carried a plentiful supply of blankets and mattresses. After all of the alarms were successfully foiled, the bedding material was used to deaden the sound of sledge-hammers breaching the wall. Once that was accomplished, the cannon, now on a special gun mount, was aimed at the vault's side. Again, the mattresses and bedding were used to deaden sound. The gun was fired time and time again until a hole 18-by-28 inches was blasted through the steel-reinforced concrete vault wall that was more than a foot thick. The hole was big enough to permit entrance of the looters and exit of the loot. The loss was not noted until the following Monday morning. Much of this story was pieced together when an uncle of one of the gunners turned informant. He lived on Long Island and was involved in assisting in the purchase of the cannons in Alexandria, Virginia. The FBI recovered the cannon used in Syracuse from the waters near the entrance to Jones Beach, Long Island.

Armored cars themselves have been the subject of many attacks. Some $700,000 was removed from an armored car parked in front of an Eastman Kodak plant in Rochester, New York. It occurred while the armored car guards were in the building. Entry into the unguarded van was made with a key that fit the armored door. In fact, the theft was so smooth that the loss was not discovered until after the crew had driven away from the building.

A faulty armored car door figured in an incident on December 2, 1973. A big containing $16,200 in $1 bills was picked up by a group of laborers who saw it drop from a Brink's armored truck. The loss was not noted by the armored car crew or by Brink's. It came to light when the police received a tip from another laborer who was not close enough to the missing package to be included in the division of the spoils made on the spot. There have been many instances of armored car robberies while the crew was in a restaurant during a meal break.

On the whole, though, considering that the armored car industry transports cash and valuables in amounts so large as to be almost incomprehensible—ranging from $10 billion to $12 billion each working day—its losses amount to the tiniest fraction of that amount.[8] In the course of these operations the industry utilizes storage facilities to keep unknown fortunes for short periods. There are no publicly available statistics on the industry's losses. There are no known figures as to its unit costs of movement or storage. There are no statistics for the industry on its research and development expenses, and, of course, on what that total is in relation to its total income. The requests of the Armored Car Sub-Committee of the LEAA Advisory Council involved suggestions for more governmental financing of what might be considered the industry's own research and development responsibilities. Alone among the subcommittees, it requested LEAA intervention on its behalf with the FBI, the local police, and state legislatures. Insofar as I have been able to ascertain, these requests have not been acted upon. Nothing in the other subcommittee's recommendations relating to the model statute for private security agencies, of for the alarm industry, pertains to the armored car companies or their employees.

10 | Law, Legislation, and Regulation

Every citizen has certain rights, including that of self-defense and a limited power of arrest, search, and seizure. The prerogatives of private security emanate from these rights and those inherent in the ownership of property. The use of private security forces for the protection of property is not limited to those countries where private property exists; they are also used where ownership is communal.

In the United States security guards are subject to the laws regulating the ownership and use of weapons. They may be armed, and if compelled to safeguard life or property, they are authorized to use their weapons. But they are limited to using only such force as is necessary. Like anyone else, private security forces are further constrained by the tort law of the individual states. While the threat of a civil suit and the possibility of a verdict awarding money damages may serve to restrain abuses, this type of lawsuit takes time to work its way through the courts, is often expensive, and almost always requires the services of an attorney. When the complainant accuses the guard or his employer of being negligent, there is the additional burden on the person suing to establish that he himself was not contributorily negligent. Tort liability as a method of control raises the question of the ability of the complainant to collect the damages awarded. Most private guards, whose actions might be the basis of the recovery, are simply too poor to have the wherewithall to pay damages. They are judgment proof. Any recovery of damages, if available, would have to come from the employer under the doctrine of *respondeat superior*. As a practical matter, most owners of property and responsible contract guard firms attempt to provide for such contingencies by the purchase of insurance. In addition there have been instances where employers interpose a defense that the guard, or the contract guard force that employed him, was an independent subcontractor. In such case, the property owner claims that he is not responsible, his point being that his contract with the guard or the contract guard agency is one in which they assumed all responsibility. However if that contract provides any duty of direction by the owner it vitiates such an independent contractor relationship. The prevailing trend of court decisions, as well as licensing and regulatory provisions seems to be against such contracted avoidance of responsibility.[1]

Public police, private police, and private citizens may all make legal arrests for felonies committed in their presence. In the case of private police and private citizens, it is vital that the felony be committed, otherwise the arrest may be considered false and may result in a lawsuit. In the case of a sworn police officer, it is sufficient that he have reasonable cause to believe that an action constituting a felony has been committed, and that the suspect was indeed the person involved. The private guard or citizen is permitted a search in connection with a lawful arrest or detention, but this search is limited to seeking arms or other weapons in the possession or control of the prisoner. There are variations of this rule used by the different states.[2] Searches by sworn officers are governed by the interpretations of the Fourth Amendment to the United States Constitution and the statutes of the various states in conformity with the amendment.

Currently, there seems to be one important difference between the duties of the public police officer and the private investigator in connection with an arrest. The case of *Miranda* v. *Arizona* sets forth the judicial requirement that each arresting officer must orally, or in writing, notify the prisoner of his right to remain silent and his right to counsel. Unless such notification is given, any statement made by the prisoner may be excluded from evidence during a trial. The courts have limited the application of this *Miranda* rule to statements obtained by sworn police, government officials, and to such private police who are commissioned under state or local law, that is, private guards and investigators who have been made deputy sheriffs or special police, or given some other official status by appointment under enabling laws. Private security officers in the employ of a governmental agency are also in this category. Statements taken by private security officers who do not come under the categories noted above, however, have been held to be admissible evidence, even though the defendants involved were not given the notice required in the *Miranda* case.[3]

In addition to regulation and control by state law, private security, since it imposes a substantial burden upon, and involves interstate commerce, is subject also to regulation by federal law. There are many statutes passed by the Congress that tangentially affect the operations of security agencies, such as wiretapping and firearm regulations, and laws concerning the impersonating of officers.

The first direct congressional enactment pertaining to private security read: "Hereafter no employee of the Pinkerton Detective Agency, or similar agency, shall be employed in any Government Service, or by any officer of the District of Columbia." As we noted earlier, this 1893 law followed the congressional hearings on violence at the Homestead plant of Carnegie Steel. A landmark annotation under this law was in the opinion of Attorney General Harry M. Doherty (later involved in the Teapot Dome scandal), on June 10, 1922.[4] The question was on the right of the United States Shipping Board Emergency Fleet Corporation to secure guards through private detective agencies for its laid up ships. Doherty held that the provision of the law was one simply to prohibit the employment of Pinkerton or similar agencies by any officer of the United States or the District of Columbia. He ruled that the employees of the Emergency Fleet Corporation were not employees of the United States, but rather of a private corporation created by law; they were therefore not restrained from hiring private detectives.

Since the Doherty ruling on the 1893 act, there have been a series of comptroller general opinions. In 1926 the Alaska Railroad was forbidden to use the Thiel Detective Service Company as a source for its guards.[5] In 1927 the hiring of individuals employed by the William J. Burns International Detective Agency by the Quartermaster Corps of the Army was barred.[6] In 1928 payments for supplying guards to protect alcohol belonging to the Panama Canal by the Dan S. Lehon Detective Agency was stopped.[7]

The most definitive of these rulings was made by Comptroller General Warren in 1946. It was made in answer to a request from the administrator of the War Assets Administration. In this opinion Warren made three points: (1) where a subcontract for guard services is made with an independent contractor of the United States, the government is not a party to the agreement, and the hiring of the guard agency therefore is not a direct employment by the government for these services in contravention of the 1893 statute; (2) that no objection would be interposed by the comptroller general to the procurement of services by direct contract with protective agencies as distinguished from detective agencies; (3) that the terms of the act of March 3, 1893 are plain and unambiguous and prohibit the employment directly by the government of employees of a detective agency "regardless of the character of the services to be performed, and the fact that the services of said agencies are not to be of a detective or investigative nature. . . ."[8]

When the restatement of that section of the United States Code was adopted in September, 1966, the 1893 statute was enacted again in slightly different form. It is still in effect and now reads: "An individual employed by the Pinkerton Detective Agency, or similar organization, may not be employed by the Government of the United States or the Government of the District of Columbia."[9]

In practice, however, this archaic provision and its tortured interpretations have been no barrier to the use of employees of Pinkerton's or other similar organizations, both directly and indirectly by the United States government. The Wackenhut Corporation, now the third largest private security organization in the country, reported that it received 20 percent of its 1967 revenues from direct contracts with the United States government, this being in addition to its subcontracts for protective services at government installations.[10] In 1966 Wackenhut was employed by a subcommittee of the House of Representatives under the chairmanship of Congressman Wayne L. Hays to determine whether persons listed as staff members of Congressman Adam Clayton Powell for his committee were "in fact real persons."[11] A 1967 Wall Street brokerage analysis of the security business as a growth industry specifically commented about the Pinkerton, Burns, and Wackenhut corporations, advising potential investors that the 1893 law was no barrier to the investment opportunities these companies offer. The appraisal points out that "Pinkerton's Security Service is a wholly owned subsidiary of Pinkerton's, is oriented exclusively to provide service to the Federal Government, and that the rulings of the Comptroller General permit such 'separately maintained subsidiary to be employed directly by the Government.' "[12]

In the recent past the Congress has adopted laws having a more direct effect on private security. It imposed security standards as a requirement for banking institutions. It also approved legislation authorizing the compulsory search of all hand luggage and other items carried by passengers boarding air flights within this country. There is no doubt that in both of these areas Federal regulations have positive results. Since the effective date of the legislation concerning bank security which was aimed at combatting holdups and burglaries, the statistics show a marked decline in these crimes at banks in relation to crimes committed against unregulated businesses. As for compulsory baggage search, it has brought about more dramatic consequences, with skyjacking, both actual and attempted, dropping sharply. According to one source, in the two years since its imposition, more than 66,000 weapons have been taken from passengers, and more than 3000 people arrested for illegal possession.[13]

None of the studies of the private security industry, and not one of the advisory committees to the Law Enforcement Assistance Administration have suggested reform or even standardization by way of Federal intervention, other than to call for the creation of government sponsored research facilities. In a number of large concerns, the security director is also the director of plant safety. In the area of safety the Congress has intervened on many occasions, legislating in such instances as mine safety and, more recently passing the Occupational Safety and Health Act of 1970. These safety-security directors find themselves administering their safety responsibilities aided by standards and regulations. The Act of 1970 provided for the creation of a National Institute for Occupational Safety and Health in the Department of Health, Education and Welfare to undertake basic research and encourage, through grants, research by academic and other qualified institutions. HEW is authorized to make grants to the states to assist them in developing their plans and expertise in the state-operated occupational and health laws. There is even provision in the 1970 act for the education of an adequate number of qualified persons to carry out the purposes of the law. Except in the case of banking and airport operations, the same security director finds no similar Federal interest or contribution in security problems.

All studies and advisory committee reports on private security suggest that more attention be given to its problems and that the industry be controlled by state legislation, licensing, and regulation. The present legislative control of private security by the states and the cities is a hodgepodge; it ranges from no controls whatever, through nominal licensing, to somewhat better, but still inadequate public supervision. Twelve states have virtually no regulations at all. The others license on various bases. Some states are involved with contract investigative agencies only; others regulate their contract guard or patrol firms; six states have provisions to license armored guard transport companies; four have regulations concerning central station alarm companies; one state requires the licensing of insurance investigators; none of the states have compulsory licensing provisions for in-house security staffs.

In those states where licensing provisions exist, they usually require an individual licensee, one of the owners, or one of the officers when a corporation is involved, to be the subject of a criminal record check. This licensee must not have been convicted of a felony or crime involving moral turpitude. In a few states all security employees of contract agencies are also required to be fingerprinted.

Fifty-two percent of the states and localities (three counties and 46 cities) that regulate private security responded to a questionnaire prepared by the principal investigators of the 1971 Rand study. A compilation of their responses shows that 15 percent of applicants at the state level and 6 percent of applicants at the local level were denied licenses in 1970. The primary reason for the denials was the "criminal record of the applicant."[14] In New Jersey, fingerprint checks of employees of private detective agencies revealed that more than 20 percent of them had arrest records.[15] These findings confirm the undoubted interest on the part of a criminal element to engage in the business of private security. These applicants, knowing of their previous convictions, aware that fingerprinting and a search would disclose their past history, nonetheless each voluntarily submitted to fingerprinting after informing the licensing agency or their prospective employer that they never had a "record." This fact raises the fair inference that many others with similar backgrounds get by the fingerprint search and obtain accreditation. It is sobering to realize that many of those found to have criminal records were first issued a uniform and badge, and in many instances a gun, and put on a business premise as its guard for a period of weeks before the fingerprints were processed and returned. It is equally worrisome to believe that similar findings would result if these fingerprinting requirements were extended to the alarm installation industry and its thousands of totally unlicensed and unregulated practitioners. Even in the case of licensed firms, only one principal is required to be cleared, while the balance of the officers and managers are, at most, listed by name.

Existing state and local licensing regulations make no provision for minimum physical requirements. They do not even impose minimum sight or hearing standards. Many of them do set the age of 21 as a minimum for security workers, while others stipulate that the starting age be 25. In no case is there a maximum age limit. With three exceptions, all of these licensing requirements are silent as to the education or literacy of security workers. One of the three requires workers to be literate, and the other two set a high-school education as a prerequisite.

The principals of licensed agencies, according to the regulations of 23 states, are required to have had previous experience, ranging from 1 to 10 years, and averaging between 2 and 3 years. Written examinations of these principals are provided for by 8 states in connection with contract guard agencies, and by 11 states when contract investigative agencies are involved. All of these requirements are far less demanding than the requirements of the 11 states that license polygraph examiners. Here the requirements usually include a bachelor's degree.

In all but a few of the licensing states and cities, the training of security personnel is not mentioned in statutes and regulations. The exceptions are in Ohio, Vermont, and St. Louis. In Ohio, where state law provides that localities may require private security personnel to be commissioned (a form of deputizing analogous to appointment as a deputy sheriff or special policeman), all commissioned employees must receive 120 hours of instruction at an accredited school. Moreover, all armed security staffs at educational institutions are required to receive the same instruction. Both accreditation and the curriculum of instruction are governed by the Ohio Peace Officers Training Council.[16] Vermont requires licensees to have completed the basic course of instruction set forth for law enforcement officers of that state, or to pass a comprehensive examination.[17] St. Louis's statutes and regulations require the attendance of all private security guards, including alarm and armored transport personnel, at special three-day courses given by the St. Louis Police Department at their training academy. One day is entirely devoted to firearm instruction. These courses are repeated periodically on a scheduled basis.[18]

Most of the existing license provisions contain requirements concerning uniforms, badges, and identification. The majority of provisions mandate that these not resemble the ones issued to or worn by sworn police. Not one of these licensing and regulatory agencies has a provision that each individual guard be required to wear a nameplate or a keyed badge number from which he can be identified. Some of the legislation requires that the individual guards obtain special handgun or concealed weapon permits, but most are silent on this point.

That these laws and regulations are insufficient is well known and understood by many in the security industry. Most anticipate the passage of new and more stringent requirements. Expecting that such new regulations will have tighter training requirements, some individuals have been rushing to obtain licenses to operate schools for training guards. One contract agency that had obtained such a license testified at Pennsylvania's 1973–1974 legislative inquiry into private security. The agency's testimony disclosed not only a keen desire to "get there first" and cash in on a possible bonanza, but also a lack of competence to conduct a training school. I myself have been sought out by strangers who had gone to great lengths to find mutual acquaintances in order to proposition me about joining with them in establishing training schools for guards. One group had no expertise in either security or education; it was simply some investors who felt guard training was a promising field for the large-scale development of a chain of schools and for a correspondence school. Many of these people are frank to say that by obtaining their licenses now they will be in the position, as an existing school, not to be subject to new and more exacting regulations.

In their "Findings and Recommendations" the principal investigators of the 1971 Rand study spelled out their conclusions that the existing regulatory agencies, state and local, have limited effectiveness. They do not have extensive data on the problems of the security industry. In fact, the findings contend that with the exception of reviewing license applications, the typical regulatory agency has very limited contact with the industry. In some cases, it has none. They very rarely invoke their post-licensing powers to correct problems. Suspensions of licenses, or their revocation are rare, as are the imposition of fines. This circumstance prevails, according to the study, not because of willful failure to take action in specific situations brought to their attention, but rather because their limited resources and ineffective channels prevent specific problems from coming to their attention. Not only is there a hodgepodge of licensing laws, there is little consistency in the controls that have been granted to the various licensing agencies. Almost every agency that responded to the inquiries of the Rand investigators recommended that some aspect of the regulation of their industry in their own jurisdiction be made stronger.[19]

Only 17 of the 42 agencies that responded to the questionnaires sent out by Rand were able to furnish detailed breakdowns of the complaints they received. The data supplied indicate that the two major items of complaint were 413 "violations of regulations" and 369 charges of "improper uniform or identification." There followed three categories of a far more serious nature: 55 instances of "shooting," 34 cases of "impersonating a police officer," and 29 cases of "theft." Other complaints ranged from 29 instances of "failure to serve as agreed" to eight "killings."[20] Since mandatory requirements to report specific instances do not exist, the fairness of this sample of abuses in private security is called further into question.

Most licensing statutes mandate the posting of a bond or insurance, but only 3 of the 42 reporting agencies maintained information on such claims. California did report getting one or two inquiries a week for the names of the bonding agent of different contract agencies, and Michigan reported a recovery in one case of $460,000 where an assault was involved.[21]

To conclude that the licensing authorities have little knowledge of the shortcomings of the private security industry does not alter the fact that such shortcomings exist. A number of them have already been detailed. Among others are the serious abuses of authority by individuals working for private security agencies. This particular abuse is partly reflected in the complaints mentioned above, which included assaults, shootings, killings, and theft. One state agency said it believed half of all the licensed agencies in its jurisdiction were violating the bugging and wiretapping laws.[22]

The paradox of the private security industry is that on the one hand it prescribes methods for the protection of individuals and property from harm and theft while on the other hand it uses for this purpose personnel that the industry itself proscribes as high risks when evaluating or surveying business operations. In other words, it employs as guards the very types of persons that it advises management are high risks when used in such places as vaults, teller cages, jewelry packaging rooms, and in the movement of small, valuable items. Need, temptation, and opportunity are among the inducing factors in our climbing crime rate. Yet the makeup of security forces is often of low-paid, low-quality, undereducated, and untrained individuals. They are entrusted with all of the assests on the premises of the business they are hired to protect. They have greater undisturbed, unobserved access to these properties than even the heads of the business.

This is especially true on weekends and holidays when they are alone on the premises. I have yet to observe guards checking fellow guards to see what they are carrying in their bags or lunch boxes, or what they have in the trunks of their cars when they leave a guarded premise at the end of their shift. Great attention has properly been paid to the problems of the crooked cop. They exist, and instances where turn-coat police were involved in stealing from premises they were supposed to be protecting have made headlines in Denver, Los Angeles, Chicago, New York, and many other cities. These policemen were recruited from a different, a better educated labor market than is used for guards, and they are paid on a much higher scale, trained intensively, supervised by experts, exposed to the procedures and penalties of the courts and the law. Yet they succumbed to the commission of crime. What would an intensive study disclose about the range of corruption within the ranks of private security?

The Rand study, recognizing that a portion of the private security industry does provide high quality personnel and equipment, made a series of recommendations that would apply to the other segments of the industry. It urged the establishment of minimum regulations, the upgrading of standards to diminish abuses with the least interference or impairment of an "individual's ability to conduct business or to work in private security." The recommendation with the highest priority was that more adequate licensing and regulation of private security be instituted at the state level, and that local areas be permitted the option of promulgating additional regulations over and above those set by the state.[23]

The principal investigators of the Rand study suggested that not only owners and corporate officers of contract security agencies be licensed, but that directors and managers of in-house forces be licensed as well. They recommended that all security employees, in-house and contract, be registered by the state. The licensing of an employee, they said, should be required *before* security operations are started, though registration with the state may take place after the employee is engaged in his activity. In this way their registration system would rely on the hiring security agency, which would be licensed, to fire an unworthy registrant from the job after his unworthiness has been proven. This procedure would allow an applicant for registration to work as a guard for weeks or months while an investigation as to his fitness was in progress. The investigators recommended registration for all in-house and contract employees who work as guards; for insurance, credit, and general investigators; for patrolmen, on foot or in vehicles; for responders to (not installers of) alarms; for armed transport guards; for polygraph examiners; and for special police.

James Kakalik and Sorrel Wildhorn, the Rand study authors, urged that all "new applicants" for licensing or registration be high-school graduates or be able to pass satisfactorily a special literacy test. They would make mandatory minimal requirements for comprehensive liability insurance and for bonding by all contract firms and employers of in-house staffs.

Minimum training was recommended to be compulsory, with quality curriculum, competence of instruction, and the hours required to be strictly controlled. Separate training programs were suggested to be tailored to major private security job categories; guards, investigators, central station alarm respondents, and supervisory personnel, with all trainees required to pass examinations. All types of private security workers were to be obliged to receive a "minimum initial training program of at least *120 hours* [emphasis in original]." Two days of compulsory annual retraining was also recommended for all security workers and supervisors.

The Rand study also urged that persons who want to serve as armed guards be specially screened, and that they complete a mandatory accredited firearms course as part of initial training. Another recommended goal was retraining, with firing range requalification at regular periods. Other suggestions were: standardizing the weapons used; placing ownership of the weapon with the agency or employer, not with the guard; forbidding the use of a concealed gun on a uniformed guard; and discouraging the use of armed guards. No mention was made of minimum physical standards. One interesting suggestion, however, was that a search be made for reliable psychological tests to screen armed guards; should none exist, the study advocated that funds be obtained to sponsor research for their development.[24]

The only other suggestions for action at the Federal level were for the use of Law Enforcement Assistance Administration funds to help develop appropriate training programs, and in this regard to set up a committee or study group to help formulate such programs.[25] Said the report:

In the interests of aiding crime prevention by providing users of private security services with information as to which systems or services would be most effective, or most cost-effective, for the intended application, we suggest that:

The Federal Government should consider funding a research center that would evaluate the effectiveness and costs of private security personnel and equipment [emphasis in original].[26]

The report specified that the research center should be financially independent of the private security industry.[27]

Publication of the five-volume Rand study at the end of 1971 caused only a ripple of interest in law enforcement circles but a furor in private security ranks, especially among the proprietors of smaller contract security agencies and the alarm industry who felt they were the targets of the report.

In October, 1972, Jerris Leonard, then administrator of the LEAA, whose money paid for the research by the Rand investigators, appointed a Private Security Advisory Council (PSAC). Members included senior representatives of major contract guard agencies, an armored car operator, manufacturers of alarm machinery, the operator of a Central Station Alarm Service, a consulting engineer, the chief of security of the largest manufacturer of computers and other machinery, a chief of police, and a sheriff. Not included were representatives of any of the existing regulatory agencies; the insurance industry; the retail industry; any branch of the transportation industry, —airlines, railroads, trucks, transit; the housing industry; Federal law enforcement agencies; unions in the private security field; the Department of Defense; the Atomic Energy Commission; NASA; state police; or quasi-governmental police such as the Governmental Guard Services. Nor were small contract guard agencies involved. Neither of the principal investigators who authored the Rand study were included either.

The Private Security Advisory Council has been operating on a basis that it must face the issues raised by the Rand study. Words to this effect have appeared in PSAC's various communications. In its first report at the end of 1972, the council recommended the creation and adoption of a "uniform code of private security regulations."[28] At the same time, it urged state and municipal governments to "refrain from being stampeded into establishing legislation," and said that it had under way a study of the type and kind of uniform legislation that should prevail throughout the United States.[29]

The council appointed four subcommittees to work on this study, and its membership was enlarged. Three years later, on February 4, 1975, PSAC's Subcommittee on Guards and Investigations released a copy of its proposed "Model Private Security Guard Licensing and Regulatory Statute." The proposed law was scheduled for review by the full advisory committee and at public hearings in Austin, Texas, in the third week of February. Distribution was made by the New England Bureau for Criminal Justice Services of Dedham, Massachusetts. This firm, whose letterhead indicates its services are "management" "training" and "evaluation," was hired in the summer of 1974 by the LEAA to assist the council in its work. The LEAA selected the firm, and no notice was given to others in the same field to enable them to bid for the contract. It is fair to assume that this Dedham company has had the opportunity for its own professional input into PSAC's model statute.

According to information the council submitted at the time it unveiled its model statute, it felt its first duty was to review the criticisms of private security contained in the Rand study. The council then went on to cite the urgent need for practical solutions to the most glaring deficiencies disclosed by the Rand investigators.

The model statute, unfortunately, fails to fulfill the need. It is an emasculated, watered-down version of the Rand study recommendations. It contains no materials not specifically targeted in that report. It is not an attempt to install basic regulations for the industry, but rather one intended to foreclose further criticism. I have previously called attention to the schism between the in-house and contract guard approach to security. I repeat that the major selling points of salesmen for contract security firms are that they are able to supply what they call "competent security staffs" at costs as much as 20 percent less than those for an in-house staff, and that in addition they relieve management of the chores of supervision. With this in mind, consider the arguments of the contract guard representatives on the council, who urged that the model statute include equal licensing requirements for both contract and in-house organizations. According to the PSAC report, it was the argument of contract guard representatives "that the ultimate goal of licensing legislation [is] to protect the general public," that it is necessary to make someone responsible for the recruiting, selecting, training, and supervising of security guards, especially armed guards, to prevent continuation of the problems cited by the Rand study. This responsibility, they are reported to have contended, should be borne equally by all employers of security guards, not just those companies who offer security services for hire.

Representatives of firms that had in-house security staffs argued that the licensing of proprietary security organizations was not necessary to correct the criticisms of the Rand study. That report, they held, was directed at security guards, not at companies employing security personnel solely for the protection of their own assets.

The model statute emerges as a tribute to compromise and consensus of those present. It requires the licensing of contract agencies and their employees, and the registering of in-house security employees.

The actual language of the model statute was the work of a drafting subcommittee consisting entirely of lawyers for contract security companies only. The committee report states that this subcommittee gradually became interchangeable with a subcommittee of the Committee of National Security Companies (CONSCO), a trade organization of contract guard agencies formed in 1974.

The model statute is silent as to any physical or mental requirements for a license to operate a private security company, except that the applicant be of legal age, a citizen or resident alien, of good moral character who has not been convicted of a felony or crime involving moral turpitude or the illegal use or possession of a dangerous weapon. It also requires that he not have been declared a mental incompetent, nor discharged from the Armed Forces under dishonorable conditions. It made habitual drunks and narcotics addicts ineligible too. Furthermore, the applicant is required to have had three years' experience as a manager or supervisor with a security organization or equivalent supervisory experience in a law enforcement or military organization. The model makes no recommendation as to his minimal educational standard. In an accompanying explanation, the PSAC said that the foregoing requirements were limited to only one person from each applying company, "the qualifying agent," but that the names of the principal corporate officers are to be filed with the license application. The reason for such a limitation, PSAC said, was to ease the burden of license applications.

While the model statute provides that a license must be issued before a new business can start, in the event of the sale or transfer of the business, it may continue while the new principal or qualifying agent makes application. It provides that the licensee shall have 30 days in which to notify the licensing authority of any change in the qualifying agent or the officers of the company "which could reasonably be expected to affect the licensee's right to a license."

The model statute provides that employees of contract agencies and in-house organizations are required to register with the state. As part of the registration form each employee must make a statement that he does not suffer from habitual drunkenness, from narcotics addiction or dependence and does "not possess any physical disability which would prevent him from performing the duties of a private security officer." Employees of contract agencies are to be registered by their employers. Unlike the licensee who is permitted 30 days before notifying authorities of a change of status, the guard has only 10 in which to disclose any change in his status that could affect his registration. To be a registered guard, the applicant must be at least 18 years old, a citizen or resident alien. He too must not have been convicted of a crime similar to the kind applicable to the licensee, nor have been discharged under dishonorable conditions from the Armed Forces, or declared mentally incompetent. Also, he must not possess "any physical disability which in the opinion of the Licensing Authority prevents him from performing the duties of a Private Security Officer."

The PSAC model statute provides that licensees—the contract agencies—can issue a temporary permit, valid for 120 days, to any private security officer prior to the issuance of a registration card by the licensing authority—the state or municipality. The licensee is required to "make reasonable and prudent inquiries" to find out if the individual meets the requirements; if he has reason to believe that he does not, "no temporary permit shall be issued by the Licensee." In other words, they are not supposed to hire as security guards individuals who fail to meet the very loose requirements.

The model law also requires that in the case of armed guards, a firearms permit must first be issued directly by the licensing authority before he may start to work in that capacity. Armed guards are required to have a high-school education or its equivalent. Before the firearms permit is issued, a statement must be submitted by a "certified trainer" that the applicant had completed three hours of training and that he qualified on a firing range by attaining an acceptable score based on the firing of at least 30 rounds. In addition, those seeking armed guard employment may be issued a temporary permit from a licensee. No physical qualifications for an armed guard, not even an eye test, are set forth.

Only 8 hours of pre-assignment training is proposed in the PSAC's model. This training is to be supplemented within the first 120 days of employment by an additional 32 hours of "in-service training." The requirement here is comparable to the 120-hour proposal for minimum training made by the principal investigators for Rand. The model statute provides that each security officer must complete an annual 8-hour refresher course. It calls for "certified trainers" and describes them as persons approved and certified by the licensing authority as qualified to administer and testify to the successful completion of the proposed law's minimum requirements.

The model is silent on other requisites for this certified trainer. It makes no mention of what education, experience, or age he would need for appointment. Nor is there any mention of whether he may be an employee of a contract agency, or that he should be an independent officer. The model statute continues on this point and says that each certified trainer "shall appoint" a training officer, certified as competent by the licensing authority, and who, in addition, must be of legal age and have at least one year supervisory experience with a private security agency or organization, with a law enforcement agency, or with the military. As an alternative to such experience, he must have a minimum of one year's experience as an instructor at "an educational institution or educational agency." The model statute then provides that the training officer shall be given authority to appoint one or more instructors to assist in the implementation of the training program. No prerequisites are spelled out for the instructor. The training officer, under the proposed statute, is privileged to instruct in person, or use a combination of personal instruction and "audio and/or visual training aids."

I believe the enactment of this model statute as written, so long in coming, would raise the standards of private security by a degree so small that it amounts to no more than paying lip service to the crucial problems of private security. I also have a negative opinion of the proposed statute's minimum requirement for comprehensive liability coverage of $100,000 per person and $300,000 per occurrence. Most responsible individuals have greater coverage on their own automobiles, which they, themselves, drive.

The Rand study recommended that localities within the states be privileged to increase the minimum requirements of any new state regulations. This model statute specifically prohibits the enactment of any local legislation, and specifically provides that such local legislation as now exists shall become ineffective within a short period after the enactment of the model state law. It makes one exception: local authorities may require the listing of names, addresses, license certificate numbers and registration numbers of those authorized by the model statute in their area, as well as copies of notice of termination, suspension, or cancellation, provided no fee be charged for this.

As noted above, the Subcommittee on Guards and Investigators, which drafted the model statute, was one of four subgroups appointed by the Private Security Advisory Council to help it in its work. Two of them—the Armored Car Subcommittee and the Manufacturing Subcommittee—have been silent since their December, 1972, reports. The latter at that time suggested a study be conducted to determine whether Underwriter Laboratories' studies and approval are adequate standards for security machinery and devices for the 1970s.[30]

The Alarm Subcommittee, the fourth subgroup, proposed a separate model statute which it presented to the full advisory council in December, 1974. The makeup of this subcommittee seems to be interchangeable with the leadership of the National Burglar and Fire Alarm Association—a circumstance remarkably similar to the interchangeability between members of the Subcommittee on Guards and Investigators and the CONSCO. Resolutions of the National Burglar and Fire Alarm Association were discussed earlier in connection with their opposition to the Cedar Rapids Police Department's operation of a central alarm system.

The model alarm statute proposed by the LEAA advisory group is not the first one in this field. Another was suggested in 1973 by the Legal Research Section of the International Association of Chiefs of Police.[31] Both of these models are heavily weighted to recognize and protect the existing "grandfather" firms. According to one sectional trade group, the Western Burglar and Fire Alarm Association, there is at least one privately owned and operating alarm company for each 40,000 citizens in each of the metropolitan areas of this country. This same association is on record recommending tax rebates for each premise equipped with an alarm installed by a Grade A central station, because such equipment, it says, decreases the cost for police protection.[32]

Neither of the model alarm statutes provide for qualifying examinations for installers and repairmen of alarms similar to those given to plumbers, electricians, barbers, beauticians, and others where expertise, or the lack of it, can affect the public good. The models do provide that licensed alarm companies be required to inspect and certify alarm installations made on a do-it-yourself basis. In connection with new devices to be introduced into the market, certification is also required by the licensed companies. Neither of these models, however, recognizes or provides for the collection and analysis of appropriate statistics on which an evaluation of alarm effectiveness by type could be made. The need for standard statistics in this area—regional and nationwide—is essential. Equally important is the creation of an appropriate unit to collect and organize this information. The creation and maintenance of materials on alarm systems and installations would have far-reaching economic impact, both on the selection of workable machines, and on the insurance industry's evaluation of machinery for premium discount purposes.

Despite the alarm industry's contention that on the average alarm systems work more than 99.14 percent of the time without a false alarm,[33] 95 percent of all alarms are false. Operation time is not a very important statistic. False alarms require the time and attention of sworn police thousands of times a year in every metropolitan area. The problem of automatic dialers has seen the increasing introduction of piecemeal legislation to control them on local and state levels. A proper model statute on alarms could save untold sums for the users who pay for them, and for the taxpayers whose police dollars are diluted by answering false calls.

A bright spot on the private security horizon has been the increasing recognition by architects and legislators that security requirements should be built into plans and specifications for new construction. The building codes and ordinances in various parts of the country are being amended to provide minimum standards for certain burglar-resistant hardware: doors, locks, windows, glazing, louvers, and so forth. Minimum standards based on security needs are also being included in the lighting specifications for public areas, such as the parking lots required for multi-occupancy structures. Unfortunately, these new specifications do not apply to existing buildings. The creation of a research center where appropriate materials could be collected and evaluated would be of enormous assistance in this developing program.

There are other unresolved legal problems involving private security. One was touched upon by the Pinkerton Law of 1893: Cross-jurisdiction between public and private security personnel. In the period of emerging sworn police forces there was an interchangeability between their use and the use of private police by governmental bodies, local, state, and national. Today the sworn police have reached a maturity tempered by almost a century and a half of evolving duties and controls. They have become jealous of their actual and perceived prerogatives. They have been concerned by the movement of some private security organizations into what they regard as the public field.

Such a case was the appointment of George Wackenhut as director of the "war on crime" by the governor of Florida in January, 1967. Though Wackenhut was to serve for $1 a year, his corporation was simultaneously engaged to supply the administrative facilities and investigative manpower for the effort. Individual Wackenhut investigators were given credentials, signed by the governor, commissioning them to conduct investigations on behalf of the state. All regular law enforcement agencies were directed to cooperate in such efforts, including the opening of their files. The assigned Wackenhut investigators were moved from the regular company offices to another building and were admonished not to use their state credentials when engaged in gathering information for private clients. In fact, they were said to have been told to start all such private inquiries with an oral disclaimer that the matter was not part of the "Governor's war on crime."[34]

When the Florida legislature failed to appropriate the requested funds for the Wackenhut investigators, and the governor failed to raise private funds for the purpose, the experiment collapsed, some four months after it started. Measurable results—as announced at the annual meeting of the Wackenhut Corporation by its president on April 24, 1967—were "17 arrests on 44 separate criminal counts" and an increase in the company's dollar volume income from private investigative work of 63 percent, when compared with the same period, the first three months, of the previous year; had the state been able to pay for the value of the services, the increase would have amounted to 208 percent. Unanswered is the question of whether the Wackenhut appointment was a lawful delegation of public power.[35] Also unanswered is whether it would be an unlawful delegation had the Wackenhut men been hired individually as independent contractors and received no credentials or other indicia of official designation. These questions remain troublesome, especially since the same company holds itself out in its annual reports and in advertisements as supplying "Police and Fire Departments with staffs and operate police departments for smaller municipalities."[36]

This area of cross-jurisdiction is not always as visible. There are numerous instances in which police officers, still active in their own departments, are open or silent partners or owners of private contract security agencies. While they may be involved in this moonlighting activity on their own off-duty time only, the knowledge of their interest by a customer or potential customer could lead to the belief that special sworn police attention would be paid to any premises the moonlighter's firm protects. There are recorded complaints by private agencies that they are losing business unfairly to such men and concerns. There are many more examples of sworn police officers moonlighting as private security guards, sometimes even in official sworn police uniform, wearing an official badge, and carrying an official gun. The presence of these trained men undoubtedly increases the security of the guarded business, but it also connotes conflict of interest and possible corruption.

The question of the rights of private individuals and organizations to confidential police records is another issue raised by the moonlighting activity. Can an investigator who obtains information working in the morning on an official matter dismiss it from his mind when in the afternoon it impinges on his obligations in a private matter? Conversely, can a private investigator employed by a public agency use that employment to obtain information on behalf of his private clients?

Information is the keystone of investigations. Security groups, both contract and in-house alike, are voracious in their need for it, especially in connection with criminal records of applicants for employment. This need was evidenced by pleas of guilty in February, 1971, by Wackenhut, Pinkerton's, Burns, Retail Credit, and others to the charge of giving unlawful gratuities to particular New York police assigned to the criminal records section for "confidential information."[37]

There is no doubt that competent, qualified private investigators have legitimate needs for what is sometimes labeled "confidential" information. Furnishing them with this material can often be of assistance also to law enforcement. I have on occasion witnessed the prompt recognition of a mug shot shown by a sworn officer to a private investigator who was thereupon able to give that officer a run-down on the suspect that led to the solution of a crime. Some of these cases did not involve the private investigator or his employer. In the case of crimes, both the sworn officer and the private investigator profit by an exchange of information.

Yet private security is involved in a practice under which reports of crime are not made to enforcement agencies and notice of its commission suppressed. This procedure has its basis in business decisions rather than in investigative or security reasons. The criminal aspect of an act is overlooked as part of a management decision. Under the common law it was a crime for a person to accept something of value under an agreement not to prosecute a known offender, or to limit or handicap the prosecution of his case. Accepting repayment for a stolen or pilfered article, or for embezzled moneys, in full or in part, in return for an agreement not to prosecute is accepting something of value. Laws against compounding exist in 46 of the 50 states today but not under the Federal law. Compounding differs from its companion crime of misprision, which makes it illegal to fail to communicate to proper authorities one's knowledge of the commission of a felony; under the Federal law, and those of a few states, misprision is a felony.[38] While prosecutions are rare under both of these laws, they have occurred.

There is no question but that a system of private justice is in use in the business community of the United States, and that private security staffs are often involved. Because it is private, its true extent is unknown, but every indicator suggests that the system must be enormous. In the retail field alone, fewer than 1 in 15 persons apprehended in the act of shoplifting is legally arrested and charged with the crime in a court of law. The consideration for not prosecuting is the return of the property. These acts of compounding are also true to an unknown degree in all areas of business when employee pilferage and embezzlement are discovered and the culprit identified. Here again the result is often a failure to report the crime, based on an agreement for full or partial restitution. Rewards paid for the return of stolen property, with no questions asked, fall into this category. It is not known just how responsible this system of private justice is for the failure to report half of all larcenies committed, a percentage recently determined by the LEAA-sponsored census study. It has resulted, however, in a two-layered system of criminal justice in America. Students of our society cannot know the true nature of the problems of crime within it—to the detriment of potential programs to overcome them.

Special questions of compounding arise when the security officer involved has a quasi-sworn status. To allow sworn police to suppress reports of crime would affect the criminal justice system. Uniform licensing and regulation of the private security industry, and compulsory, adequate training of its staff, will raise security personnel to a new position vis-à-vis the sworn police and the citizen, though they will not reach the status in law of a special officer, or a special deputy, or, as in Texas, that of a special Texas Ranger. An entire area of the private security world has its officers so deputized. Many state's and local laws bestow on these special deputies police powers beyond that of a citizen, yet not quite at the level of full-time, sworn police. Many of them, as in the case of commissioned officers in Ohio, the railroad police, and others, are trained at a level far beyond the norm of the private security guard. Other groups that often enjoy similar special status are the security officers in large retail establishments. In some jurisdictions, like New York City, security guards at hospitals are commissioned special police. In Texas, selected security employees of railroads, oil producers, and cattle ranches are given the status of special Texas Rangers. Under this status they are legally able to carry concealed firearms as an exception to the new, strict gun-control law there. Depending on the state, many of these deputized security officers, by virtue of their status, may obtain information from police files otherwise limited to sworn law enforcement agencies. In other jurisdictions the designation carries with it the right to wear a special badge and a uniform, similar to the ones worn by duly sworn uniformed police. Security guards with their shoulder patches as deputy sheriffs, so evident in the Las Vegas casinos, are in this category.

So long as these problems of law remain unresolved, they serve as a hindrance to the proper growth of private security and to its own understanding of its rights and duties. In the unresolved area of private justice it can well escalate problems similar to those raised by traffic ticket fixing. It retards private security from achieving acceptable professional status.

11 | Conclusions

Business managers use private security as a tool of last resort. They are forced into using it by the pressure of economic or legal necessity. It is only with reluctance that they take the step of employing private security to stem obvious threats to themselves, their property, their employees, their customers and their corporate well-being. In some instances private security becomes an obligatory supplement to their insurance coverage, a device to keep the coverage and the costs commensurate with their own appraisal of the risks involved. When required to provide security by law, or as dictated by custom or contracts, such as with the Department of Defense, their usual attitude is to adhere as closely as possible to what is specified—and no more. But for the potential risk, most managers would forego security and its costs, and the savings would go toward profits.

Clearly, most business executives buy private security as cheaply as possible, as they do all other standard commodities. Unfortunately, they generally know so little about private security that they are not able to distinguish between available grades, nor can they select what is best suited to their needs. In short, they have failed to pay this phase of their business the intelligent attention they apply in many other areas. They have not developed for security the knowledge, tools, and other resources needed to assess its value accurately. They have not learned where and when to use private security—other than for cosmetic purposes.

Business has at stake some $50 billion a year: that is the total of its losses to crime, its cost for private security and insurance, and its portion of taxes used to combat crime and operate the criminal justice system. Yet in many instances business cannot trace these losses back to their individual source. It cannot say with the degree of positiveness necessary to prosecute a criminal case when or where it was robbed. Almost 15 percent of that $50 billion, some $7 billion, is attributable to embezzlement and employee pilferage. These are acts that occur under business's own roof, within its own family, and can in no way be ascribed to neglect or any other deficiency on the part of law enforcement or the criminal justice system. Losses from embezzlement and pilferage are constantly increasing, but many business enterprises have no real way of knowing what they lost, or when, two important factors in determining not only "who took it," but how to stop it from being taken.

Managers who conclude that it is too expensive to install appropriate systems of control—marking goods so that they can be traced, establishing decentralized counts, taking inventory more than once a year—intensify the problems of crime, law enforcement, and their own system of private security. No retail store or chain can say with any certainty what is lost to shoplifting, to pilferage, to spoilage, and to inefficiency—a statement that does not augur well for any reduction in these totals. An effective control that could pinpoint losses, the time of the losses, and where they occurred would do more to reduce them than all of the new mechanized tags and other anti-shoplifting devices put together.

The transportation industry's problems are heralded with the fact that only 15 percent of goods lost while in the custody of motor carriers are recorded as being stolen or hijacked. What about the other 85 percent? That is reported as having "mysteriously disappeared." How can the police and prosecutors be called upon to check this outflow when the custodians cannot say if the goods are lost, where they were lost, or, in many cases, whether they ever had the goods in the first place? Under these conditions, convictions of known thieves found in possession of stolen property are almost impossible to obtain. Law enforcement in its anxiety to combat crime in this area has underway elaborate cargo theft programs, including one involving training to improve the investigative ability of law enforcement officers in this field and to help these officers develop crime prevention plans for transportation facilities. Other measures in the planning stage are designed to train state and local prosecutors in the trial techniques of stolen goods cases. Yet the LEAA, the sponsor of these programs, misses the major opportunity by a wide margin. Gearing its efforts to control the 15 percent of known loss, the assistance administration simply ignores the "mysterious disappearance" of 85 percent of the goods. Of course the 85 percent pertains to an area where self-help by the cargo transporters is a necessary precondition to improvement. These losses and the recourse by business to insurance on its freight adds to the eventual price of all goods sold.

Retail and transportation are not the only areas of business where losses occur in a vacuum of little or no concurrent control, to emerge in accountant's reports, so much later, and with such little support, that a write-off is the only action possible. Manufacturing, wholesaling, and service industries also suffer enormous losses each year. But here again, the necessary adjustments to business operations—to reflect losses on a timely basis and to indicate on a flow chart where they are occurring—can only be achieved by the senior managers. No one on the security level has the leverage to bring about a fundamental reconsideration regarding security, and authorize the expenditures for the necessary research and operational changes to make security effective. The benefits of such revisions would undoubtedly be larger than those that could be attributed to security alone, because new systems would reflect a greater control at all operating points.

Existing statistics show that business is the choice target of most crime in which the motive is economic. The joint Bureau of the Census—Law Enforcement Assistance Administration Study of Unreported Crime bears this out. The statement by the Department of Commerce that there are four million apprehensions a year in retail stores alone is corroborative evidence. Not only does business support the criminal justice structure through its taxes, it also spends about $4 billion a year on security, security devices, and machinery. Indeed, business employs more security manpower than exists on all the law enforcement rolls of sworn police and investigators.

Yet relatively little is known about private security, its staffs and their training and effectiveness. There is a similar paucity of understandable data on the effectiveness of security machinery and devices. Nowhere is there a collected body of knowledge, scholars, and research capable of effecting a disinterested appraisal or criticism of the private security system. There have been individual projects on one aspect or another of private security, but no institution of continuing interest in this area has been created to serve as a source of data and scholastic inquiry. The LEAA funded the Rand study which in 1971 recommended the creation of a research center. The LEAA's original advisory council recommended in December of 1972 that the assistance administration itself become the clearinghouse for factual data on private security. Currently, LEAA takes the position that its present advisory council cannot agree that the creation of such a research center and institute is justified at this time. And so it continues to procrastinate.

The insurance industry which covers many of the losses should be particularly concerned, because it is vitally involved with private security. It has a vested interest in improving the effectiveness of private security measures. It uses security investigators in its own defense against fraudulent claims—and there are so many of those that the U.S. Chamber of Commerce estimates they account for 15 percent of premium costs. In the writing or particular coverage, insurance companies offer premium discounts of up to 70 percent for the installation and use of certain security devices and services. These items have not been changed in years, however, and their viability has been challenged by many, including the Rand investigators. Understandably then, insurers profit immeasurably from any reduction in crime against business through more effective security devices. Such a reduction would show up on the insurance company's books as profit.

Individually and as a group insurance companies have made sizable financial contributions to research and training in the field of traffic control in an effort to cut automobile accident claims. Yet they have not participated to any great extent in the work of the groups involved with private security. No representative of the insurance industry is a member of any of the LEAA advisory groups, and the Advisory Committee on Federal Crime Insurance has not met in years.

Another reflection of the insurance industry's interest in security and crime control is the fact that they are the collectors and custodians of detailed information vital to the general field of loss to crime. They probably have more solid data on amounts of loss and methods of loss than do the police. Insurance companies are aware of many losses not reported to the authorities, losses adjusted by their customers with their consent as part of the system of private justice. Their records could be a tool of great consequence in the continuing effort to obtain better statistics regarding losses to business from crime. This potential should be the subject of intensive study by private security, law enforcement, and the insurance industry.

At the present time the only apparent interest in progress toward changes in the private security field is being generated at the security manager level. This is evident in the activities of the several industry organizations and associations. Foremost among them is the American Society for Industrial Security. Its members are mainly the security directors of the larger in-house forces, and include many whose firms are contractors for the Department of Defense, NASA and the AEC. The society publishes an informative magazine, *Security Management,* and sponsors extensive seminar meetings and training sessions of three or more days' duration.

As we have noted, the contract guard firms formed their own organization—CONSCO—in 1974, and the alarm firms have their own national organization, the National Burglar and Fire Alarm Association. The International Association of Chiefs of Police, which includes as nonvoting associate members many security managers, inaugurated a Committee on Private Security in 1974, and the Private Security Advisory Council of LEAA was first set up in 1972; it has four major subcommittees, with some individuals serving on two or three of them at the same time.

Yet the combined efforts of all these groups have been less than effective. Two of the LEAA subcommittees have finally circulated proposed model statutes for the state licensing of contract private security firms, the registration of in-house security guards, and the licensing of alarm firms. In their present version these proposed models tend to favor the status quo. They provide for repeal of all contradictory local legislation, and would, I believe, have little effect on raising the standards of selection, training, or usefulness of private security. There can be no harsher evaluation of the efforts of these subcommittees than to refer to the rising losses due to crime.

There also seems to be a lack of knowledge of the work of these committees within the private security industry, as evidenced by the transcript of the testimony of Neal Holmes, president of Allied Security of Pittsburgh. Holmes, who employs some 2000 guards, told the Committee of the Pennsylvania House of Representatives on April 19, 1974:

Basically, I'd like to just bring one thing to your attention, that the major agencies throughout the United States, Pinkerton, Burns, Wackenhut, Allied, who account for approximately $1 billion in revenues through the United States have formed a national association that is known as the L.E.A.A. Association. It's the Law Enforcement Assistance Administration Association and the purpose of this association was set up so that we could set national standards for training, hiring, supervising of guards and within the next month, we will have out a pamphlet outlining our thoughts of a training program for guards, armed and unarmed, and in-house as well as contract security guards which we would like to see accepted on a national basis, that we as an association are going forward state to state with this law because we feel there must be an enactment but we feel that we should have some say in this enactment because we are supposed to have the expertise and if we come up with something that is good, that it's going to be acceptable by all states and this is what we would like to get, a national standard, much like the bar association and other professional associations have. So, I just want to make one comment and that is if you would bear with anything that you plan to do for the next 30 or 60 days, we will be contacting you people in Harrisburg with this finalized form which I think will have some great thoughts for you to utilize.[1]

Leaving aside the professional protestations expressed, the "great thoughts" promised by the spokesman for the security group did not arrive in time to help the legislative efforts in Pennsylvania. The House members who sat through the long hearings introduced a bill aimed at tighter licensing and control of security, including strict regulations on the use of firearms by guards. Their bill, however, was superseded by one introduced by some state senators, who did not attend the hearings. The Senate version was adopted and became law on October 10, 1974, as Act 235 of the General Assembly of the Commonwealth of Pennsylvania. The main thrust of the new law is the control of "lethal weapons" and the training and certification of guards who use them. It has no effect whatever on the remainder of the security industry, its guards or investigators. The law has a certain irony. It accomplishes precisely the opposite of legislative intention; to make it illegal for private guards to carry dummy guns. As enacted, the law prohibits individuals "certified" from carrying inoperative or dummy weapons. In early drafts "individuals certified" were to include all guards armed and unarmed. As enacted certification, however, applies only to those trained and qualified as entitled to carry weapons. So now Pennsylvania forbids trained weapon handlers from carrying dummy guns, and, by clear implication, all unarmed guards not certified to handle real weapons may carry dummy guns.

There seems to be every indication that eventually meaningful legislation will be forthcoming at the federal and state levels of government to establish guidelines for the private security industry that will be in closer accord with the public interest. The sample model statutes on alarm systems and the licensing of guards discussed in the previous chapter do not meet these objectives. It may well be that these sample laws will be further amended before being proffered as a basis for legislation, but with input for both models coming primarily from industry sources, these model statutes as they now stand will certainly run into head winds at legislative hearings. Solid research and statistical information are needed to convince lawmakers of the soundness of any proposals related to private security.

There are a number of important areas—besides licensing and regulation—where legislative or regulatory agency decisions must sooner or later be brought to bear on the private security industry. Some of these decisions may have far-reaching influence on the operation of business generally, and the definition of civil rights.

Of these problems, private justice is the most pervasive. The failure to report all crimes, for whatever reason, affects the basis of research in both sociology and psychology. It also shakes the foundation of the legal theory of "equal justice under law." An agreement not to prosecute a crime for a consideration—which includes the repayment of all or a portion of what was stolen—violates the compounding statutes of most states, and is a crime itself. While I do not urge the repeal of these compounding statutes, or those on misprision, neither do I advocate their enforcement to the nth degree. But private justice needs to be carefully scrutinized by those involved with the goal of creating a formal method of handling such cases. Should restitution, in full or in part, be accepted as an ample deterrent, and the case allowed to rest there? Should each instance of restitution require review by a court, or another agency created for that purpose? The present practice of hushing up the embezzlement and letting the swindler bargain his way free with restitution is an ugly blot on our system of justice. It prevents the proper appraisal of the full nature of crime and its impact on society. It also perpetuates in the business system many who have been found lacking in financial integrity and turns them loose without penalty of any kind to repeat their defalcations upon successive employers.

A two-tiered hierarchy exists within the private security world. Many of its guards and investigators are given special status by being made deputy sheriffs, special officers, commissioned private police, or given other titles that carry increased police power. Some of those with special status are entitled as a matter of state or local law to access to regular police files and information. This raises the question of using future licensing and regulation statutes to establish special deputy status for all private security personnel in recognition of their new status of selection and training. I endorse the suggestion made by the principal investigators of the Rand study that a nationwide review be undertaken of deputization and the commissioning of private police in order to determine their parameters and their value.

There are legitimate reasons why private security should have limited access to police records. Properly controlled, such access can be *pro bono publico,* and not wrongfully invade civil rights. Recognizing the wide percentage of untutored employees of private security, however, I find it difficult to argue that access be granted to all. Still, many private security investigators possess credentials—background and training—equal to or superior to many of their sworn police counterparts. A method of evaluation can be devised to segregate those qualified and grant them legal, limited access so as to avoid hypocrisy and subterfuge.

The relationship between the two police groups, public and private, requires differentiation so that clear, uniform spheres of prerogatives, and rights can replace those that are now too vague. One I have already mentioned: the degree of access private forces should have to public records. Another involves the moonlighting of sworn police in private security posts. Is moonlighting to be barred, condoned, or regulated by statute? The potential for abuse of this practice exists, along with the potential for corruption. So does the potential for lawsuits, in the event of negligence, against the municipalities that permit it. Should sworn police be allowed to moonlight in private security jobs in civilian clothes? in their official uniform with their official badge and gun? or in the uniform supplied by their private employer? Should sworn police be permitted to own and, on their own time, operate a private security agency? What then happens to the requirement that sworn police are subject to emergency call? Is there a difference in prerogatives and rights when the moonlighting duty in uniform involves the handling of traffic in a shopping center, at a football game, at a wedding reception?

Conversely, should private police be hired to perform functions that are normally filled by the duly constituted police? Should they be permitted to supply an entire police department for a small community? Should they be hired to conduct investigations for public bodies?

With regard to the last question, Congress should recognize reality and repeal the Pinkerton Law, because it obviously serves no present purpose and because it is obviously not being honored.

The Federal Communications Commission is a regulatory agency that has a direct impact on private security in its function of assigning radio communications channels. By its rule the private security industry shares allotted wave bands with taxi dispatchers, plumbers, TV repair crews, and others. Putting a call on the air on one of these busier bands, even a May-day call for help, becomes a problem. As a function associated with the prevention of crime, a more suitable assignment of an appropriate band should be made.

Model statutes and legislative decisions on these foregoing problems will not change private security practices and the need for understanding them by the business community. Many business leaders have overlooked or misinterpreted recommendations on these issues from their own security directors. Others have been too busy. Still more are not interested, except when losses rise and affect their balance sheets. But business cannot continue to entrust its entire wealth to the most unlettered, untutored, least trained, poorest paid, and physically marginal of all its employees, and then point to law enforcement and its shortcomings and claim them to be the cause of their rising losses to crime. True risk management cannot be limited to surface overview, but must go beyond the equation between insurance and private guards and test the value of these guards as to quality and integrity.

Instead of waiting for the new basic physical requirements and training minimums to become part of private security control legislation, research should begin now on security employee selection. Positions in private security hitherto always filled by men could, in many cases, be filled by the use of better qualified women in both the guard and investigator categories.

Moreover, security duties and responsibilities should be redefined so as to make each of these positions as interesting and challenging as possible. In this regard, training and training guidelines are critical. I disagree with the testimony that equates a guard with the mechanical dummy set up on a highway to wave a red flag continuously as a detour warning. Minimum training will produce minimum results. The lack of guard training is surely related to losses.

The private security supervisor is the most handicapped by the lack of adequately trained personnel. Unfortunately, he, too, has had little in the way of formal instruction. With many firms using on-the-job training as the most viable method of obtaining the greatest results for their security dollar, the use of the supervisor as the training officer is quite common. In many instances this practice becomes a case of the halt leading the blind. Nor is the use of the few training films available an adequate substitute. Each requires interpolation by a trained supervisor to adapt filmed situations and instructions to particular circumstances.

Other than a few short seminars that try to cover all aspects of private security in three or four sessions, there are no outside institutions that senior or middle security management can attend. Other than a few short how-to manuals, there is little literature available on the subject. Many large companies expose their security managers to company meetings, seminars, retreats, and other classroom or round-table sessions on topics that range from marketing to budgets, from traffic to pension programs, from business planning to computer appreciation. Few of the line or staff managers, however, are ever exposed to similar sessions conducted by the security staff on loss prevention, security training, the importance of anticrime controls, and the reporting of suspicious circumstances. None of the graduate schools of business have courses on the subject. Yet if marketing sessions or planning sessions have a tangible return, a security session would have a greater impact because it would be dealing with company personnel and company problems related to internal losses. But invariably sessions on security are ineffective because they are unsupported by senior management.

There is no source of disinterested expertise on security that can be called in by business management for advice prior to authorizing investment in security machinery and equipment. This equipment does not come with easily understood labels giving horsepower, outputs per minute, or other standard indexes of capability. Safe and vault manufacturers can specify the length of time the contents of a particular box can withstand the heat of fire, but they cannot make claims about resistance to break-in, especially when the key can be turned, or the combination dialed by a conniving employee, or by an honest one with a gun in his ribs. On security matters, business managers today are forced to rely on the advice of their staff chief of security, who accumulates his information through word of mouth from his colleagues in other companies. This advice and the sales descriptions and claims are poor substitutes for properly gathered data based on laboratory tests and experience records verified by police, insurance, and other authorities. Such material does not exist at the present time. The need for an appropriate rating organization, for example, is intensified by the burgeoning market of security devices. While I do not doubt that there are persons and firms of integrity in this field, neither do I doubt that there are also charlatans selling relatively useless equipment at inflated prices. Some of this equipment, because of its propensity for malfunction and false alarm, has caused problems for the police without increasing the security of the premises on which it has been installed.

In conclusion there is a need for an institute for private security, for research, for evaluation, as a teaching facility, independent of the private security industry. With proper tools, researchers, investigators, faculty, technicians and librarians, such an institute can assemble the existing materials and literature, and objectively evaluate them for the benefit of all users. It would be a source to which a legislature could turn when considering corrective measures for security problems.

Such an institute or research center could also formulate training criteria, curriculums, and guidelines on the basis of study and research and not, as is now being done, as an exercise in consensus in short committee meetings. It could set up its guidelines for the best results possible, not simply to meet minimum legislative requirements. It could serve as a place to train the trainers, as well as all interested in the myriad aspects of private security.

The agenda for such an institute could be rich and varied: individual projects designed to seek optimum ways to use manpower; training materials; standards for security equipment; the cataloguing and dissemination of information about all equipment and methods found to have immediate practical value. The need for a data bank of pertinent security statistics is urgent—data ranging from a proper census of an industry and its divisions to loss data to false alarm statistics correlated to individual types of installations. In such a data bank would lie the answer to many of the problems now troubling the industry.

Such an institute would also serve as a meeting and discussion center in which the security needs of business management and its requirements could be addressed. Here, too, the relationship of private security and public law enforcement could be analyzed and defined. It would serve equally as a bridge to some of the work being undertaken in the field of law enforcement by a number of institutions of higher learning, and it would be a significant resource for the graduate schools of business and business administration.

Ultimately, with the accumulation of sufficient materials and the training of an adequate staff, the institute could examine the cost effectiveness of specific private security techniques in individual situations. Standards set by the operation of such an institute would undoubtedly be superior to those fixed by minimum licensing regulations. Returns in private security efficiency and productivity could equate to the savings of billions of dollars to business, and thus to the consumer.

Appendixes

TRENDS IN SELECTED PROTECTIVE-SERVICES EMPLOYMENT[a]

Category	1950	1960	1967	1975 (projected)
Public police and other public law enforcement personnel (all governments)	199,000[b]	260,000[c]–266,000[b]	363,000[c]	489,000[d]
Private police and detectives	21,000[b]	20,000[b]– 27,000[c]	33,000[c]	29,000[d]
Guards, watchmen, doorkeepers, and bridge tenders				
Private	...	245,000[c]	256,000[c]	263,000[d]
Public	...	85,000[c]	109,000[c]	152,000[d]
Total	261,000[b]	282,000[b]–330,000[c]	365,000[c]	415,000[d]
Total guards and private police	282,000[b]	302,000[b]–357,000[c]	398,000[c]	444,000[d]

[a]All figures rounded to nearest thousand.

[b]From Census of Population publications.

[c]From Bureau of Labor Statistics publications.

[d]From Bureau of Labor Statistics projections.

(*Source: 1971 Rand study of private police industry for the Department of Justice*)

Type of Security Personnel or Organization	Numbers of People		Expenditures ($ millions)	
	Security Personnel	Total Employment	Payroll Expenditures	Total Expenditures or Revenues
Public Law Enforcement				
Local police (city, county, township)	324,000[a]	432,000[b]	3,040[c]	3,326[b]
Reserve local police	N/A	N/A	N/A	N/A
Special local law-enforcement agencies	N/A	N/A	N/A	N/A
State police or highway patrol	39,000[a]	}54,000[b]	}455[c]	}621[b]
Special state law-enforcement agencies	N/A			
Federal law-enforcement agencies	N/A[d]	36,000[b,d]	344[c]	492[b]
Total Public Law Enforcement	395,000[e]	523,000[c]	3,839[c]	4,430[b]
Public (Government) Guards (all governments)	120,000[e]	N/A	N/A	~1,000
Total Public Sector (police and guards)	515,000	N/A	N/A	~5,400
Private Sector Security				
In-house detectives and investigators	23,900[e]	N/A	N/A	N/A
In-house guards	198,500[e]	N/A	N/A	N/A
Subtotal in-house security	222,400[e]	N/A	N/A	~1,600[f]
Contract detectives	8,100[e]	N/A	N/A	N/A
Contract guards	59,400[e]	N/A	N/A[h]	N/A[i]
Subtotal contract guards and detectives	67,500[e]	~110,000[g]	435[h]	620[i]
Patrolmen in contract agencies	N/A (included in contract guards)	N/A (included in contract guards)	N/A	N/A (included in contract guards)
Armored-car services		10,000[g]	73[h]	128[j]
Central station alarm services		N/A (included in contract guards)	N/A	120[k]
Total Private Sector	289,900[e]	N/A	N/A	~2,500
Security Equipment	N/A	N/A	N/A	~800
Grand Total	804,000	N/A	N/A	~8,700

[a] Sources: FBI, *1969 Uniform Crime Reports*, and telephone conversations with personnel at International Association of Chiefs of Police. Figures are for sworn officers. Local police total shown includes 287,000 sworn officers in cities and suburbs and 37,000 officers in county sheriff departments. State figures include state police and state highway patrol officers.

[b] Source: *Expenditure and Employment Data for the Criminal Justice System 1968-69*, LEAA, U.S. Department of Justice, December 1970. Expenditure data are for FY 1968-69, and employment data are for October 1969.

[c] Source: Bureau of the Census publications *(Census of Governments* for various years, *Public Employment in 1968*, and *Governmental Finances)*.

[d] The 36,000 federal law-enforcement employees include all employees of only five agencies: FBI, Secret Service, Immigration and Naturalization Service, Bureau of Narcotics and Dangerous Drugs, and Bureau of Customs. But only a fraction of these employees are actually investigators or law-enforcement officers with police powers. From Hearings of the Committee on Government Operations, *Unmet Training Needs of the Federal Investigator and the Consolidated Federal Law Enforcement Training Center*, House Report No. 91-1429, U.S. Government Printing Office, 1970, it is estimated that the federal government's investigative force exceeds 50,000 employees.

[e] Source: Bureau of Labor Statistics publications and unpublished data. Excludes part-time employees unless their primary occupation is security-related.

[f] This estimate derives from two sources: Predicasts, Inc., and a Rand estimate, both of which are discussed in Chapter IV of R-870-DOJ.

[g] Sources: *1967 Census of Business: County Business Patterns for 1968 and 1969*. Includes part-time employees. See footnote e above.

[h] Assuming payroll is 57 percent of revenues, as estimated in the *1967 Census of Business*.

[i] Source: *1967 Census of Business* data extrapolated to 1969, utilizing revenue growth ratios equal to those achieved by large contract detective agencies and protective service firms.

[j] Source: *1967 Census of Business* data extrapolated to 1969, using revenue growth rates equal to those achieved by large armored-car firms.

[k] Source: Predicasts, Inc., Special Study 56, *Security Systems, 1970*.

(Source: 1971 Rand study of private police industry for the Department of Justice)

A COMPARISON OF PRIVATE SECURITY SPENDING ESTIMATES
($ millions)

Source	1949	1958	1959	1963	1966	1967	1968	1969	1970	1973	1978
Overall spending or payroll[a]											
Census of Population (Occup. Charact.)[b]	640	..	1124	..	..	..			..	..	..
Predicasts, Inc., *Special Study 56*, 3/5/70	..	1170	1280	1730	..	2666	2900	3500	3500	4400	6350
Wall St. Journal, "Selling Security," 8/4/70	..	..	..	..	..	..	..	..	3000	..	..
Newsweek, "To Catch a Thief," 7/27/70	..	..	..	..	1200	..	..	..	2000	..	..
Barron's, "Safety and Growth," 10/17/66	..	..	..	..	..	..	..	..	..	..	..
Forbes, "Creeping Capitalism," 9/1/70	..	..	..	..	..	..	..	..	2000	..	..
Purchased security services and equipment											
Barron's, "Profits in Protection," 2/20/61	..	..	250–300	..	..	..	..	..	..	..	..
Predicasts, Inc.	..	511	..	780	..	1272	1395	..	1773	2340	3670
In-house security services spending											
Predicasts, Inc.	..	659	..	950	..	1394	1505	..	1727	2060	2680
Contract guard and investigative services revenues and payrolls											
Predicasts, Inc.											
Revenues	..	177	..	289	..	481	530	..	682	910	1425
Payrolls	..	107	..	194	..	339	375	..	470	613	910
Census of Business and County Business Patterns											
Revenues	..	177	..	289	..	445	..	..	..	..	..
Payrolls	..	107	..	194	..	312	417	490	..	..	..

[a] Expenditures not adjusted to compensate for changes in the purchasing power of the dollar.

[b] Total reported earnings in occupational categories of guard, watchman, doorkeeper, private policeman and detective, crossing watchman, and bridge tender. The estimate was obtained by averaging two estimates, each obtained as follows: (1) median earnings x number of wage and salary earners summed over the occupational categories mentioned above, and (2) number of wage earners x average wage in each wage or salary category, summed over all wage categories and over the occupational categories mentioned above.

[c] Includes guard, investigative, and armored-car services, monitoring and detection systems, plus crime-deterrent and fire-control equipment.

(*Source: 1971 Rand study of private police industry for the Department of Justice*)

REVENUE TRENDS OF LARGE PUBLICLY OWNED PRIVATE PROTECTION FIRMS[a]

Firm	Revenue ($ millions)							Comp. Annual Growth Rate, 1965-69 (% per year)
	1963	1964	1965	1966	1967	1968	1969	
Guard and Investigative Services								
Pinkerton's, Inc.	42.7	64.1	66.7	71.3	82.8	99.4	120.5	15.8
Wm. J. Burns Intl. Detective Agency, Inc.	41.0	43.2	48.2	55.9	66.5	82.8	97.1	19.0
Wackenhut Corporation	9.6	10.8	17.8	22.4	29.0	36.7	48.5	28.4
Walter Kidde and Co. (Globe Security Systems)[b]	....	....	22.8	25.3	29.0	39.4	46.3	19.4
Baker Industries, Inc. (Wells Fargo Security Guard)[c]	....	....	3.3	5.8	8.1	11.7	15.8	45.5[d]
Total	93.3	118.1	158.8	180.7	235.4	270.0	328.0	....
Industrywide total	289[e]	....	....	....	445[e]	530[f]	620[g]	....
Percent of industrywide total	36	....	....	....	51	51	53	....
Central Station Alarm Services								
American District Telegraph Co.	70.9	74.9	78.7	81.8	87.4	93.3[h]	97.2[h]	5.5
Baker Industries, Inc. (Wells Fargo Alarm Services)	....	....	3.3	5.8	8.1	11.6	13.6	45.5[d]
Holmes Electric Protective Co.	....	....	....	....	....	15.0	17.5	....
Total	70.9	74.9	82.0	87.6	95.5	119.9[h]	128.8[h]	....
Industrywide total	80[f]	....	....	....	....	110[f]	120[f]	....
Armored-Car Services								
Brink's, Inc.	....	....	40.6	44.5	48.9	56.7	64.0	12.1
Baker Industries, Inc. (Wells Fargo Armored Service)[j]	....	....	2.6	4.7	6.6	9.8	13.0	45.5[i]
Loomis	....	....	6.1	7.1	8.3	10.0	12.7	20.6
Total	....	....	49.3	56.3	63.8	76.5	89.7	....
Industrywide total	67.3[e]	....	87.0[h]	....	90.6[e]	115.0[h]	128[k]	....
Percent of industrywide total	....	....	57	....	....	67	70	....

[a]Data in this table have not been adjusted to compensate for the reduced purchasing power of the dollar over time; between 1959 and 1965, that purchasing power declined about 8 percent, while it declined an additional 14 percent between 1965 and 1969.

[b]Guard services and equipment only.

[c]Wells Fargo Security Guard Group only (part of Wells Fargo Protective Services Division). Data prior to 1968 assume that the Security Guard Group revenues are 27 percent of total revenues of Baker Industries, Inc.

[d]Annual growth rate for entire corporation. Total income was $54.9 million in 1969 and $11.9 million in 1965. The large growth rates were due, in part, to acquisitions.

[e]Source: Census of Business, op. cit.

[f]Source: Predicasts, Inc., op. cit.

[g]Source: 1967 Census of Business data extrapolated to 1969, using revenue growth ratios equal to those achieved by large contract guard and investigative agencies.

[h]At least 80 percent of the ADT total revenues are attributable to central station alarm services.

[i]Wells Fargo Alarm Services Group only (part of Wells Fargo Protective Services Division). Revenues prior to 1968 are assumed to be 27 percent of total revenues of Baker Industries, Inc.

[j]Wells Fargo Armored Service Group only (part of Wells Fargo Protective Services Division). Revenues prior to 1968 are assumed to be 22 percent of total revenues of Baker Industries, Inc.

[k]Source: 1967 Census of Business data extrapolated to 1969, using revenue growth ratios equal to those achieved by large armored-car firms.

(Source: 1971 Rand study of private police industry for the Department of Justice)

SALES OF PRIVATE SECURITY SERVICES AND EQUIPMENT

Product	Sales ($ millions)					Compound Average Annual Growth (%)			
	1958	1963	1968	1973	1978	1958-63	1963-68	1968-73	1973-78
Guard and investigative services	177	289	530	910	1425	...	...	...	...
Armored-car services	42	68	115	190	290	...	...	...	...
Total protective services	219	357	645	1100	1715	10.2	12.6	11.3	9.3
Fixed security equipment	69	91	144	215	320	...	...	...	...
Lighting equipment	23	49	91	160	265	...	...	...	...
Total deterrent equipment	92	140	235	375	585	8.8	11.0	9.8	9.3
Monitoring and detection systems	117	165	270	450	700	7.1	10.4	10.7	9.2
Fire-control equipment	83	118	245	415	670	7.3	15.7	11.1	10.1
Total	511	780	1395	2340	3670	8.8	12.4	10.9	9.4

(Source: 1971 Rand study of private security industry for the Department of Justice)

	Licensing of Contract Security Businesses			Licensing or Registration of Employees of Contract Security Businesses			No State Level Regulation	Other
	Investi-gative	Guard	Patrol	Investi-gative	Guard	Patrol		
Alabama	L							
Alaska	L							
Arizona							✓	
Arkansas	L			L				License polygraph examiners
California	L	L	L					License certain insurance adjustors, central alarm agencies, armored transport companies, repossessors, and polygraph examiners
Colorado	L							
Connecticut	L	L	L	R	R	R		License special police; license armored transport agencies and register their employees
Delaware	L	L	L	R	R	R		License polygraph examiners
Florida	L	L	L					License polygraph examiners and repossessors
Georgia								License polygraph examiners
Hawaii	L	L	L					
Idaho							✓	
Illinois	L	L	L	R	R	R		License polygraph examiners
Indiana	L	L	L	R	R	R		
Iowa	L	L	L					
Kansas	L							
Kentucky								License special police and polygraph examiners
Louisiana	L	L	L					
Maine	L							
Maryland	L	L	L	R				License special police
Massachusetts	L	L	L					
Michigan	L	L	L	R	R	R		License special police; license central alarm and armored transport agencies and register their employees
Minnesota	L	L	L					License armored transport agencies
Mississippi								License polygraph examiners
Missouri							✓	
Montana							✓	
Nebraska	L	L	L	L				License central alarm, armored transport agencies, and repossessors
Nevada	L		L	R		R		License process servers, repossessors, and polygraph examiners
New Hampshire							✓	
New Jersey	L	L	L	R	R	R		
New Mexico	L	L	L	R	R	R		License polygraph examiners
New York	L	L	L	R	R	R		
North Carolina	L	L	L					License special police
North Dakota	L	L	L					License polygraph examiners
Ohio	L	L	L	R	R	R		
Oklahoma							✓	
Oregon							✓	
Pennsylvania	L	L	L	R	R	R		
Rhode Island							✓	
South Carolina	L			L				
South Dakota							✓	
Tennessee	L	L	L					
Texas	L	L	L	R				License central alarm, armored car agencies, and polygraph examiners
Washington							✓	
Vermont	L							
Virginia								License polygraph examiners
Washington							✓	
West Virginia	L	L	L					
Wisconsin	L	L	L	L	L	L		
Wyoming							✓	
TOTAL	34	25	26	17	11	12	12	

L = License
R = Registration

(Source: 1971 Rand study of private police industry for the Department of Justice)

201

Index of Crime, United States, 1960–1973

Population [1]	Total Crime Index	Violent [2] crime	Property [2] crime	Murder and nonnegligent manslaughter	Forcible rape	Robbery	Aggravated assault	Burglary	Larceny-theft	Auto theft
Number of offenses:										
1960—179,323,175	3,352,800	286,220	3,066,600	9,050	17,050	107,410	152,720	903,400	1,836,800	326,400
1961—182,953,000	3,455,500	287,120	3,168,400	8,680	17,080	106,240	155,130	940,400	1,893,800	334,200
1962—185,822,000	3,717,400	299,150	3,418,200	8,490	17,410	110,410	162,850	984,800	2,068,700	364,800
1963—188,531,000	4,071,200	314,490	3,756,700	8,580	17,510	116,000	172,400	1,076,000	2,274,800	406,000
1964—191,334,000	4,522,800	361,850	4,161,000	9,300	21,250	129,860	200,940	1,201,600	2,489,300	470,200
1965—193,818,000	4,695,500	384,340	4,311,200	9,900	23,230	138,130	213,090	1,270,200	2,546,900	494,100
1966—195,587,000	5,175,500	426,880	4,748,300	10,970	25,620	157,350	232,890	1,396,500	2,793,700	558,100
1967—197,864,000	5,849,200	496,150	5,353,000	12,160	27,410	202,100	254,490	1,616,500	3,080,500	656,100
1968—199,861,000	6,656,900	590,640	6,066,200	13,720	31,410	261,780	283,720	1,841,100	3,447,800	779,300
1969—201,921,000	7,343,300	657,050	6,686,200	14,670	36,880	297,650	307,850	1,962,900	3,849,700	873,600
1970—203,184,772	8,024,100	733,530	7,290,500	15,890	37,690	348,460	331,480	2,183,800	4,183,500	923,300
1971—206,256,000	8,509,800	810,680	7,699,100	17,670	41,940	386,150	364,920	2,376,300	4,379,900	942,900
1972—208,232,000	8,173,400	828,820	7,344,600	18,550	46,480	374,790	389,000	2,352,800	4,109,600	882,200
1973—209,851,000	8,638,400	869,470	7,768,900	19,510	51,000	382,680	416,270	2,540,900	4,304,400	923,600
Percent change 1960–1973 [3]	+157.6	+203.8	+153.3	+115.6	+199.2	+256.3	+172.6	+181.3	+134.3	+183.0
Rate per 100,000 inhabitants:										
1960	1,869.7	159.6	1,710.1	5.0	9.5	59.9	85.2	503.8	1,024.3	182.0
1961	1,888.8	156.9	1,731.8	4.7	9.3	58.1	84.8	514.0	1,035.2	182.7
1962	2,000.5	161.0	1,889.5	4.6	9.4	59.4	87.6	530.0	1,113.3	196.3
1963	2,159.4	166.8	1,992.6	4.5	9.3	61.5	91.4	570.7	1,206.6	215.3
1964	2,363.6	188.9	2,174.7	4.9	11.1	67.9	105.0	628.0	1,301.0	245.7
1965	2,422.6	198.3	2,224.3	5.1	12.0	71.3	109.9	655.4	1,314.0	254.9
1966	2,646.0	218.2	2,427.7	5.6	13.1	80.4	119.1	714.0	1,428.4	285.3
1967	2,956.2	250.8	2,705.4	6.1	13.9	102.1	128.6	817.0	1,556.9	331.6
1968	3,331.8	295.5	3,036.2	6.9	15.7	131.0	142.0	921.2	1,725.1	389.9
1969	3,636.7	325.4	3,311.3	7.3	18.3	147.4	152.5	972.1	1,906.5	432.7
1970	3,949.2	361.0	3,588.1	7.8	18.6	171.5	163.1	1,074.8	2,059.0	454.4
1971	4,125.8	393.0	3,732.8	8.6	20.3	187.2	176.9	1,152.1	2,123.5	457.2
1972	3,925.2	398.0	3,527.1	8.9	22.3	180.0	186.8	1,129.9	1,973.6	423.7
1973	4,116.4	414.3	3,702.1	9.3	24.3	182.4	198.4	1,210.8	2,051.2	440.1
Percent change 1960–1973 [3]	+120.2	+159.6	+116.5	+86.0	+155.8	+204.5	+182.9	+140.3	+100.3	+141.8

[1] Population is Bureau of the Census provisional estimates as of July 1, except Apr. 1, 1960 and 1970, census.

[2] Violent crime is offenses of murder, forcible rape, robbery and aggravated assault. Property crime is offenses of burglary, larceny-theft, and auto theft.

[3] Percent change and crime rates calculated prior to rounding number of offenses. Revised estimates and rates based on changes in reporting practices.

(*Source: 1974 FBI uniform crime reports for the United States*)

Offense Analysis 1973—Percent Distribution, Average Value, and Percent Change Over 1972

[4,343 agencies; Chicago, Detroit, Los Angeles, New York, Philadelphia   1973 estimated population 128,611,000]

Classification	Number of offenses 1973	Percent change over 1972	Percent distribu- tion [1]	Average value
ROBBERY				
TOTAL	328,782	+1.3	100.0	$261
Highway	159,665	−1.1	48.6	167
Commercial house	56,043	+8.2	17.0	398
Gas or service station	12,204	−17.1	3.7	175
Chain store	18,348	+36.1	5.6	329
Residence	36,673	−4.2	11.2	339
Bank [2]	1,871	−2.0	.6	4,653
Miscellaneous	43,978	+2.7	13.4	170
BURGLARY—BREAKING OR ENTERING				
TOTAL	1,842,812	+6.7	100.0	337
Residence (dwelling):				
Night	538,421	+3.2	29.2	339
Day	601,702	+8.5	32.7	352
Nonresidence (store, office, etc.):				
Night	587,068	+6.4	31.9	331
Day	115,621	+16.7	6.3	288
LARCENY-THEFT (EXCEPT AUTO THEFT)				
TOTAL	3,175,300	+3.3	100.0	140
By type:				
Pocket-picking	31,670	−2.9	1.0	101
Purse-snatching	68,584	−1.2	2.2	62
Shoplifting	344,283	+6.1	10.8	28
From autos (except accessories)	553,643	+3.9	17.4	160
Auto accessories	508,157	−4.7	16.0	73
Bicycles	535,913	+3.1	16.9	58
From buildings	532,192	+1.0	16.8	246
From coin-operated machines	41,001	+8.7	1.3	44
All others	559,857	+13.3	17.6	247
By value:				
$50 and over	1,549,377	+14.1	48.8	267
Under $50	1,625,923	−5.2	51.2	20
Auto theft				1,095

[1] Because of rounding, the percentages may not add to total.
[2] For total U.S., bank robbery decreased from 2,618 offenses in 1972 to 2,521 in 1973 or 3.7 percent.

(*Source: 1974 FBI uniform crime reports for the United States*)

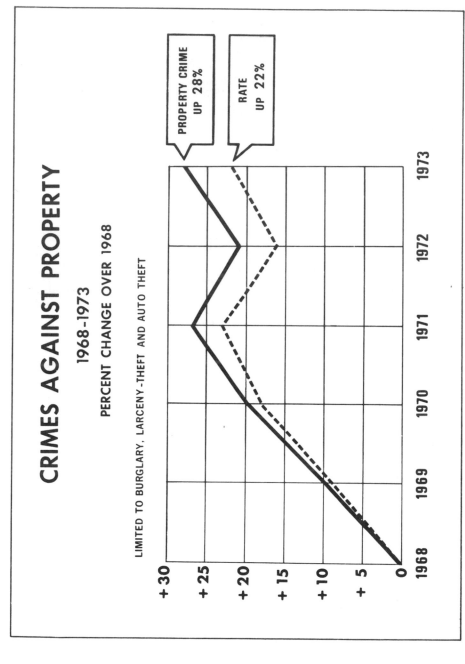

CRIMES AGAINST PROPERTY

1968-1973

PERCENT CHANGE OVER 1968

LIMITED TO BURGLARY, LARCENY-THEFT AND AUTO THEFT

PROPERTY CRIME UP 28%

RATE UP 22%

+30					
+25					
+20					
+15					
+10					
+5					
0					

1968   1969   1970   1971   1972   1973

(*Source: 1974 FBI uniform crime reports for the United States*)

Crimes Against Property 1968–1973
(Percent change over 1968)

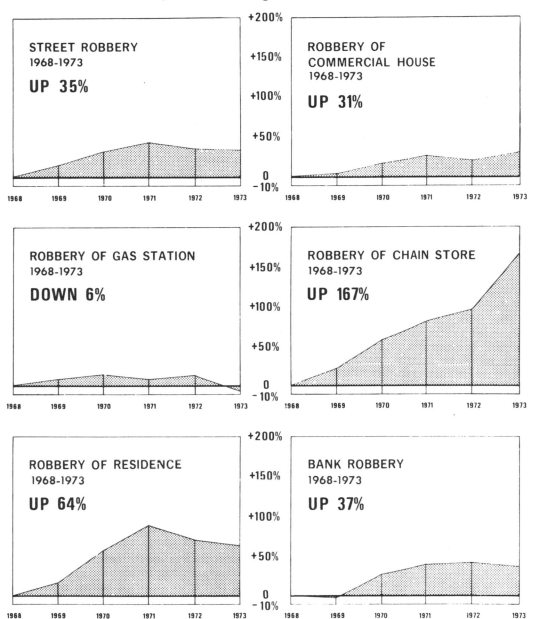

STREET ROBBERY
1968-1973

UP 35%

ROBBERY OF
COMMERCIAL HOUSE
1968-1973

UP 31%

ROBBERY OF GAS STATION
1968-1973

DOWN 6%

ROBBERY OF CHAIN STORE
1968-1973

UP 167%

ROBBERY OF RESIDENCE
1968-1973

UP 64%

BANK ROBBERY
1968-1973

UP 37%

(Source: 1974 FBI uniform crime reports for the United States)

Commercial Victimization Rates, by Type of Victimization and City

(Rate per 1,000 establishments, based on surveys during the months July through November 1972 of victimizations during the previous 12 months)

Type of Victimization

	Burglary	Completed Burglary	Attempted Burglary	Robbery	Completed Robbery	Attempted Robbery
Atlanta	741	544	197	157	120	37
Baltimore	578	397	181	135	112	23
Cleveland	367	269	97	77	58	19
Dallas	355	273	82	48	40	9
Denver	443	313	130	54	44	11
Newark	631	455	176	98	59	39
Portland	355	259	96	39	28	11
St. Louis	531	345	186	94	62	32

NOTE: Detail may not add to the total shown because of rounding. In general, small differences between any two figures in this table are not statistically significant because of sampling.

(*Source: 1974 U.S. Department of Commerce—the cost of crimes against business*)

Terms and Definitions for Intrusion Alarm Systems

prepared for
National Institute of Law Enforcement and Criminal Justice
Law Enforcement Assistance Administration
U.S. Department of Justice

by

G. N. Stenbakken
W. E. Phillips
Electronic Technology Division
and
S. E. Bergsman
Technical Analysis Division
National Bureau of Standards

ACCESS CONTROL.—The control of pedestrian and vehicular traffic through entrances and exits of a PROTECTED AREA or premises.

ACCESS MODE.—The operation of an ALARM SYSTEM such that no ALARM SIGNAL is given when the PROTECTED AREA is entered; however, a signal may be given if the SENSOR, ANNUNCIATOR, or CONTROL UNIT is tampered with or opened.

ACCESS/SECURE CONTROL UNIT.—See CONTROL UNIT.

ACCESS SWITCH.—See AUTHORIZED ACCESS SWITCH.

ACCUMULATOR.—A circuit which accumulates a sum. For example, in an audio alarm control unit, the accumulator sums the amplitudes of a series of pulses, which are larger than some threshold level, subtracts from the sum at a predetermined rate to account for random background pulses, and initiates an alarm signal when the sum exceeds some predetermined level. This circuit is also called an integrator; in digital circuits it may be called a counter.

ACTIVE INTRUSION SENSOR.—An active sensor which detects the presence of an intruder within the range of the sensor. Examples are an ULTRASONIC MOTION DETECTOR, a RADIO FREQUENCY MOTION DETECTOR, and a PHOTOELECTRIC ALARM SYSTEM. See also PASSIVE INTRUSION SENSOR.

ACTIVE SENSOR.—A sensor which detects the disturbance of a radiation field which is generated by the sensor. See also PASSIVE SENSOR.

ACTUATING DEVICE.—See ACTUATOR.

ACTUATOR.—A manual or automatic switch or sensor such as HOLDUP BUTTON, MAGNETIC SWITCH, or thermostat which causes a system to transmit an ALARM SIGNAL when manually activated or when the device automatically senses an intruder or other unwanted condition.

AIR GAP.—The distance between two magnetic elements in a magnetic or electromagnetic circuit, such as between the core and the armature of a relay.

ALARM.—An ALARM DEVICE or an ALARM SIGNAL.

ALARM CIRCUIT.—An electrical circuit of an alarm system which produces or transmits an ALARM SIGNAL.

ALARM CONDITION.—A threatening condition, such as an intrusion, fire, or holdup, sensed by a DETECTOR.

ALARM DEVICE.—A device which signals a warning in response to a ALARM CONDITION, such as a bell, siren, or ANNUNCIATOR.

ALARM DISCRIMINATION.—The ability of an alarm system to distinguish between those stimuli caused by an INTRUSION and those which are a part of the environment.

ALARM LINE.—A wired electrical circuit used for the transmission of ALARM SIGNALS from the protected premises to a MONITORING STATION.

ALARM RECEIVER.—See ANNUNCIATOR.

ALARM SENSOR.—See SENSOR.

ALARM SIGNAL.—A signal produced by a CONTROL UNIT indicating the existence of an ALARM CONDITION.

ALARM STATE.—The condition of a DETECTOR which causes a CONTROL UNIT in the SECURE MODE to transmit an ALARM SIGNAL.

ALARM STATION.—(1) A manually actuated device installed at a fixed location to transmit an ALARM SIGNAL in response to an ALARM CONDITION, such as a concealed HOLDUP BUTTON in a bank teller's cage. (2) A well-marked emergency control unit, installed in fixed locations usually accessible to the public, used to summon help in response to an ALARM CONDITION. The CONTROL UNIT contains either a manually actuated switch or telephone connected to fire or police headquarters, or a telephone answering service. See also REMOTE STATION ALARM SYSTEM.

ALARM SYSTEM.—An assembly of equipment and devices designated and arranged to signal the presence of an ALARM CONDITION requiring urgent attention such as unauthorized entry, fire, temperature rise, etc. The system may be LOCAL, POLICE CONNECTION, CENTRAL STATION or PROPRIETARY. (For individual alarm systems see alphabetical listing by type, e.g., INTRUSION ALARM SYSTEM.)

ANNUNCIATOR.—An alarm monitoring device which consists of a number of visible signals such as "flags" or lamps indicating the status of the DETECTORS in an alarm system or systems. Each circuit in the device is usually labelled to identify the location and condition being monitored. In addition to the visible signal, an audible signal is usually associated with the device. When an alarm condition is reported, a signal is indicated visibly, audibly, or both. The visible signal is generally maintained until reset either manually or automatically.

ANSWERING SERVICE.—A business which contracts with subscribers to answer incoming telephone calls after a specified delay or when scheduled to do so. It may also provide other services such as relaying fire or intrusion alarm signals to proper authorities.

AREA PROTECTION.—Protection of the inner space or volume of a secured area by means of a VOLUMETRIC SENSOR.

AREA SENSOR.—A sensor with a detection zone which approximates an area, such as a wall surface or the exterior of a safe.

AUDIBLE ALARM DEVICE.—(1) A noise-making device such as a siren, bell, or horn used as part of a local alarm system to indicate an ALARM CONDITION. (2) A bell, buzzer, horn or other noisemaking device used as a part of an ANNUNCIATOR to indicate a change in the status or operating mode of an alarm system.

AUDIO DETECTION SYSTEM.—See SOUND SENSING DETECTION SYSTEM.

AUDIO FREQUENCY (SONIC).—Sound frequencies within the range of human hearing, approximately 15 to 20,000 Hz.

AUDIO MONITOR.—An arrangement of amplifiers and speakers designed to monitor the sounds transmitted by microphones located in the PROTECTED AREA. Similar to an ANNUNCIATOR, except that supervisory personnel can monitor the protected area to interpret the sounds.

AUTHORIZED ACCESS SWITCH.—A device used to make an alarm system or some portion or zone of a system inoperative in order to permit authorized access through a PRO-

TECTED PORT. A SHUNT is an example of such a device.

B. A.—Burglar alarm.

BEAM DIVERGENCE.—In a PHOTO-ELECTRIC ALARM SYSTEM, the angular spread of the light beam.

BREAK ALARM.—(1) An ALARM CONDITION signaled by the opening or breaking of an electrical circuit. (2) The signal produced by a break alarm condition (sometimes referred to as an open circuit alarm or trouble signal, designed to indicate possible system failure).

BUG.—(1) To plant a microphone or other SOUND SENSOR or to tap a communication line for the purpose of SURREPTITIOUS listening or AUDIO MONITORING; loosely, to install a sensor in a specified location. (2) The microphone or other sensor used for the purpose of surreptitious listening.

BUILDING SECURITY ALARM SYSTEM.—The system of PROTECTIVE SIGNALING devices installed at a premise.

BURGLAR ALARM (B. A.) PAD.—A supporting frame laced with fine wire or a fragile panel located with FOIL or fine wire and installed so as to cover an exterior opening in a building, such as a door, or skylight. Entrance through the opening breaks the wire or foil and initiates an ALARM SIGNAL. See also GRID.

BURGLAR ALARM SYSTEM.—See INTRUSION ALARM SYSTEM.

BURGLARY.—The unlawful entering of a structure with the intent to commit a felony or theft therein.

CABINET-FOR-SAFE.—A wooden enclosure having closely spaced electrical GRIDS on all inner surfaces and CONTACTS on the doors. It surrounds a safe and initiates an alarm signal if an attempt is made to open or penetrate the cabinet.

CAPACITANCE.—The property of two or more objects which enables them to store electrical energy in an electric field between them. The basic measurement unit is the farad. Capacitance varies inversely with the distance between the objects, hence the change of capacitance with relative motion is greater the nearer one object is to the other.

CAPACITANCE ALARM SYSTEM.—An

alarm system in which a protected object is electrically connected as a CAPACITANCE SENSOR. The approach of an intruder causes sufficient change in CAPACITANCE to upset the balance of the system and initiate an ALARM SIGNAL. Also called proximity alarm system.

CAPACITANCE DETECTOR.—See CAPACITANCE SENSOR.

CAPACITANCE SENSOR.—A sensor which responds to a change in CAPACITANCE in a field containing a protected object or in a field within a protected area.

CARRIER CURRENT TRANSMITTER.—A device which transmits ALARM SIGNALS from a sensor to a CONTROL UNIT via the standard ac power lines.

CENTRAL STATION.—A control center to which alarm systems in a subscriber's premises are connected, where circuits are supervised, and where personnel are maintained continuously to record and investigate alarm or trouble signals. Facilities are provided for the reporting of alarms to police and fire departments or to other outside agencies.

CENTRAL STATION ALARM SYSTEM.—An alarm system, or group of systems, the activities of which are transmitted to, recorded in, maintained by, and supervised from a CENTRAL STATION. This differs from PROPRIETARY ALARM SYSTEMS in that the central station is owned and operated independently of the subscriber.

CIRCUMVENTION.—The defeat of an alarm system by the avoidance of its detection devices, such as by jumping over a pressure sensitive mat, by entering through a hole cut in an unprotected wall rather than through a protected door, or by keeping outside the range of an ULTRASONIC MOTION DETECTOR. Circumvention contrasts with SPOOFING.

CLOSED CIRCUIT ALARM.—See CROSS ALARM.

CLOSED CIRCUIT SYSTEM.—A system in which the sensors of each zone are connected in series so that the same current exists in each sensor. When an activated sensor breaks the circuit or the connecting wire is cut, an alarm is transmitted for that zone.

CLUTCH HEAD SCREW.—A mounting screw with a uniquely designed head for which the installation and removal tool is not commonly available. They are used to install alarm system components so that removal is inhibited.

CODED-ALARM SYSTEM.—An alarm system in which the source of each signal is identifiable. This is usually accomplished by means of a series of current pulses which operate audible or visible ANNUNCIATORS or recorders or both, to yield a recognizable signal. This is usually used to allow the transmission of multiple signals on a common circuit.

CODED CABLE.—A multiconductor cable in which the insulation on each conductor is distinguishable from all others by color or design. This assists in identification of the point of origin or final destination of a wire.

CODED TRANSMITTER.—A device for transmitting a coded signal when manually or automatically operated by an ACTUATOR. The actuator may be housed with the transmitter or a number of actuators may operate a common transmitter.

CODING SIREN.—A siren which has an auxiliary mechanism to interrupt the flow of air through its principal mechanism, enabling it to produce a controllable series of sharp blasts.

COMBINATION SENSOR ALARM SYSTEM.—An alarm system which requires the simultaneous activation of two or more sensors to initiate an ALARM SIGNAL.

COMPROMISE.—See DEFEAT.

CONSTANT RINGING DROP (CRD).—A relay which when activated even momentarily will remain in an ALARM CONDITION until RESET. A key is often required to reset the relay and turn off the alarm.

CONSTANT RINGING RELAY (CRR).—See CONSTANT RINGING DROP.

CONTACT.—(1) Each of the pair of metallic parts of a switch or relay which by touching or separating make or break the electrical current path. (2) A switch-type sensor.

CONTACT DEVICE.—A device which when actuated opens or closes a set of electrical contacts; a switch or relay.

CONTACT MICROPHONE.—A microphone designed for attachment directly to a surface of a PROTECTED AREA or object; usually used to detect surface vibrations.

CONTACT VIBRATION SENSOR.—See VIBRATION SENSOR.

CONTACTLESS VIBRATING BELL.—A VIBRATING BELL whose continuous operation depends upon application of an alternating current, without circuit-interrupting contacts such as those used in vibrating bells operated by direct current.

CONTROL CABINET.—See CONTROL UNIT.

CONTROL UNIT.—A device, usually ELECTRONIC, which provides the interface between the alarm system and the human operator and produces an ALARM SIGNAL when its programmed response indicates an ALARM CONDITION. Some or all of the following may be provided for: power for sensors, sensitivity adjustments, means to select and indicate ACCESS MODE or SECURE MODE, monitoring for LINE SUPERVISION and TAMPER DEVICES, timing circuits, for ENTRANCE and EXIT DELAYS, transmission of an alarm signal, etc.

COVERT.—Hidden and protected.

CRD.—See CONSTANT RINGING DROP.

CROSS ALARM.—(1) An ALARM CONDITION signaled by crossing or shorting an electrical circuit. (2) The signal produced due to a cross alarm condition.

CROSSOVER.—An insulated electrical path used to connect foil across window dividers, such as those found on multiple pane windows, to prevent grounding and to make a more durable connection.

CRR.—Constant ringing relay. See CONSTANT RINGING DROP.

DARK CURRENT.—The current output of a PHOTOELECTRIC SENSOR when no light is entering the sensor.

DAY SETTING.—See ACCESS MODE.

DEFEAT.—The frustration, counteraction, or thwarting of an ALARM DEVICE so that it fails to signal an alarm when a protected area is entered. Defeat includes both CIRCUMVENTION and SPOOFING.

DETECTION RANGE.—The greatest distance at which a sensor will consistently detect an intruder under a standard set of conditions.

DETECTOR.—(1) A sensor such as those used to detect INTRUSION, equipment malfunctions or failure, rate of temperature rise, smoke or fire. (2) A demodulator, a device for recovering the modulating function or signal from a modulated wave, such as that used in a modulated photoelectric alarm system. See also PHOTOELECTRIC ALARM SYSTEM, MODULATED.

DIALER.—See TELEPHONE DIALER, AUTOMATIC.

DIFFERENTIAL PRESSURE SENSOR.—A sensor used for PERIMETER PROTECTION which responds to the difference between the hydraulic pressures in two liquid-filled tubes buried just below the surface of the earth around the exterior perimeter of the PROTECTED AREA. The pressure difference can indicate an intruder walking or driving over the buried tubes.

DIGITAL TELEPHONE DIALER.—See TELEPHONE DIALER, DIGITAL.

DIRECT CONNECT.—See POLICE CONNECTION.

DIRECT WIRE BURGLAR ALARM CIRCUIT (DWBA).—See ALARM LINE.

DIRECT WIRE CIRCUIT.—See ALARM LINE.

DOOR CORD.—A short, insulated cable with an attaching block and terminals at each end used to conduct current to a device, such as FOIL, mounted on the movable portion of a door or window.

DOOR TRIP SWITCH.—A MECHANICAL SWITCH mounted so that movement of the door will operate the switch.

DOPPLER EFFECT (SHIFT).—The apparent change in frequency of sound or radio waves when reflected from or originating from a moving object. Utilized in some types of MOTION SENSORS.

DOUBLE-CIRCUIT SYSTEM.—An ALARM CIRCUIT in which two wires enter and two wires leave each sensor.

DOUBLE DROP.—An alarm signaling method often used in CENTRAL STATION ALARM SYSTEMS in which the line is first opened to produce a BREAK ALARM and then shorted to produce a CROSS ALARM.

DROP.—(1) See ANNUNCIATOR. (2) A light indicator on an annunciator.

DURESS ALARM DEVICE.—A device which produces either a SILENT ALARM or LOCAL ALARM under a condition of personnel stress such as holdup, fire, illness, or other panic or emergency. The device is normally manually operated and may be fixed or portable.

DURESS ALARM SYSTEM.—An alarm system which employes a DURESS ALARM DEVICE.

DWBA.—Direct wire burglar alarm. See ALARM LINE.

E-FIELD SENSOR.—A PASSIVE SENSOR which detects changes in the earth's ambient electric field caused by the movement of an intruder. See also H-FIELD SENSOR.

ELECTRICAL.—Related to, pertaining to, or associated with electricity.

ELECTROMAGNETIC.—Pertaining to the relationship between current flow and magnetic field.

ELECTROMAGNETIC INTERFERENCE (EMI).—Impairment of the reception of a wanted electromagnetic signal by an electromagnetic disturbance. This can be caused by lightning, radio transmitters, power line noise and other electrical devices.

ELECTROMECHANICAL BELL.—A bell with a prewound spring-driven striking mechanism, the operation of which is initiated by the activation of an electric tripping mechanism.

ELECTRONIC.—Related to, or pertaining to, devices which utilize electrons moving through a vacuum, gas, or semiconductor, and to circuits or systems containing such devices.

EMI.—See ELECTROMAGNETIC INTERFERENCE.

END OF LINE RESISTOR.—See TERMINAL RESISTOR.

ENTRANCE DELAY.—The time between actuating a sensor on an entrance door or gate and the sounding of a LOCAL ALARM or transmis-

sion of an ALARM SIGNAL by the CONTROL UNIT. This delay is used if the AUTHORIZED ACCESS SWITCH is located within the PROTECTED AREA and permits a person with the control key to enter without causing an alarm. The delay is provided by a timer within the CONTROL UNIT.

E.O.L.—End of line.

EXIT DELAY.—The time between turning on a control unit and the sounding of a LOCAL ALARM or transmission of an ALARM SIGNAL upon actuation of a sensor on an exit door. This delay is used if the AUTHORIZED ACCESS SWITCH is located within the PROTECTED AREA and permits a person with the control key to turn on the alarm system and to leave through a protected door or gate without causing an alarm. The delay is provided by a timer within the CONTROL UNIT.

FAIL SAFE.—A feature of a system or device which initiates an alarm or trouble signal when the system or device either malfunctions or loses power.

FALSE ALARM.—An alarm signal transmitted in the absence of an ALARM CONDITION. These may be classified according to causes: environmental, e.g., rain, fog, wind, hail, lightning, temperature, etc.; animals, e.g., rats, dogs, cats, insects, etc.; man-made disturbances, e.g., sonic booms, EMI, vehicles, etc.; equipment malfunction, e.g., transmission errors, component failure, etc.; operator error; and unknown.

FALSE ALARM RATE, MONTHLY.—The number of false alarms per installation per month.

FALSE ALARM RATIO.—The ratio of FALSE ALARMS to total alarms; may be expressed as a percentage or as a simple ratio.

FENCE ALARM.—Any of several types of sensors used to detect the presence of an intruder near a fence or any attempt by him to climb over, go under, or cut through the fence.

FIELD.—The space or area in which there exists a force such as that produced by an electrically charged object, a current, or a magnet.

FIRE DETECTOR (SENSOR).—See HEAT SENSOR and SMOKE DETECTOR.

FLOOR MAT.—See MAT SWITCH.

FLOOR TRAP.—A TRAP installed so as to detect the movement of a person across a floor space, such as a TRIP WIRE SWITCH or MAT SWITCH.

FOIL.—Thin metallic strips which are cemented to a protected surface (usually glass in a window or door), and connected to a closed electrical circuit. If the protected material is broken so as to break the foil, the circuit opens, initiating an alarm signal. Also called tape. A window, door, or other surface to which foil has been applied is said to be taped or foiled.

FOIL CONNECTOR.—An electrical terminal block used on the edge of a window to join interconnecting wire to window FOIL.

FOOT RAIL.—A HOLDUP ALARM DEVICE, often used at cashiers' windows, in which a foot is placed under the rail, lifting it, to initiate an ALARM SIGNAL.

FREQUENCY DIVISION MULTIPLEXING (FDM).—See MULTIPLEXING, FREQUENCY DIVISION.

GLASSBREAK VIBRATION DETECTOR.—A VIBRATION DETECTION SYSTEM which employs a CONTACT MICROPHONE attached to a glass window to detect cutting or breakage of the glass.

GRID.—(1) An arrangement of electrically conducting wire, screen, or tubing placed in front of doors or windows or both which is used as a part of a CAPACITANCE SENSOR. (2) a lattice of wooden dowels or slats concealing fine wires in a closed circuit which initiates an ALARM SIGNAL when forcing or cutting the lattice breaks the wires. Used over accessible openings. Sometimes called a protective screen. See also BURGLAR ALARM PAD. (3) A screen or metal plate, connected to earth ground, sometimes used to provide a stable ground reference for objects protected by a CAPACITANCE SENSOR. If placed against the walls near the protected object, it prevents the sensor sensitivity from extending through the walls into areas of activity.

HEAT DETECTOR.—See HEAT SENSOR.

HEAT SENSOR.—(1) A sensor which responds to either a local temperature above a selected value, a local temperature increase which is at a rate of increase greater than a preselected rate (rate of rise), or both. (2) A sensor which responds to infrared radiation from a remote source such as a person.

H-FIELD SENSOR.—A PASSIVE SENSOR which detects changes in the earth's ambient magnetic field caused by the movement of an intruder. See also E-FIELD SENSOR.

HOLDUP.—A ROBBERY involving the threat to use a weapon.

HOLDUP ALARM DEVICE.—A device which signals a holdup. The device is usually SURREPTITIOUS and may be manually or automatically actuated, fixed or portable. See DURESS ALARM DEVICE.

HOLDUP ALARM SYSTEM, AUTOMATIC.—An alarm system which employs a holdup alarm device, in which the signal transmission is initiated solely by the action of the intruder, such as a money clip in a cash drawer.

HOLDUP ALARM SYSTEM, MANUAL.—A holdup alarm system in which the signal transmission is initiated by the direct action of the person attacked or of an observer of the attack.

HOLDUP BUTTON.—A manually actuated MECHANICAL SWITCH used to initiate a duress alarm signal; usually constructed to minimize accidental activation.

HOOD CONTACT.—A switch which is used for the supervision of a closed safe or vault door. Usually installed on the outside surface of the protected door.

IMPEDANCE.—The opposition to the flow of alternating current in a circuit. May be determined by the ratio of an input voltage to the resultant current.

IMPEDANCE MATCHING.—Making the IMPEDANCE of a TERMINATING DEVICE equal to the impedance of the circuit to which it is connected in order to achieve optimum signal transfer.

INFRARED (IR) MOTION DETECTOR.—A sensor which detects changes in the infrared light radiation from parts of the PROTECTED AREA. Presence of an intruder in the area changes the infrared light intensity from his direction.

INFRARED (IR) MOTION SENSOR.—See

INFRARED MOTION DETECTOR.

INFRARED SENSOR.—See HEAT SENSOR, INFRARED MOTION DETECTOR, and PHOTOELECTRIC SENSOR.

INKING REGISTER.—See REGISTER, INKING.

INTERIOR PERIMETER PROTECTION.—A line of protection along the interior boundary of a PROTECTED AREA including all points through which entry can be effected.

INTRUSION.—Unauthorized entry into the property of another.

INTRUSION ALARM SYSTEM.—An alarm system for signaling the entry or attempted entry of a person or an object into the area or volume protected by the system.

IONIZATION SMOKE DETECTOR.—A SMOKE DETECTOR in which a small amount of radioactive material ionizes the air in the sensing chamber, thus rendering it conductive and permitting a current to flow through the air between two charged electrodes. This effectively gives the sensing chamber an electrical conductance. When smoke particles enter the ionization area, they decrease the conductance of the air by attaching themselves to the ions causing a reduction in mobility. When the conductance is less than a predetermined level, the detector circuit responds.

IR.—Infrared.

JACK.—An electrical connector which is used for frequent connect and disconnect operations; for example, to connect an alarm circuit at an overhang door.

LACING.—A network of fine wire surrounding or covering an area to be protected, such as a safe, vault, or glass panel, and connected into a CLOSED CIRCUIT SYSTEM. The network of wire is concealed by a shield such as concrete or paneling in such a manner that an attempt to break through the shield breaks the wire and initiates an alarm.

LIGHT INTENSITY CUTOFF.—In a PHOTOELECTRIC ALARM SYSTEM, the percent reduction of light which initiates an ALARM SIGNAL at the photoelectric receiver unit.

LINE AMPLIFIER.—An audio amplifier which is used to provide preamplification of an audio ALARM SIGNAL before transmission of the signal over an ALARM LINE. Use of an amplifier extends the range of signal transmission.

LINE SENSOR (DETECTOR).—A sensor with a detection zone which approximates a line or series of lines, such as a PHOTOELECTRIC SENSOR which senses a direct or reflected light beam.

LINE SUPERVISION.—Electronic protection of an ALARM LINE accomplished by sending a continuous or coded signal through the circuit. A change in the circuit characteristics, such as a change in IMPEDANCE due to the circuit's having been tampered with, will be detected by a monitor. The monitor initiates an alarm if the change exceeds a predetermined amount.

LOCAL ALARM.—An alarm which when activated makes a loud noise (see AUDIBLE ALARM DEVICE) at or near the PROTECTED AREA or floods the site with light or both.

LOCAL ALARM SYSTEM.—An alarm system which when activated produces an audible or visible signal in the immediate vicinity of the protected premises or object. This term usually applies to systems designed to provide only a local warning of INTRUSION and not to transmit to a remote MONITORING STATION. However, local alarm systems are sometimes used in conjunction with a REMOTE ALARM.

LOOP.—An electric circuit consisting of several elements, usually switches, connected in series.

MAGNETIC ALARM SYSTEM.—An alarm system which will initiate an alarm when it detects changes in the local magnetic field. The changes could be caused by motion of ferrous objects such as guns or tools near the MAGNETIC SENSOR.

MAGNETIC CONTACT.—See MAGNETIC SWITCH.

MAGNETIC SENSOR.—A sensor which responds to changes in magnetic field. See also MAGNETIC ALARM SYSTEM.

MAGNETIC SWITCH.—A switch which consists of two separate units: a magnetically-actuated switch, and a magnet. The switch is usually mounted in a fixed position (door jamb or window frame) opposing the magnet, which is fastened to a hinged or sliding door, window, etc. When the movable section is opened, the magnet moves with it, actuating the switch.

MAGNETIC SWITCH, BALANCED.—A MAGNETIC SWITCH which operates using a balanced magnetic field in such a manner as to resist DEFEAT with an external magnet. It signals an alarm when it detects either an increase or decrease in magnetic field strength.

MATCHING NETWORK.—A circuit used to achieve IMPEDANCE MATCHING. It may also allow audio signals to be transmitted to an ALARM LINE while blocking direct current used locally for LINE SUPERVISION.

MAT SWITCH.—A flat area switch used on open floors or under carpeting. It may be sensitive over an area of a few square feet or several square yards.

McCULLOH CIRCUIT (LOOP).—A supervised single wire LOOP connecting a number of CODED TRANSMITTERS located in different PROTECTED AREAS to a CENTRAL STATION receiver.

MECHANICAL SWITCH.—A switch in which the CONTACTS are opened and closed by means of a depressible plunger or button.

MERCURY FENCE ALARM.—A type of MERCURY SWITCH which is sensitive to the vibration caused by an intruder climbing on a fence.

MERCURY SWITCH.—A switch operated by tilting or vibrating which causes an enclosed pool of mercury to move, making or breaking physical and electrical contact with conductors. These are used on tilting doors and windows, and on fences.

MICROWAVE ALARM SYSTEM.—An alarm system which employs RADIO FREQUENCY MOTION DETECTORS operating in the MICROWAVE FREQUENCY region of the electromagnetic spectrum.

MICROWAVE FREQUENCY.—Radio frequencies in the range of approximately 1.0 to 300 GHz.

MICROWAVE MOTION DETECTOR.— See RADIO FREQUENCY MOTION DETEC-TOR.

MODULATED PHOTOELECTRIC ALARM SYSTEM.—See PHOTOELECTRIC ALARM SYSTEM, MODULATED.

MONITOR CABINET.—An enclosure which houses the ANNUNCIATOR and associated equipment.

MONITOR PANEL.—See ANNUNCIATOR.

MONITORING STATION.—The CENTRAL STATION or other area at which guards, police, or commercial service personnel observe ANNUNCIATORS and REGISTERS reporting on the condition of alarm systems.

MOTION DETECTION SYSTEM.—See MOTION SENSOR.

MOTION DETECTOR.—See MOTION SENSOR.

MOTION SENSOR.—A sensor which responds to the motion of an intruder. See also RADIO FREQUENCY MOTION DETECTOR, SONIC MOTION DETECTOR, ULTRASONIC MOTION DETECTOR, AND INFRARED MOTION DETECTOR.

MULTIPLEXING.—A technique for the concurrent transmission of two or more signals in either or both directions, over the same wire, carrier, or other communication channel. The two basic multiplexing techniques are time division multiplexing and frequency division multiplexing.

MULTIPLEXING, FREQUENCY DIVISION (FDM).—The multiplexing technique which assigns to each signal a specific set of frequencies (called a channel) within the larger block of frequencies available on the main transmission path in much the same way that many radio stations broadcast at the same time but can be separately received.

MULTIPLEXING, TIME DIVISION (TDM).—The multiplexing technique which provides for the independent transmission of several pieces of information on a time-sharing basis by sampling, at frequent intervals, the data to be transmitted.

NEUTRALIZATION.—See DEFEAT.

NICAD.—(Contraction of "nickel cadmium".) A high performance, long-lasting rechargeable battery, with electrodes made of nickel and cadmium, which may be used as an emergency power supply for an alarm system.

NIGHT SETTING.—See SECURE MODE.

NONRETRACTABLE (ONE-WAY) SCREW.—A screw with a head designed to permit installation with an ordinary flat bit screwdriver but which resists removal. They are used to install alarm system components so that removal is inhibited.

NORMALLY CLOSED (NC) SWITCH.—A switch in which the CONTACTS are closed when no external forces act upon the switch.

NORMALLY OPEN (NO) SWITCH.—A switch in which the CONTACTS are open (separated) when no external forces act upon the switch.

NUISANCE ALARM.—See FALSE ALARM.

OBJECT PROTECTION.—See SPOT PROTECTION.

OPEN-CIRCUIT ALARM.—See BREAK ALARM.

OPEN-CIRCUIT SYSTEM.—a system in which the sensors are connected in parallel. When a sensor is activated, the circuit is closed, permitting a current which activates an ALARM SIGNAL.

PANIC ALARM.—See DURESS ALARM DEVICE.

PANIC BUTTON.—See DURESS ALARM DEVICE.

PASSIVE INTRUSION SENSOR.—A passive sensor in an INTRUSION ALARM SYSTEM which detects an intruder within the range of the sensor. Examples are a SOUND SENSING DETECTION SYSTEM, a VIBRATION DETECTION SYSTEM, an INFRARED MOTION DETECTOR, and an E-FIELD SENSOR.

PASSIVE SENSOR.—A sensor which detects natural radiation or radiation disturbances, but does not itself emit the radiation on which its operation depends.

PASSIVE ULTRASONIC ALARM SYSTEM.—An alarm system which detects the sounds in the ULTRASONIC FREQUENCY range caused by an attempted forcible entry into a protected structure. The system consists of mi-

crophones, a CONTROL UNIT containing an amplifier, filters, an ACCUMULATOR, and a power supply. The unit's sensitivity is adjustable so that ambient noises or normal sounds will not initiate an ALARM SIGNAL; however, noise above the preset level or a sufficient accumulation of impulses will initiate an alarm.

PERCENTAGE SUPERVISION.—A method of LINE SUPERVISION in which the current in or resistance of a supervised line is monitored for changes. When the change exceeds a selected percentage of the normal operating current or resistance in the line, an ALARM SIGNAL is produced.

PERIMETER ALARM SYSTEM.—An alarm system which provides perimeter protection.

PERIMETER PROTECTION.—Protection of access to the outer limits of a PROTECTED AREA, by means of physical barriers, sensors on physical barriers, or exterior sensors not associated with a physical barrier.

PERMANENT CIRCUIT.—An ALARM CIRCUIT which is capable of transmitting an ALARM SIGNAL whether the alarm control is in ACCESS MODE or SECURE MODE. Used, for example, on foiled fixed windows, TAMPER SWITCHES, and supervisory lines. See also SUPERVISORY ALARM SYSTEM, SUPERVISORY CIRCUIT, and PERMANENT PROTECTION.

PERMANENT PROTECTION.—A system of alarm devices such as FOIL, BURGLAR ALARM PADS, or LACINGS connected in a permanent circuit to provide protection whether the CONTROL UNIT is in the ACCESS MODE or SECURE MODE.

PHOTOELECTRIC ALARM SYSTEM.—An alarm system which employs a light beam and PHOTOELECTRIC SENSOR to provide a line of protection. Any interruption of the beam by an intruder is sensed by the sensor. Mirrors may be used to change the direction of the beam. The maximum beam length is limited by many factors, some of which are the light source intensity, number of mirror reflections, detector sensitivity, BEAM DIVERGENCE, fog, and haze.

PHOTOELECTRIC ALARM SYSTEM, MODULATED.—A photoelectric alarm system in which the transmitted light beam is modulated in a predetermined manner and in which the receiving equipment will signal an alarm unless it receive the properly modulated light.

PHOTOELECTRIC BEAM TYPE SMOKE DETECTOR.—A SMOKE DETECTOR which has a light source which projects a light beam across the area to be protected onto a photoelectric cell. Smoke between the light source and the receiving cell reduces the light reaching the cell, causing actuation.

PHOTOELECTRIC DETECTOR.—See PHOTOELECTRIC SENSOR.

PHOTOELECTRIC SENSOR.—A device which detects a visible or invisible beam of light and responds to its complete or nearly complete interruption. See also PHOTOELECTRIC ALARM SYSTEM and PHOTOELECTRIC ALARM SYSTEM, MODULATED.

PHOTOELECTRIC SPOT TYPE SMOKE DETECTOR.—A SMOKE DETECTOR which contains a chamber with covers which prevent the entrance of light but allow the entrance of smoke. The chamber contains a light source and a photosensitive cell so placed that light is blocked from it. When smoke enters, the smoke particles scatter and reflect the light into the photosensitive cell, causing an alarm.

POINT PROTECTION.—See SPOT PROTECTION.

POLICE CONNECTION.—The direct link by which an alarm system is connected to an ANNUNCIATOR installed in a police station. Examples of a police connection are an ALARM LINE, or a radio communications channel.

POLICE PANEL.—See POLICE STATION UNIT.

POLICE STATION UNIT.—An ANNUNCIATOR which can be placed in operation in a police station.

PORTABLE DURESS SENSOR.—A device carried on a person which may be activated in an emergency to send an ALARM SIGNAL to a MONITORING STATION.

PORTABLE INTRUSION SENSOR.—A sensor which can be installed quickly and which does not require the installation of dedicated wiring for the transmission its ALARM SIGNAL.

POSITIVE NONINTERFERING (PNI) AND SUCCESSIVE ALARM SYSTEM.—An alarm system which employs multiple alarm transmitters on each ALARM LINE (like McCULLOH LOOP) such that in the event of simultaneous operation of several transmitters, one of them takes control of the alarm line, transmits its full signal, then release the alarm line for successive transmission by other transmitters which are held inoperative until they gain control.

PRESSURE ALARM SYSTEM.—An alarm system which protects a vault or other enclosed space by maintaining and monitoring a predetermined air pressure differential between the inside and outside of the space. Equalization of pressure resulting from opening the vault or cutting through the enclosure will be sensed and will initiate an ALARM SIGNAL.

PRINTING RECORDER.—An electromechanical device used at a MONITORING STATION which accepts coded signals from alarm lines and converts them to an alphanumeric printed record of the signal received.

PROPRIETARY ALARM SYSTEM.—An alarm system which is similar to a CENTRAL STATION ALARM SYSTEM except that the ANNUNCIATOR is located in a constantly manned guard room maintained by the owner for his own internal security operations. The guards monitor the system and respond to all ALARM SIGNALS or alert local law enforcement agencies or both.

PROTECTED AREA.—An area monitored by an alarm system or guards, or enclosed by a suitable barrier.

PROTECTED PORT.—A point of entry such as a door, window, or corridor which is monitored by sensors connected to an alarm system.

PROTECTION DEVICE.—(1) A sensor such as a GRID, FOIL, CONTACT, or PHOTOELECTRIC SENSOR connected into an INTRUSION ALARM SYSTEM. (2) A barrier which inhibits INTRUSION, such as a grille, lock, fence or wall.

PROTECTION, EXTERIOR PERIMETER.—A line of protection surrounding but somewhat removed from a facility. Examples are

217

fences, barrier walls, or patrolled points of a perimeter.

PROTECTION OFF.—See ACCESS MODE.

PROTECTION ON.—See SECURE MODE.

PROTECTIVE SCREEN.—See GRID.

PROTECTIVE SIGNALING.—The initiation, transmission, and reception of signals involved in the detection and prevention of property loss due to fire, burglary, or other destructive conditions. Also, the electronic supervision of persons and equipment concerned with this detection and prevention. See also LINE SUPERVISION and SUPERVISORY ALARM SYSTEM.

PROXIMITY ALARM SYSTEM.—See CAPACITANCE ALARM SYSTEM.

PUNCHING REGISTER.—See REGISTER, PUNCH.

RADAR ALARM SYSTEM.—An alarm system which employs RADIO FREQUENCY MOTION DETECTORS.

RADAR (RADIO DETECTING AND RANGING).—See RADIO FREQUENCY MOTION DETECTOR.

RADIO FREQUENCY INTERFERENCE (RFI).—ELECTROMAGNETIC INTERFERENCE in the radio frequency range.

RADIO FREQUENCY MOTION DETECTOR.—A sensor which detects the motion of an intruder through the use of a radiated radio frequency electromagnetic field. The device operates by sensing a disturbance in the generated RF field caused by intruder motion, typically a modulation of the field referred to as a DOPPLER EFFECT, which is used to initiate an ALARM SIGNAL. Most radio frequency motion detectors are certified by the FCC for operation as "field disturbance sensors" at one of the following frequencies: 0.915 GHz (L-Band), 2.45 GHz (S-Band), 5.8 GHz (X-Band), 10.525 GHz (X-Band), and 22.125 GHz (K-Band). Units operating in the MICROWAVE FREQUENCY range are usually called MICROWAVE MOTION DETECTORS.

REED SWITCH.—A type of MAGNETIC SWITCH consisting of contacts formed by two thin moveable magnetically actuated metal vanes or reeds, held in a normally open position within a sealed glass envelope.

REGISTER.—An electromechanical device which marks a paper tape in response to signal impulses received from transmitting circuits. A register may be driven by a prewound spring mechanism, an electric motor, or a combination of these.

REGISTER, INKING.—A register which marks the tape with ink.

REGISTER, PUNCH.—A register which marks the tape by cutting holes in it.

REGISTER, SLASHING.—A register which marks the tape by cutting V-shaped slashes in it.

REMOTE ALARM.—An ALARM SIGNAL which is transmitted to a remote MONITORING STATION. See also LOCAL ALARM.

REMOTE STATION ALARM SYSTEM.—An alarm system which employes remote ALARM STATIONS usually located in building hallways or on city streets.

REPORTING LINE.—See ALARM LINE.

RESET.—To restore a device to its original (normal) condition after an alarm or trouble signal.

RESISTANCE BRIDGE SMOKE DETECTOR.—A SMOKE DETECTOR which responds to the particles and moisture present in smoke. These substances reduce the resistance of an electrical bridge grid and cause the detector to respond.

RETARD TRANSMITTER.—A CODED TRANSMITTER in which a delay period is introduced between the time of actuation and the time of signal transmission.

RFI.—RADIO FREQUENCY INTERFERENCE.

Rf MOTION DETECTOR.—See RADIO FREQUENCY MOTION DETECTOR.

ROBBERY.—The felonious or forcible taking of property by violence, threat, or other overt felonious act in the presence of the victim.

SECURE MODE.—The condition of an alarm system in which all sensors and CONTROL UNITS are ready to respond to an intrusion.

SECURITY MONITOR.—See ANNUNCIATOR.

SEISMIC SENSOR.—A sensor, generally buried under the surface of the ground for PERIME-

TER PROTECTION, which responds to minute vibrations of the earth generated as an intruder walks or drives within its DETECTION RANGE.

SENSOR.—A device which is designed to produce a signal or offer indication in response to an event or stimulus within its detection zone.

SENSOR, COMBUSTION.—See IONIZATION SMOKE DETECTOR, PHOTOELECTRIC BEAM TYPE SMOKE DETECTOR, PHOTOELECTRIC SPOT TYPE SMOKE DETECTOR and RESISTANCE BRIDGE SMOKE DETECTOR.

SENSOR, SMOKE.—See IONIZATION SMOKE DETECTOR, PHOTOELECTRIC BEAM TYPE SMOKE DETECTOR, PHOTOELECTRIC SPOT TYPE SMOKE DETECTOR and RESISTANCE BRIDGE SMOKE DETECTOR.

SHUNT.—(1) A deliberate shorting-out of a portion of an electric circuit. (2) A key-operated switch which removes some portion of an alarm system for operation, allowing entry into a PROTECTED AREA without initiating an ALARM SIGNAL. A type of AUTHORIZED ACCESS SWITCH.

SHUNT SWITCH.—See SHUNT.

SIGNAL RECORDER.—See REGISTER.

SILENT ALARM.—A REMOTE ALARM without an obvious local indication that an alarm has been transmitted.

SILENT ALARM SYSTEM.—An alarm system which signals a remote station by means of a silent alarm.

SINGLE CIRCUIT SYSTEM.—An ALARM CIRCUIT which routes only one side of the circuit through each sensor. The return may be through either ground or a separate wire.

SINGLE-STROKE BELL.—A bell which is struck once each time its mechanism is activated.

SLASHING REGISTER.—See REGISTER, SLASHING.

SMOKE DETECTOR.—A device which detects visible or invisible products of combustion. See also IONIZATION SMOKE DETECTOR, PHOTOELECTRIC BEAM TYPE SMOKE DETECTOR, PHOTOELECTRIC SPOT TYPE SMOKE DETECTOR, and RESISTANCE

BRIDGE SMOKE DETECTOR.

SOLID STATE.—(1) An adjective used to describe a device such as a semiconductor transistor or diode. (2) A circuit or system which does not rely on vacuum or gas-filled tubes to control or modify voltages and currents.

SONIC MOTION DETECTOR.—A sensor which detects the motion of an intruder by his disturbance of an audible sound pattern generated within the protected area.

SOUND SENSING DETECTION SYSTEM.—An alarm system which detects the audible sound caused by an attempted forcible entry into a protected structure. The system consists of microphones and a CONTROL UNIT containing an amplifier, ACCUMULATOR, and a power supply. The unit's sensitivity is adjustable so that ambient noises or normal sounds will not initiate an ALARM SIGNAL. However, noises above this preset level or a sufficient accumulation of impulses will initiate an alarm.

SOUND SENSOR.—A sensor which responds to sound; a microphone.

SPACE PROTECTION.—See AREA PROTECTION.

SPOOFING.—The defeat or compromise of an alarm system by "tricking" or "fooling" its detection devices such as by short circuiting part or all of a series circuit, cutting wires in a parallel circuit, reducing the sensitivity of a sensor, or entering false signals into the system. Spoofing contrasts with CIRCUMVENTION.

SPOT PROTECTION.—Protection of objects such as safes, art objects, or anything of value which could be damaged or removed from the premises.

SPRING CONTACT.—A device employing a current-carrying cantilever spring which monitors the position of a door or window.

STANDBY POWER SUPPLY.—Equipment which supplies power to a system in the event the primary power is lost. It may consist of batteries, charging circuits, auxiliary motor generators or a combination of these devices.

STRAIN GAUGE ALARM SYSTEM.—An alarm system which detects the stress caused by the weight of an intruder as he moves about a building. Typical uses include placement of the strain gauge sensor under a floor joist or under a stairway tread.

STRAIN GAUGE SENSOR.—A sensor which, when attached to an object, will provide an electrical response to an applied stress upon the object, such as a bending, stretching or compressive force.

STRAIN SENSITIVE CABLE.—An electrical cable which is designed to produce a signal whenever the cable is strained by a change in applied force. Typical uses including mounting it in a wall to detect an attempted forced entry through the wall, or fastening it to a fence to detect climbing on the fence, or burying it around a perimeter to detect walking or driving across the perimeter.

SUBSCRIBER'S EQUIPMENT.—That portion of a CENTRAL STATION ALARM SYSTEM installed in the protected premises.

SUBSCRIBER'S UNIT.—A CONTROL UNIT of a CENTRAL STATION ALARM SYSTEM.

SUPERVISED LINES.—Interconnecting lines in an alarm system which are electrically supervised against tampering. See also LINE SUPERVISION.

SUPERVISORY ALARM SYSTEM.—An alarm system which monitors conditions or persons or both and signals any deviation from an established norm or schedule. Examples are the monitoring of signals from guard patrol stations for irregularities in the progression along a prescribed patrol route, and the monitoring of production or safety conditions such as sprinkler water pressure, temperature, or liquid level.

SUPERVISORY CIRCUIT.—An electrical circuit or radio path which sends information on the status of a sensor or guard patrol to an ANNUNCIATOR. For INTRUSION ALARM SYSTEMS, this circuit provides LINE SUPERVISION and monitors TAMPER DEVICES. See also SUPERVISORY ALARM SYSTEM.

SURREPTITIOUS.—COVERT, hidden, concealed, or disguised.

SURVEILLANCE.—(1) Control of premises for security purposes through alarm systems, closed circuit television (CCTV), or other monitoring methods. (2) Supervision or inspection of industrial processes by monitoring those conditions which could cause damage if not corrected. See also SUPERVISORY ALARM SYSTEM.

TAMPER DEVICE.—(1) Any device, usually a switch, which is used to detect an attempt to gain access to intrusion alarm circuitry, such as by removing a switch cover. (2) A monitor circuit to detect any attempt to modify the alarm circuitry, such as by cutting a wire.

TAMPER SWITCH.—A switch whch is installed in such a way as to detect attempts to remove the enclosure of some alarm system components such as control box doors, switch covers, junction box covers, or bell housings. The alarm component is then often described as being "tampered".

TAPE.—See FOIL.

TAPPER BELL.—A SINGLE-STROKE BELL designed to produce a sound of low intensity and relatively high pitch.

TELEPHONE DIALER, AUTOMATIC.—A device which, when activated, automatically dials one more pre-programmed telephone numbers (e.g., police, fire department) and relays a recorded voice or coded message giving the location and nature of the alarm.

TELEPHONE DIALER, DIGITAL.—An automatic telephone dialer which sends its message as a digital code.

TERMINAL RESISTOR.—A resistor used as a TERMINATING DEVICE.

TERMINATING CAPACITOR.—A capacitor sometimes used as a terminating device for a CAPACITANCE SENSOR antenna. The capacitor allows the supervision of the sensor antenna, especially if a long wire is used as the sensor.

TERMINATING DEVICE.—A device which is used to terminate an electrically supervised circuit. It makes the electrical circuit continuous and provides a fixed IMPEDANCE reference (end of line resistor) against which changes are measured to detect an ALARM CONDITION. The impedance changes may be caused by a sensor, tampering, or circuit trouble.

TIME DELAY.—See ENTRANCE DELAY and EXIT DELAY.

TIME DIVISION MULTIPLEXING (TDM).—See MULTIPLEXING, TIME DIVI-

SION.

TIMING TABLE.—That portion of CENTRAL STATION equipment which provides a means for checking incoming signals from Mc-CULLOH CIRCUITS.

TOUCH SENSITIVITY.—The sensitivity of a CAPACITANCE SENSOR at which the ALARM DEVICE will be activated only if an intruder touches or comes in very close proximity (about 1 cm or $^1/_2$ in.) to the protected object.

TRAP.—(1) A device, usually a switch, installed within a protected area, which serves as secondary protection in the event a PERIMETER ALARM SYSTEM is successfully penetrated. Examples are a TRIP WIRE SWITCH placed across a likely path for an intruder, a MAT SWITCH hidden under a rug, or a MAGNETIC SWITCH mounted on an inner door. (2) A VOLUMETRIC SENSOR installed so as to detect an intruder in a likely traveled corridor or pathway within a security area.

TRICKLE CHARGE.—A continuous direct current, usually very low, which is applied to a battery to maintain it at peak charge or to recharge it after it has been partially or completely discharged. Usually applied to nickel cadmium (NICAD) or wet cell batteries.

TRIP WIRE SWITCH.—A switch which is actuated by breaking or moving a wire or cord installed across a floor space.

TROUBLE SIGNAL.—See BREAK ALARM.

UL.—See UNDERWRITERS LABORATORIES, INC.

UL CERTIFICATED.—For certain types of products which have met UL requirements, for which it is impractical to apply the UL Listing Mark or Classification Marking to the individual product, a certificate is provided which the manufacturer may use to identify quantities of material for specific job sites or to identify field installed systems.

UL LISTED.—Signifies that production samples of the product have been found to comply with established Underwriters Laboratories requirements and that the manufacturer is authorized to use the Laboratories' Listing Marks on the listed products which comply with the requirements, contingent upon the follow-up services as a check of compliance.

ULTRASONIC.—Pertaining to a sound wave having a frequency above that of audible sound (approximately 20,000 Hz). Ultrasonic sound is used in ultrasonic detection systems.

ULTRASONIC DETECTION SYSTEM.—See ULTRASONIC MOTION DETECTOR and PASSIVE ULTRASONIC ALARM SYSTEM.

ULTRASONIC FREQUENCY.—Sound frequencies which are above the range of human hearing; approximately 20,000 Hz and higher.

ULTRASONIC MOTION DETECTOR.—A sensor which detects the motion of an intruder through the use of ULTRASONIC generating and receiving equipment. The device operates by filling a space with a pattern of ultrasonic waves; the modulation of these waves by a moving object is detected and initiates an ALARM SIGNAL.

UNDERDOME BELL.—A bell most of whose mechanism is concealed by its gong.

UNDERWRITERS LABORATORIES, INC. (UL).—A private independent research and testing laboratory which tests and lists various items meeting good practice and safety standards.

VIBRATING BELL.—A bell whose mechanism is designed to strike repeatedly and for as long as it is activated.

VIBRATING CONTACT.—See VIBRATION SENSOR.

VIBRATION DETECTION SYSTEM.—An alarm system which employs one or more CONTACT MICROPHONES or VIBRATION SENSORS which are fastened to the surfaces of the area or object being protected to detect excessive levels of vibration. The contact microphone system consists of microphones, a CONTROL UNIT containing an amplifier and an ACCUMULATOR, and a power supply. The unit's sensitivity is adjustable so that ambient noises or normal vibrations will not initiate an ALARM SIGNAL. In the vibration sensor system, the sensor responds to excessive vibration by opening a switch in a CLOSED CIRCUIT SYSTEM.

VIBRATION DETECTOR.—See VIBRATION SENSOR.

VIBRATION SENSOR.—A sensor which responds to vibrations of the surface on which it is mounted. It has a NORMALLY CLOSED

SWITCH which will momentarily open when it is subjected to a vibration with sufficiently large amplitude. Its sensitivity is adjustable to allow for the different levels of normal vibration, to which the sensor should not respond, at different locations. See also VIBRATION DETECTION SYSTEM.

VISUAL SIGNAL DEVICE.—A pilot light, ANNUNCIATOR or other device which provides a visual indication of the condition of the circuit or system being supervised.

VOLUMETRIC DETECTOR.—See VOLUMETRIC SENSOR.

VOLUMETRIC SENSOR.—A sensor with a detection zone which extends over a volume such as an entire room, part of a room, or a passageway. ULTRASONIC MOTION DETECTORS and SONIC MOTION DETECTORS are examples of volumetric sensors.

WALK TEST LIGHT.—A light on motion detectors which comes on when the detector senses motion in the area. It is used while setting the sensitivity of the detector and during routine checking and maintenance.

WATCHMAN'S REPORTING SYSTEM.— A SUPERVISORY ALARM SYSTEM arranged for the transmission of a patrolling watchman's regularly recurrent report signals from stations along his patrol route to a central supervisory agency.

ZONED CIRCUIT.—A circuit which provides continual protection for parts or zones of the PROTECTED AREA while normally used doors and windows or zones may be released for access.

ZONES.—Smaller subdivisions into which large areas are divided to permit selective access to some zones while maintaining other zones secure and to permit pinpointing the specific location from which an ALARM SIGNAL is transmitted.

Notes

CHAPTER 1.
The Business of Private Security

1. U.S. Department of Commerce, Bureau of Domestic Commerce, *Preliminary Staff Report; The Economic Impact of Crimes Against Business* (Washington: Government Printing Office [hereafter GPO], 1972). As the 1968 *Report of the President's Commission on Law Enforcement and the Administration of Justice* notes on page 3: "The only comprehensive study of the cost of crime ever undertaken in this country was made by The Wickersham Commission (U. S. National Commission on Law Observance and Enforcement, *Report on Cost of Crime* . . .). It set forth in detail a conceptual framework for discussing the economic cost of crime and recommended that further studies be made. . . . However, except in the area of statistics concerning the costs of the criminal justice system . . . the lack of knowledge about which the Wickersham Commission complained 30 years ago is almost as great today."
2. Dept. of Commerce, Bureau of Domestic Commerce, *Preliminary Staff Report* (Washington: GPO, 1972), p. 1.
3. Idem, *The Cost of Crimes Against Business* (Washington: GPO, 1974).
4. Ibid.
5. Dept. of Commerce, *Preliminary Staff Report*, p. 5.
6. Herbert Edelhertz, *Nature, Impact and Prosecution of White Collar Crime* (Washington: National Institute of Law Enforcement and Criminal Justice, 1970), under the direction of Henry S. Ruth, Jr.

7. Chamber of Commerce of the United States, *A Handbook on White Collar Crime* (Washington: 1974), p. 5.
8. U.S. Department of Justice, Federal Bureau of Investigation, *Uniform Crime Reports* (Washington: GPO, 1950–1973).
9. International Business Machines Corporation, *Data Security and Data Processing,* 6 vols. (White Plains, N.Y.: IBM, 1974), 3:18.
10. Law Enforcement Assistance Administration, U.S. Department of Justice, press release, April, 1974.
11. Ibid.
12. Dept. of Justice, LEAA, *Sourcebook of Criminal Justice Statistics, 1973,* (Washington: LEAA, 1974), p. 68.
13. Ibid, p. 68.
14. Notes taken at an IACP convention committee meeting in Washington, Sept. 23, 1974.
15. Unpublished memorandum, dated April 15, 1974, issued by Office of Director, Private Police Services Project, Governor's Office of Human Resources, Chicago, Ill.
16. Dept. of Justice, LEAA, *Sourcebook,* p. 68.
17. Insurance Services Office, *Summary Burglary Insurance Experience— Accident Years 1965 through 1969* (New York, N.Y.: ISO, 1970), exhibit 54, sheet 1.
18. U.S. Senate, Select Committee on Small Business, *Report of the Small Business Administration* (Washington: GPO, 1969), printed as Document 91–14, of U.S. Senate. Transcⅰipt of hearings printed separately.
19. James S. Kakalik and Sorrel Wildhorn, *Private Police in the United States,* 5 vols. (Santa Monica: Rand Corporation 1971). This work is a report of a study by the Rand Corporation, Santa Monica, California, made under Grant NI-70-057 by the National Institute of Law Enforcement and Criminal Justice, Law Enforcement Assistance Administration, Department of Justice.
20. Dept. of Justice, LEAA, *Sourcebook,* p. 68.
21. Ibid.
22. Dept. of Commerce, Bureau of Domestic Commerce, *Cost of Crimes Against Business,* states: "About four million shoplifters are apprehended each year" (p. 19).
23. Kakalik and Wildhorn, *Private Police,* vol. 2, p. 66.
24. Ibid., vol. 2, pp. 79–80.
25. Ibid.
26. Dept. of Justice, LEAA, *Sourcebook,* p. 68.
27. Kakalik and Wildhorn, *Private Police,* vol. 2, p. 94.
28. U.S. Chamber of Commerce, *Handbook on White Collar Crime,* pp. 4–5.

CHAPTER 2.
Security Before 1830

1. John Wade, *A Treatise on the Police and Crimes of the Metropolis* (London, 1829; reprint ed., Montclair, N.J.: Patterson Smith, 1972), p. 78.
2. Charles Reith, *The Blind Eye of History,* (London: Faber & Faber, 1942).
3. Wade, *Treatise on the Police,* p. 193.
4. W. L. Melville-Lee, *A History of Police in England,* (London: 1901; reprint ed., Montclair, N.J.: Patterson Smith, 1971), p. 200.
5. Jerome Hall, *Theft, Law and Society,* 2nd ed. (New York: Bobbs-Merrill, 1952), p. 73.
6. Ibid. Statute quoted is *4 George I C11, Sec. 4.*
7. *Encyclopaedia Britannica,* 14th ed., vol. 18, p. 158.
8. Hall, *Theft, Law and Society,* p. 77.
9. Leon Radzinowicz, *A History of English Criminal Law and Its Administration from 1750,* (London: Stevens & Son, 1950), vol. 3, pp. 507–533.
10. Wade, *Treatise on the Police,* p. 193.
11. Hall, *Theft, Law and Society,* p. 58.

CHAPTER 3.
Private Security and the First Police Century

1. Alden Hatch, *American Express* (New York: Doubleday, 1950), p. 15.
2. Ibid., pp. 35 and 134.
3. James D. Horan, *The Pinkertons* (New York: Crown Publishers, 1967), p. 23.
4. Ibid., p. 24.
5. Allan Pinkerton, *The Gypsies and the Detectives; A Double Life and the Detectives; Bucholz and the Detectives; Claude Melnotte as a Detective; The Spiritualists and the Detectives; The Mississippi Outlaws and the Detectives; Strikers, Communists, Tramps, and Detectives; The Spy of the Rebellion; The Bank-Robbers and the Detectives; The Rail-road Forger and the Detectives; Criminal Reminiscences and Detective Sketches; The Expressman and the Detectives; The Somnambulist and the Detectives; The Model Town and the Detectives; The Burglar's Fate and the Detectives; The Molly Maguires and the Detectives; Professional Thieves and the Detectives; Thirty Years a*

Detective. All these books were published by G. W. Carleton & Co., New York, between 1870 and 1884.

6. Horan, *The Pinkertons,* p. 31.

7. Burton J. Hendrick, *The Life of Andrew Carnegie,* 2 vols. (New York: Doubleday Doran, 1932), vol. 1, p. 389. These volumes were presented to me personally in 1941 by the late Mrs. Andrew Carnegie, together with her husband's bookplates. I had occasion to visit with her professionally. She also presented me with a copy of the *Autobiography of Andrew Carnegie* printed in 1920 by Houghton Mifflin. In giving me these books, she remarked that as a reader of history, I would like the Hendrick book better. The Hendrick version had her approval.

8. Ibid., vol. 1, p. 389.

9. Ibid.

10. Ibid., vol. 1, p. 396.

11. Ibid., vol. 1, p. 399.

12. U.S. House of Representatives, 52nd Congress, 2nd Session, 1892–1893, *Report 2447.*

13. 27 Statute 591, 5 U.S. Code 53, enacted March 3, 1893, reads in part as follows: "Hereafter no employee of the Pinkerton Detective Agency, or similar agency, shall be employed in any Government Service, or by any officer of the District of Columbia." This section was revised in 1966 as part of Public Law 89–554, and is now cited as Section 3108, Title 5, U.S.C.A.; in this version it reads: "An individual employed by Pinkerton Detective Agency, or similar organization, may not be employed by the Government of the United States, or by the Government of the District of Columbia."

14. Melvyn Dubofsky, *We Shall Be All, A History of the I.W.W.,* (New York: Quadrangle, 1969), pp. 96–105.

15. James S. Kakalik and Sorrel Wildhorn, *Private Police in the United States,* 5 vols. Report of study by the Rand Corporation (Santa Monica: Rand Corporation, 1971), vol. 2, at p. 93.

16. Jay Monaghan, *The Book of the American West* (New York: Julian Messner, 1963), p. 272.

17. Horan, *The Pinkertons,* p. 262.

18. Ibid., pp. 363 and 383–384.

19. Ibid., p. 50.

20. Ibid., pp. 238–239.

21. Samuel Dash, Robert E. Knowlton, and Richard F. Schwartz, *The Eavesdroppers* (New Brunswick: Rutgers University Press, 1959), pp. 23–28.

22. Roger Burlingame, *Henry Ford,* (1955, Alfred A. Knopf; reprint ed., New York: Quadrangle, 1970), p. 138.

23. Ibid.
24. *Newsday* (Nassau County, New York), Feb. 2, 1975.

CHAPTER 4.
The Private Security Boom: World War II to the Present

1. *First Annual Report of the Attorney General of the United States: Federal Law Enforcement and Criminal Justice Activities,* (Washington: GPO, 1972), p. 331.
2. Ibid., pp. 330–331.
3. James S. Kakalik, and Sorrel Wildhorn, *Private Police in the United States,* 5 vols. Report of study by the Rand Corporation (Santa Monica: Rand Corporation, 1971), vol. 2, pp. 88–90.
4. *Attorney General's Report,* p. 13.
5. Ibid.
6. Ibid.
7. Ibid., p. 505.
8. Ibid., pp. 177 and 329.
9. Ibid., p. 169.
10. Select Committee on Small Business of the U.S. Senate, *Report of the Small Business Administration,* (Washington: GPO, 1969). Printed as Document 91–14 of U.S. Senate.
11. Ibid.
12. *United States of America* v. *Grinnell Corporation, American District Telegraph Company, Holmes Electric Protective Company and Automatic Fire Alarm Company of Delaware,* 236 F. Supp. 244, dated November 27, 1964, Decision and Opinion by U.S. District Court Judge Wyzanski.
13. Kakalik and Wildhorn, *Private Police,* vol. 2, p. 80.
14. Ibid., vol. 2, p. 128.
15. Jack B. Weinstein and Tom J. Farer, *State Credit Card Crime Act and Report* (New York: American Express, 1967). Privately printed.
16. *State Laws Against Piracy of Sound Recordings: A Handbook for Enforcement and Prosecution,* (New York: Recording Industry Association of America, 1974).

CHAPTER 5.
Guards

1. *Investment Opportunities in the Security Protection and Investigative Services Industry,* an appraisal issued to its customers by Burnham and

Co., New York (September, 1970), p. 6; James S. Kakalik and Sorrel Wildhorn, *Private Police in the United States,* 5 vols. (Santa Monica: Rand Corporation 1971), vol. 2, p. 55.

2. *The New York Times,* Real Estate Section, Sunday, Oct. 13, 1974.
3. Ibid.
4. John Wade, *A Treatise on the Police and Crimes of the Metropolis* (London, 1829; reprint ed., Montclair, N.J.: Patterson Smith, 1972), p. 193.
5. U.S. Department of Commerce, Bureau of Domestic Commerce, *Economic Impact of Crimes Against Business* (Washington: GPO 1972).
6. Arthur C. Kaufman, *Combatting Shoplifting* (New York: National Retail Merchants Association, 1974).
7. Dept. of Commerce, *Economic Impact of Crimes,* p. 11.
8. Kaufman, *Combatting Shoplifting,* p. 4.
9. *Women's Wear Daily,* Oct. 18, 1973.
10. Dept. of Commerce, *Economic Impact of Crimes.*
11. Ibid. See also U.S. Department of Commerce, Bureau of Domestic Commerce, *The Cost of Crimes Against Business* (Washington: GPO, 1974).
12. Dept. of Commerce, *Economic Impact of Crimes*
13. U.S. Department of Commerce, *Commerce Today,* July 8, 1974. p. 13.
14. Ibid.
15. Dept. of Commerce, *Economic Impact of Crimes.*
16. Dept. of Commerce, *Commerce Today.*
17. *Commerce Today.*
18. Kakalik and Wildhorn, *Private Police,* vol. 2, p. 96; *Investment Opportunities,* p. 5; and *Crime Protection: A Growth Industry,* an appraisal issued to its customers by Bear Stearns & Co., New York (October, 1967), p. 9.

CHAPTER 6.
Security Personnel Practices

1. James S. Kakalik and Sorrel Wildhorn, *Private Police in the United States,* 5 vols. (Santa Monica: Rand Corporation, 1971), vol. 2, pp. 133–143.
2. Ibid.
3. House of Representatives of the Commonwealth of Pennsylvania, *Hearings of Select Committee to Investigate Necessity for Legislation in re Private Security Guards,* James B. Kelly of Pittsburgh, chairman. Hearings held on October 12, 25, and 26, and November 15, 1973, and on March 27, April 4, 5, 18, and 19, 1974.

4. Ibid., pp. 70–74.
5. Ibid., pp. 48 and 66.
6. Ibid., p. 114.
7. Kakalik and Wildhorn, *Private Police,* vol. 1, p. viii.
8. Pennsylvania House of Representatives, *Hearings of Select Committee,* pp. 105 and 115.
9. Ibid., p. 68.
10. Ibid., pp. 120 and 127.
11. Ibid., pp. 67–68.
12. Ibid., p. 17.
13. Kakalik and Wildhorn, *Private Police,* vol. 1, p. 32.
14. Ibid., vol. 2, pp. 153, 176, and 182.
15. Pennsylvania House of Representatives, *Hearings of Select Committee,* p. 95.
16. Ibid., pp. 32, 33.
17. Ibid., pp. 111, 112.
18. U.S. Department of Commerce, Bureau of Domestic Commerce, *Economic Impact of Crimes Against Business,* (Washington: 1972), p. 3.
19. Kakalik and Wildhorn, *Private Police,* vol. 2, pp. 150–152.
20. Ibid.
21. Ibid., vol. 2, p. 192.
22. Arthur Niederhoffer and Abraham S. Blumberg, *The Ambivalent Force: Perspectives on the Police* (New York: Ginn and Co., 1970).

CHAPTER 7.
Fraud Investigation

1. James S. Kakalik and Sorrel Wildhorn, *Private Police in the United States,* 5 vols. (Santa Monica: Rand Corporation), vol. 2, pp. 102–103.
2. U.S. Department of Commerce, Bureau of Domestic Commerce, *The Cost of Crimes Against Business,* (Washington: 1974), p. 3.
3. Jack B. Weinstein and Tom J. Farer, *State Credit Card Crime Act and Report,* (New York: American Express, 1967), privately printed.
4. Chamber of Commerce of the United States, *A Handbook on White Collar Crime* (Washington: 1974), p. 6.
5. *Insurance Crime Prevention Institute,* an advertising brochure distributed by the Westport, Conn., organization.
6. C. Arthur Williams, Jr., and Richard M. Heins, *Risk Management and Insurance,* 2nd ed., (New York: McGraw-Hill, 1971), p. 325.
7. Kakalik and Wildhorn, *The Private Police,* vol. 2, pp. 19–26.
8. Ibid., vol. 2, p. 25.

9. Chamber of Commerce, *Handbook on White Collar Crime,* p. 6.
10. Jerome Hall, *Theft, Law and Society,* 2nd ed. (New York. Bobbs-Merrill, 1952), p. 311.
11. Ibid.
12. Kakalik and Wildhorn, *Private Police,* vol. 4, p. 33.
13. Samuel Dash, Robert Knowlton, and Richard F. Schwartz, *The Eavesdroppers* (New Brunswick, N.J.: Rutgers University Press, 1959), p. 271.
14. Stephen Barlay, *The Secrets Business* (New York: Crowell, 1973), p. 96.
15. Donn B. Parker, *Computer Abuse* (Menlo Park, Calif.: Stanford Research Institute, 1973), p. 99.
16. International Business Machines Corporation, *Data Security and Data Processing,* 5 vols. (White Plains, N.Y.: IBM, 1974), vol. 1, p. 7.
17. Parker, *Computer Abuse,* pp. 92 and 100.
18. Ibid., p. 104.
19. Ibid., pp. 93 and 100.
20. Ibid., p. 94.
21. Ibid.
22. U.S. Senate Select Committee on Small Business, *Criminal Redistribution Systems and Their Economic Impact on Small Business,* 2 vols. (Washington: Gov't Printing Off., 1973). Hearings before the Select Committee, U.S. Senate, 93rd Congress, 1st Session, 1973.

CHAPTER 8.
Security Equipment

1. Part of Report of Manufacturing Sub-Committee of the Private Security Advisory Council to LEAA, *The Builders Hardware Industries' Place in the Security Manufacturing Industry* dated Dec. 12, 1972.
2. James S. Kakalik and Sorrel Wildhorn, *Private Police in the United States,* 5 vols. (Washington: 1971), vol. 2, p. 58.
3. *United States of America* v. *Grinnell Corporation, American District Telegraph Company, Holmes Electric Protective Company and Automatic Fire Alarm Company of Delaware,* 236 F.Supp. 244, dated November 27, 1964, Opinion by U.S. District Court Judge Wyzanski.
4. *Private Police,* ref. vol. 2, p. 115.
5. Robert J. Cohen, "False Alarm Legislation in Seattle," *Police Chief* (September, 1974).
6. Clark H. Alsop, "San Jose Gets Proposal for Alarm Ordinance," *Police Chief* (September, 1974).
7. Kakalik and Wildhorn, *Private Police,* vol. 2, p. 62.

8. *Catalog of Alarm Device Manufacturing Co.,* a division of the Pittway Corp., Syosset, N.Y.
9. George J. Matias, *Report of the Second Year of Operation—Installation and Evaluation of a Large-Scale Burglar Alarm System for a Municipal Police Department* (Cedar Rapids: Police Department, undated). Matias was chief of police and project director at the time.
10. Letter entitled "Background Information on the Cedar Rapids Project in Support of a Resolution Submitted to the International Association of Chiefs of Police by the National Burglar and Fire Alarm Association" dated August 21, 1974.
11. Ibid.
12. Ibid.
13. Matias, *Report of the Second Year of Operation.*
14. Alsop, *San Jose Gets Proposal for Alarm Ordinance.* See 6 above.
15. John Wade, *A Treatise on the Police and Crimes of the Metropolis,* (London: 1829; reprint ed., Montclair, N.J.: Patterson Smith, 1972), p. 193.

CHAPTER 9.
Armored Car Services

1. U.S. Department of Justice, Law Enforcement Assistance Association, *Report of Armored Car Sub-Committee of Private Security Advisory Council,* Oct. 10, 1972.
2. Ibid.
3. James S. Kakalik and Sorrel Wildhorn, *Private Police in the United States,* 5 vols. (Santa Monica: Rand Corporation, 1971), vol. 2, p. 69.
4. *Investment Opportunities in the Security Protection and Investigative Services Industry,* an appraisal issued to its customers by Burnham and Co., New York, N.Y. (September, 1970), p. 17.
5. Ibid. Also, Kakalik and Wildhorn, *Private Police,* vol. 2, p. 69.
6. Dept. of Justice, LEAA, *Report of Armored Car Sub-Committee.*
7. *The New York Times,* October 24, 1974.
8. Dept. of Justice, *LEAA, Report of Armored Car Sub-Committee.*

CHAPTER 10.
Law, Legislation and Regulation

1. "Private Police Forces: Legal Powers and Limitations," *University of Chicago Law Review* 38 (Spring Issue, 1971) p. 555.

2. Ibid.
3. Ibid. Also, "Law and Social Order," *Arizona State Law Review* (1972) p. 600.
4. Opinion of the Attorney General of the United States, June 10, 1922, cited as 34 Op. A.G. 241.
5. Decision, Comptroller General A12129, dated February 23, 1926.
6. Decision, Comptroller General A18856, dated July 1, 1927.
7. Decision, Comptroller General A24043, dated August 24, 1928.
8. Decision, Comptroller General B60794, dated November, 1946.
9. Public Law 89–554, Sec. 3108, Title 5, USCA.
10. James S. Kakalik and Sorrel Wildhorn, *Private Police in the United States,* 5 vols. (Santa Monica: Rand Corporation, 1971), vol. 2, p. 89.
11. *The New York Times,* December 20, 1966.
12. *Crime Protection: A Growth Industry,* an appraisal issued to its customers by Baer Stearns & Co., New York, N.Y., dated October, 1967.
13. *Newsday* (Nassau County, N.Y.) Feb. 13, 1975.
14. Kakalik and Wildhorn, *Private Police,* vol. 1, p. 55.
15. Ibid., vol. 3, p. 57.
16. Ibid., vol. 3, p. 141.
17. Ibid., vol. 3, p. 153.
18. Ibid., vol. 3, pp. 177–178.
19. Ibid., vol. 1, p. 38.
20. Ibid., vol. 1, p. 54.
21. Ibid., vol. 3, p. 39.
22. Ibid., vol. 1, p. 55.
23. Ibid., vol. 2, p. 74.
24. Ibid.
25. Ibid., vol. 1, p. 87.
26. Ibid., vol. 1, p. 105.
27. Ibid., vol. 1, p. 107.
28. Private Security Advisory Committee, *Report* to LEAA, proposed press release entitled "Private Security Advisory Council to LEAA Calls for Uniform Security Code," Dec. 20, 1972.
29. Ibid., p. 1.
30. Ibid., p. 2.
31. International Association of Chiefs of Police, Legal Research Section, *Model Burglar and Holdup Alarm Systems Ordinance* (Washington: IACP, 1973).
32. Enclosure with letter of October 1, 1974, to Members of Western Burglar and Fire Alarm Association, signed E. A. Westphal, Chairman, Information Committee.
33. Ibid.

34. T. Frankel, "The Governor's Private Eyes," *Boston University Law Review,* 49 (1969), p. 627.
35. Ibid.
36. Wackenhut Corporation, *Annual Report,* 1971.
37. *New York Times,* Feb. 21, 1971.
38. "Compounding Crimes: Time for Enforcement?" 27 *Hastings Law Journal* (1975).

CHAPTER 11.
Conclusions

1. House of Representatives of the Commonwealth of Pennsylvania, *Hearings of Select Committee to Investigate Necessity for Legislation in re Private Security Guards;* Session of April 19, 1974, pp. 70, 71.

Bibliography

Barlay, Stephen. *The Secrets of Business*. New York: Crowell, 1974.

Blackstock, Paul W. *Agents of Deceit*. New York: Quadrangle, 1966.

Burlingame, Roger. *Henry Ford*. New York: Alfred A. Knopf, 1955.

Cameron, Mary Owen. *The Booster and the Snitch: Department Store Shoplifting*. New York, N.Y.: Free Press, 1964.

Carnegie, Andrew. *Autobiography*. Edited by J. S. Van Dyke. New York: Houghton Mifflin, 1924.

Chamberlin, Jo Hubbard. *Careers in the Protective Services*. New York: Henry Z. Walck, 1963.

Cook, Fred J. *The Pinkertons*. New York: Doubleday, 1974.

Cressy, Donald R. "The Criminal Violation of Financial Trust." *American Sociological Review* (December 1950).

Curtis, Bob. *Security Control: External Theft*. New York: Chain Store Publishing Corp., 1971.

Dash, Samuel; Knowlton, Robert E., Schwartz, Richard F. *The Eavesdroppers*. New Brunswick: Rutgers University Press, 1959.

Dorman, Michael. *Payoff*. New York: David McKay, 1972.

Drago, Harry Sinclair. *Outlaws on Horseback*. New York: Dodd, Mead, 1964.

Dubofsky, Melvyn. *We Shall Be All: A History of the I.W.W.* New York: Quadrangle, 1969.

Edelhertz, Herbert. *Nature, Impact and Prosecution of White Collar Crime*. Washington: National Institute of Law Enforcement and Criminal Justice, 1970.

Fooner, Michael, *Interpol*. Chicago: Henry Regnery Co., 1973.

Gellerman, Saul W. *Motivation and Productivity*. New York: American Management Association, 1963.

Hall, Jerome. *Theft, Law and Society*. 2nd ed. Indianapolis: Bobbs-Merrill, 1952.

Hatch, Alden. *American Express*. New York: Doubleday, 1950.

Hendrick, Burton. *The Life of Andrew Carnegie*. New York: Doubleday Doran, 1932.

Horan, James D. *The Pinkertons*. New York: Crown Publishers, 1967.

International Business Machine Corporation. *Data Security and Data Processing*. White Plains, N.Y.: IBM, 1974.

Jeffries, Fern. *Private Policing: A Bibliography*, Centre of Criminology, University of Toronto, November, 1973.

Kakalik, James S., and Wildhorn, Sorrel. *Private Police in the United States*. 5 vols. Santa Monica: Rand Corporation, Report of a study by the Rand Corp. 1971.

Kaufmann, Arthur C. *Combating Shoplifting*. New York: National Retail Merchants Association, 1974.

Klockars, Carl B. *The Professional Fence*. New York: Free Press, 1974.

Meltzer, Milton. *Brother, Can You Spare a Dime*. New York: Alfred A. Knopf, 1969.

Melville Lee, W. L. *A History of Police in England*. London: Methuen, 1901; reprint ed. Montclair N.J.: Patterson Smith, 1971.

Momboisse, Raymond M. *Industrial Security for Strikes, Riots and Disasters*. Springfield, Ill.: Charles C. Thomas, 1968.

Nevins, Allen and Hill, Frank E. *Ford*. Charles Scribner's Sons, 1957.

Niederhoffer, Arthur and Blumberg, Abraham S. *The Ambivalent Force: Perspectives on the Police*. New York: Ginn, 1970.

Oliver, Eric, and Wilson, John. *Security Manual*. London: Gower Press, 1969.

Oughton, Frederick. *Fraud and White Collar Crime*. London: Elek Books, Ltd., 1971.

Peel, John Donald. *The Story of Private Security*. Springfield, Ill.: Chas. C. Thomas, 1971.

Pinkerton, Allan. *Criminal Reminiscences and Detective Sketches*. G. W. Carleton, 1879; reprint ed. Garrett Press, 1969.

Pinkerton, Allan. *Professional Thieves and the Detective*. G. W. Carleton, 1881; reprint ed. Ams Press, New York: 1973.

Pinkerton, Allan. *The Molly Maguires and the Detectives*. G. W. Dillingham, 1887.

Pinkerton, Allan. *Thirty Years a Detective*. Philadelphia: W. H. Thompson, 1884.

Radzinowicz, Leon. *A History of English Criminal Law and Its Administration from 1750*. London: Stevens & Sons, 1950.

Recording Industry Association of America. *State Laws Against Piracy of Sound Recordings: A Handbook for Enforcement and Prosecution*. New York: 1974.

Reith, Charles. *The Blind Eye of History*. London: Faber & Faber, 1952.

Report of the Proceedings, *Private Policing and Security in Canada: A*

Workshop. Convened by the Centre of Criminology, University of Toronto, October, 1973.

Rowan, Richard Wilmer. *"The Pinkertons": A Detective Dynasty*. Boston: Little, Brown, 1931.

Selznick, Philip. *Law, Society, and Industrial Justice*. New York: Russell Sage Foundation, 1969.

U.S. Attorney General, First Annual Report, *Federal Law Enforcement and Criminal Justice Activities*. Washington: Gov't Printing Office 1972.

U.S. Congress, Senate Select Committee on Small Business, *Crime Against Small Business: A Report of the Small Business Administration*. Washington: Gov't Printing Office 1969. Sen. Doc. 91–14.

U.S. Congress, Senate Select Committee on Small Business, *Criminal Redistribution Systems and Their Economic Impact on Small Business*. 2 vols. Washington: 1973.

U.S. Congress, Senate Select Committee on Small Business, *Impact of Crime on Small Business–1969*. Washington: Gov't Printing Office 1969.

Wade, John. *A Treatise on the Police and Crimes of the Metropolis*. Montclair, N.J.: Patterson Smith, 1972. Reprint from 1829 ed.

Ward, Milburn Robert, Jr. *The Story Behind Private Investigation*. New York: Vantage Press, 1957.

Weinstein, Jack B., and Farer, Tom J. *State Credit Card Crime Act and Report*. New York: American Express, 1967. Privately printed.

Westin, Alan F., and Baker, Michael A. *Databanks in a Free Society*. New York: Quadrangle, 1972.

Williams, C. Arthur, Jr., and Heins, Richard M. *Risk Management and Insurance*. 2nd ed. New York: McGraw-Hill, 1971.

Law Review Articles

Compounding Crimes: Time for Enforcement? 1975. 27 Hastings Law Journal.

Greening of the Board Room. 1973. Columbia Law, Law and Social Problems, vol. 10, p. 15.

Private Assumption of the Police Function Under the Fourth Amendment. 1971. Boston University Law Review, vol. 51, p. 464.

Private Police Forces: Legal Powers and Limitations. 1971. Univ. of Chicago Law Review, vol. 38, p. 555.

Private Police Practices and Problems. 1972. Arizona State Law Review, Law and the Social Order, p. 585.

Police Use of Remote Camera Systems for Surveillance of Public Streets.
1972. Columbia Human Rights Law Review, vol. 4, p. 143.
Regulation of Private Police. 1967. Southern California Law Review, vol.
40, p. 540.
Shoplifting: Protection for Merchants in Wisconsin. 1973. Marquette Law
Review, vol. 57, p. 141.
The Development of the Private Sector of the Criminal Justice System.
1971. Univ. of Minnesota Law & Society Review, vol. 6, p. 267.
The Governor's Private Eyes. 1969. Boston Univ. Law Review, vol. 49, p.
627.

Periodicals

Criminology—quarterly; official publication of American Society of Crimi-
nology. Beverly Hills, Calif.: Sage Publications, Inc.
F.B.I. Law Enforcement Bulletin—monthly. Washington: U.S. Department
of Justice, Federal Bureau of Investigation.
International Criminal Police Review—quarterly official publication of the
International Criminal Police Organization (Interpol). Saint-Cloud,
Paris.
Security Gazette—monthly. London: Security Gazette, Ltd.
Security Management—bimonthly. Washington; American Society for In-
dustrial Security.
Security World—monthly. Los Angeles, Calif.: Security World Publishing
Co., Inc.
Systems Technology & Science for Law Enforcement & Security—
monthly. Mt. Airy, Md.: Lomond Systems, Inc.
The Police Chief—monthly. Gaithersburg, Md.: International Association
of Chiefs of Police.

Index